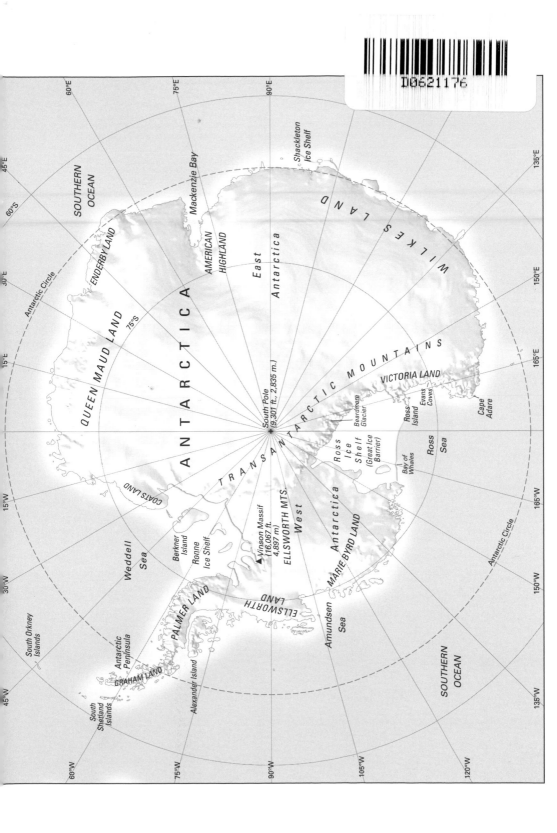

SOUTHERN
OCEAN

60°E

75°E

90°E

Shackleton
Ice Shelf

135°E

Mackenzie Bay

WILKES LAND

45°E

ENDERBY LAND

AMERICAN
HIGHLAND

East
Antarctica

150°E

Antarctic Circle

30°E

QUEEN MAUD LAND

75°S

ANTARCTICA

TRANSANTARCTIC MOUNTAINS

VICTORIA LAND

165°E

15°E

South Pole
(9,301 ft., 2,835 m.)

Evans
Coves

Beardmore
Glacier

Ross
Island

Cape
Adare

COATS LAND

Ross
Ice
Shelf
(Great Ice
Barrier)

Ross
Sea

15°W

Berkner
Island

Bay of
Whales

166°W

Weddell
Sea

Ronne
Ice Shelf

Vinson Massif
(16,067 ft.
4,897 m)
ELLSWORTH MTS.

West
Antarctica

MARIE BYRD LAND

150°W

30°W

ELLSWORTH
LAND

Antarctic Circle

South Orkney
Islands

PALMER LAND

Amundsen
Sea

45°W

Antarctic
Peninsula

Alexander Island

105°W

SOUTHERN
OCEAN

60°W

South
Shetland
Islands

GRAHAM LAND

135°W

75°W

90°W

120°W

60°S

Antarctic Circle

15°E

Return to Antarctica

Terra Nova stuck in the pack ice, December, 1910.

RETURN TO ANTARCTICA

THE AMAZING ADVENTURE OF SIR CHARLES WRIGHT ON ROBERT SCOTT'S JOURNEY TO THE SOUTH POLE

Adrian Raeside

John Wiley & Sons Canada, Ltd.

Library and Archives Canada Cataloguing in Publication

Raeside, Adrian, 1957–
        Return to Antarctica : the amazing adventure of Sir Charles Wright on Robert Scott's journey to the South Pole / Adrian Raeside.

Includes bibliographical references and index.
ISBN 978-0-470-15380-2

        1. Wright, Charles S. (Charles Seymour), 1887-1975—Travel—Antarctica. 2. Scott, Robert Falcon, 1868–1912—Travel—Antarctica. 3. British Antarctic ("Terra Nova") Expedition (1910-1913). 4. Antarctica—Discovery and exploration—British. I. Title.

G850.1910.W75R34 2009   919.8'904   C2009-902926-X

Production Credits
Cover Design and Interior Design: Michael Chan
Printer: Tri-graphic

Editorial Credits
Editor: Don Loney
Project Coordinator: Pauline Ricablanca

John Wiley & Sons Canada, Ltd.
6045 Freemont Blvd.
Mississauga, Ontario
L5R 4J3

Printed in Canada

1 2 3 4 5 TG 13 12 11 10 09

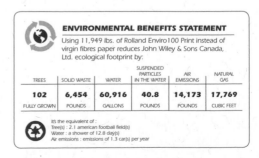

ENVIRONMENTAL BENEFITS STATEMENT

Using 11,949 lbs. of Rolland Enviro100 Print instead of virgin fibres paper reduces John Wiley & Sons Canada, Ltd. ecological footprint by:

TREES	SOLID WASTE	WATER	SUSPENDED PARTICLES IN THE WATER	AIR EMISSIONS	NATURAL GAS
102	6,454	60,916	40.8	14,173	17,769
FULLY GROWN	POUNDS	GALLONS	POUNDS	POUNDS	CUBIC FEET

It's the equivalent of :
Tree(s) : 2.1 american football field(s)
Water : a shower of 12.8 day(s)
Air emissions : emissions of 1.3 car(s) per year

CONTENTS

Adélie and chick, Cape Adare.

PREFACE

Christchurch, New Zealand December 12, 2008
I'm standing in front of one of the many statues of Captain Robert Falcon Scott scattered about the globe. Christchurch's Scott is sculpted from marble; it's cold, lifeless and rock-hard. Which seems appropriate, considering that the real Captain Scott is cold, lifeless and rock-hard, and still lying out on the Ross Ice Shelf.

I grew up surrounded by the Scott Expedition. I had three relatives who were there with Scott. My grandfather Sir Charles "Silas" Wright, my great uncle Sir Raymond Priestley and my great uncle Thomas Griffith "Griff" Taylor.

Physicist and glaciologist Silas Wright accompanied Scott on his 1911 march to the South Pole, getting to within 283 miles of the Pole before being turned back by Scott. Geologist Raymond Priestley was on the ill-fated Northern Party, and geologist Griffith Taylor was with Silas in the Western Mountains.

Silas navigated for the search party that went back out on the Ice Barrier to look for Scott after his Polar Party had failed to return from the South Pole, and it was Silas who spotted the small mound of snow covering the tent that contained the frozen remains of Captain Robert Scott, Edward Wilson and Henry "Birdie" Bowers. If it hadn't been for Silas's sharp eyes, the world might never have known what happened to Scott and his Polar Party.

Like Scott himself, the statue has a chequered history. In 1914 the Christchurch city fathers commissioned Scott's widow, artist and sculptor Kathleen Scott, to create a bronze sculpture of her husband—Christchurch being the *Terra Nova*'s second-to-last port of call before the expedition sailed for the Antarctic. Unfortunately, with the outbreak of the Great War, armament factories were gobbling up all available copper to help provide a steady rain of shells on the German trenches, so the statue was created in marble instead. On completion, it was disassembled for shipment to New Zealand, but prior to its leaving England, a dispute arose between Kathleen Scott and the City of Christchurch over the final bill, resulting in Mrs. Scott withholding a few vital pieces of Captain Scott pending resolution of the dispute. The statue remains incomplete to this day. Even in death, Scott was dogged by chronic funding problems.

I grew up in New Zealand, surrounded by pieces of the 1910 Scott Expedition. Large, framed Ponting* photographs of icicle-encrusted men in beards stared down at me from the walls of the family home. Occasional visits by my grandfather would add a few anecdotes to my rather vague understanding of the trip, but for the most part, my knowledge of the Scott Expedition was drawn from tatty 1930s-era English history textbooks, all of which gushed over Scott's accomplishments: "He died a glorious death!" or the more classic "He died a hero's death!" Like any sadistic schoolboy going through the "how many ants can you fry with a magnifying glass" period, I gobbled it up. No British adventure would be complete without a lingering (and, hopefully, gruesome) death. My schoolmates were unimpressed that I had a grandfather and two great-uncles on the expedition, and who could blame them? The history texts barely mentioned those who accompanied Scott to the South Pole. The same dismissive attitude was meted out to Scott's rival, Roald Amundsen, who reached the South Pole weeks before Scott and returned home without even a case of piles. He was shuffled to history's bleachers by the inconvenient fact that he didn't eviscerate himself on the ice.

As I got older, I began to notice discrepancies between what I had been taught in school and the stories relayed by my grandfather. Illustrations in my history textbooks of a lantern-jawed, clean-shaven Scott and

---

*Herbert Ponting was the official photographer on the Expedition

his companions didn't match the photographs of the grizzled, starving, frostbitten explorers I had grown up with.

After my grandfather's death in 1975, his papers, diaries and memoirs passed to his daughter, Patricia Wright—my aunt, a brilliant wildlife artist in her own right, who drew the pen and ink illustrations in this book—had the role of family archivist thrust upon her. Upon her passing in 2005, my brother, Nicholas, and I came into possession of numerous polar artifacts and boxes of material, much of which had remained unopened for decades. What we discovered was a fascinating account of the expedition and the individual members, along with letters and photographs that hadn't seen the light of day for almost a century. Collectively, they revealed a side to the expedition that I—not to mention the world at large—was unaware of, and one that raised more questions than answers.

Which is why I'm in Christchurch about to board the *Kapitan Khlebnikov*, an Antarctic-bound icebreaker, leaving from the same harbour my grandfather sailed from ninety-eight years earlier.

This is my grandfather's story and my journey to discover what really happened on Captain Robert Falcon Scott's 1910 Expedition to the South Pole.

Adrian Raeside

Standing, from left: Griff Taylor, Cherry-Garrard, Day, Nelson, Lt. Teddy Evans, Oates, Atkinson, Capt. Scott, Silas Wright, Keohane, Gran, Lashly, Hooper, Forde, Anton and Demetri. Sitting, from left: Birdie Bowers, Meares, Debenham, Dr. Wilson, Simpson, PO Taff Evans and Crean.

Terra Nova hut at Cape Evans, 1911

PART I

650 – 1911
DISCOVERY OF ANTARCTICA AND
SILAS'S ARRIVAL AT CAPE EVANS

1. THE LAST UNEXPLOITED PLACE ON EARTH

I would sooner fail than not be among the greatest.

—John Keats

The ancient Greeks were convinced there was a continent on the southern end of the planet, theorising that something had to balance the continent in the North. But they were also convinced there was a Golden Fleece, hot-looking homicidal girls hanging out on rocks and a creature that was half man, half bull.

The earliest record of there actually being anything at the southern end of the planet is from Polynesian explorer Ui-te-Rangiora, who described an ice-strewn ocean *circa* AD 650. His mates back at the luau put it down to an overindulgence of kava and ignored him.

Fast-forward one thousand years.

In 1772, French explorer Yves-Joseph de Kerguélen-Trémarec bumped into a large island at latitude 50° south. Assuming it was the rumoured southern continent, he named it after himself and went home for brandy and prostitutes. He was wrong; it was only a pile of guano-covered rocks situated halfway between Australia and South Africa and not the southern continent, which was just as well, as "de Kerguélen-Trémarecica" just doesn't roll off the tongue as easily as "Antarctica" and besides, no one could have spelled it anyway.

The Spanish, taking a break from burning heretics, were the next to turn up, sailing around Isla de San Pedro, 1,500 miles from the Antarctic land mass, and claiming it for Spain. Unfortunately, no sooner had they left for home than Captain James Cook also discovered it, renamed it South Georgia Island and claimed it for England.

British cartographers were convinced there was a large land mass in the Southern Hemisphere and James Cook had been dispatched by the Admiralty to locate it and annex it for Britain.

Annex (adj.): To massacre the local inhabitants, cart away all their stuff and shoot anything that might look good mounted on the wall.

Unlike his predecessors, who were just looking for economic opportunities, Cook was a scholar as well as a brilliant navigator and carried on board his ships *Resolution* and *Adventure* a number of artists, naturalists and astronomers, along with Larcum Kendall's chronometer, which greatly aided him in fixing longitude. Up to now, figuring out where you were on the ocean had been a rather hit-or-miss affair—usually leading to more misses than hits. Englishman John Harrison invented the original chronometer, which spawned numerous copies, Kendall's being one.

Cook also took along Joseph Priestley's device for obtaining fresh water from sea water by impregnating sea water with fixed air (the precursor to what we now know as soda water).

The revolutionary ideas dreamed up by Joseph Priestley (a distant relative of mine) were considered heretical and resulted in his being verbally attacked in the House of Commons, burned in effigy, brutalised by cartoonists (bastards) and denounced from pulpits, culminating in his house being burned to the ground by an angry mob during the anti-Catholic Gordon riots of 1780.

He was snubbed by the Royal Society (a.k.a. science academy) and was forced to resign his membership. At age sixty-one, he chucked it all in and fled with his family to America, where he died after a failed experiment with Priestley Cola.

Cook was the first European to actually sight the continent of Antarctica, during his 1772–75 voyage. Well, not exactly the continent, more like the pack ice that surrounded it. Skirting the edge of the pack ice, Cook wasn't impressed: all he could see was ice and he never actually laid eyes on the continent. Not that it mattered; his report on the abundance of furry sea life lounging about on the ice was all the merchants waiting at home needed to hear, and the sealing rush was on.

Cook returned to the Southern Ocean on his 1776–80 voyage, with orders to explore the Pacific Coast and find the rumoured Northwest Passage connecting the Atlantic to the Pacific. He sailed from London at the same time as the American colonies declared their independence. However, his task was considered of such international importance that Benjamin Franklin thoughtfully issued Cook a letter of safe conduct in case he had the misfortune to run into any American privateers along the way.

Once again, Cook didn't set foot on shore, but the accurate charts he produced of the surrounding coastline proved most helpful to the sealing ship captains. So helpful were they that by 1830 almost all the fur seals had been wiped out and the sealers turned their attention to reducing the abundant local whale population.

From the records of the Peterhead Whale and Seal Fishery Co.:
No. of seals killed between 1790 and 1861: 1,628,760
No. of whales killed between 1790 and 1861: 4,259

At the other end of the planet, Arctic exploration was becoming passé. Nobody had yet reached the geographic North Pole, but anyone who owned a fur-lined parka and could lay their hands on a ship turned up on the ice floes to have a portrait-worthy encounter with an Inuit family, kill a polar bear (or vice versa) and sail home, along with enough seal skins to enable them to live the rest of their port-sodden lives in relative comfort. The Arctic was close, and to be there wasn't much of a hardship to the English, the mean temperature in the Arctic being similar to the temperature in the drawing-rooms of most English country houses. In fact, the Arctic might have been slightly warmer.

Early Arctic exploration wasn't done entirely for scientific reasons, although there is a science in figuring out how many seal skins one can stuff into the hold of a ship, while leaving enough space for a few dozen barrels of whale oil without having to throw the drinks trolley (and the steward) overboard. But early Arctic exploration was mostly about being the first to be there and surviving to come back and tell about it—a successful polar explorer was the rock star of the period. The lecture circuit, girls, a bigger ship, bigger girls ... The Arctic made many careers, including that of English explorer Sir John Franklin, who became more famous in death than in life, and to this day is the Elvis of Arctic explorers—and just as dead.

The trip from London to the Arctic was a relatively easy one, involving a short hop across the North Atlantic. Antarctica was an altogether tougher proposition. Ten thousand miles from the London gentlemen's clubs, the financial cost to mount your average pillaging expedition was generally prohibitive, and many voyages to the southern continent never left the dock. Those voyagers who actually did make it to Antarctica never set foot on land, as anything worth killing lived in the ocean.

That changed in 1897 when a Belgian expedition under the command of Adrien-Victor-Joseph-de Gerlache de Gomery sailed south in *Belgica*, a ship that was not much longer than his name. Among the crew were Russian and Romanian scientists, along with a young Roald Amundsen and Dr. Frederick Cook, both of whom would go on to play future roles in the geographic unveiling of Antarctica. Unaware of the shortness of the Austral summer, they dawdled on their way south, arriving in the Bellingshausen Sea off the Antarctic Peninsula much too late in the season. *Belgica* and her crew spent eleven months trapped in the ice and are credited with being the first party to spend a winter on the Antarctic continent—although it was purely accidental. They had a miserable time of it, and had it not been for the resourcefulness of Dr. Cook in adapting tents, diet and clothing, they'd be just another set of ice-scoured wooden crosses sticking out of the snow.

Dr. Frederick Cook

Born in Hortonville, New York, in 1865, Cook had an addiction to polar exploration and spent more than twenty years in either the Antarctic or the Arctic. Credited with saving the crew of *Belgica*, he claimed to have reached the North Pole in 1908, one year before Admiral Robert Peary, and was supposedly the first to reach the summit of Alaska's Mount McKinley, the highest peak in North America.

To pass the time while trapped in the ice, *Belgica*'s men conducted a series of experiments on skis vs. snowshoes—snowshoes being preferred for climbing glaciers or pulling sledges. Curiously, this was the last polar expedition to use snowshoes for many decades, which was something Silas Wright remarked upon, twelve years later, from the Beardmore Glacier, when he wrote: "Wish I had moccasins & snowshoes down here, as I would like to convince Capt. Scott of their superiority over ski. They could have been used with advantage for 2/3rds. of the distance."

Two people died during de Gomery's expedition. There were a few cases of insanity, which were delicately ascribed to "polar ennui" and scurvy, which was cured by Dr. Cook's prescription of fresh seal meat. Although the crew didn't appreciate it at the time, the lessons learned during their eleven months trapped in the ice were to prove most useful to the explorers who followed.

Royal Geographical Society: Founded in 1830 to promote the advancement of geographical science—and as a discreet place to drink one's face off. William IV put the "Royal" in the Royal Geographical Society. Explorers David Livingstone, Sir Henry Morton Stanley, Robert Scott, Sir Ernest Shackleton, John Hunt and Sir Edmund Hillary have all been members, as well as Sir Charles "Silas" Wright and Sir Raymond Priestley—who was secretary from 1961 to 1963.

De Gomery was followed by Norwegian Carsten Borchgrevink, who for years had been soliciting funds towards mounting a scientific expedition to Victoria Land in the Ross Sea, a place he had become familiar with during his time bashing in seals's heads. But the all-powerful Royal Geographical Society (RGS) was taking an interest in Antarctica, and Borchgrevink, as an outsider (not British), was given the cold shoulder. Fortunately, he was able to sell the rights to his upcoming story to British newspaper publisher Sir George Newnes for £40,000, which really pissed off Sir Clements Markham, the RGS chair, who felt that money should have been given to his society, which, by coincidence, was short exactly £40,000 needed to mount its very own, and very British, Antarctic expedition.

But Borchgrevink was way ahead of the RGS. In 1898, he sailed south on *Southern Cross*, carrying with him an assortment of British and Norwegian scientists as well as two Finns, who were expert skiers and charged with the care of the ninety dogs mustered from Greenland and Siberia that were crammed onto *Southern Cross*'s deck. Borchgrevink landed at Cape Adare at the entrance to the Ross Sea and set up a prefabricated hut, where he carried out numerous zoological, geological, magnetic and meteorological observations. While there, he sledged on the Great Ice Barrier as far as 78° south—at that time the farthest south anyone had ever been. By the onset of winter, there was a nasty falling-out between Borchgrevink and his men, with conditions inside their hut becoming increasingly strained. Borchgrevink retreated to the hut's attic space, where he presumably slept with a pistol under his pillow and one eye open.

Borchgrevink's *Southern Cross hut* is still standing, and is the oldest man-made dwelling on the Antarctic continent.

On his return to London in 1900, Borchgrevink was chagrined to find that Royal Geographical Society president Sir Clements Markham had been trash-talking him in his absence and he had become a leper to London society. Although his was the first truly scientific expedition, nobody was interested in hearing his findings. Besides, the RGS had scraped up enough money for its very own National Antarctic Expedition to reach the geographic South Pole. Helping Markham in his fundraising was the fact that two more "foreign" expeditions were being planned:

1. The German Antarctic Expedition (which would lose one crew member from beriberi).
2. The Swedish South Polar Expedition 1901−04 (which would lose the entire ship).

The Discovery Expedition

Sir Clements Markham, whose only previous polar experience had been on a futile search for the ill-fated Franklin Expedition in the Arctic some years earlier, took personal charge of mounting the 1901 British Antarctic Expedition—now fully underwritten by the RGS, which even commissioned a ship for the expedition, HMS *Discovery*. This was the first time a British ship was specifically designed for polar exploration. Up to this point, polar explorers had had to improvise with whatever scow was surplus to the booming sealing trade—HMS *Discovery* was to be the ultimate ride.

But building a ship from scratch proved to be a far more expensive proposition than Markham had anticipated. The Dundee Ship Building Company was the lowest bidder at £33,700 (minus engines), and the actual construction was a tortuous affair for the shipyard. Nobody at the RGS had any experience in designing ships, and the cooks in the kitchen kept changing plans and cutting corners, which not only added to the cost but also compromised the ship's original design.

Finally, in March 1901, *Discovery* was launched. At 121 feet long, she had a 2-foot-thick hull and a bow of 8-foot-thick oak, with further outside strengthening of galvanised steel plating. Her hull was flatter than it should have been for a sailing vessel, as she was designed to ride up on the ice and crush it, rather than bust through it. With the lack of a keel, *Discovery* rolled up to 50 degrees in anything more than a light chop. (Similar in fact to a certain Russian icebreaker.)

None of this mattered to the fossils in the RGS. They weren't going any farther south than the society's wine cellar. It would be Captain Robert Falcon Scott, Ernest Shackleton and a collection of scientists, including Dr. Edward Wilson, who would be making the trip south on *Discovery*. Only three members of the crew had any previous experience on the ice, including Louis Charles Bernacchi, who had been one of the ten men in Borchgrevink's Southern Cross Expedition. Bernacchi was keen to offer helpful advice to Markham on Antarctic survival but was told in no uncertain terms to sod off. This was a Royal Geographical Society

HMS *Discovery* in the Ross Sea off the Great Ice Barrier. Painting by Bruce Clark.

expedition and the British were experts at exploration. Two-thirds of the world atlas was coloured in British pink, and once Scott reached the South Pole, it was almost certain that cartographers would be rendering the Antarctic continent in the same dye. To the surprise of many at the RGS, Markham insisted the previously unknown Robert Scott command the expedition.

Robert Falcon Scott

Born on June 30, 1868, in Plymouth, England, one of six children—two boys, four girls. His grandfather owned a brewery, which eventually went bankrupt. No mean feat in a military town. His father, a church warden and magistrate, had a quick temper—a personality trait that Scott inherited.

The family fell on hard times and the children were farmed out to various boarding schools. At the age of twelve, Scott went to Stubbington House to cram for entry into the naval cadet college, HMS *Britannia*. Scott was considered a "delicate boy" and rather shy, and his time there was unpleasant. Drilled by Royal Marine pensioners, he was beaten on a regular basis and usually finished near the bottom of his class.

Scott's career in the Royal Navy was lacklustre and appeared to be going nowhere, until he caught the eye of Sir Clements Markham. Markham, who was known to frequent tropical locations in the company of young midshipmen on loan from the Royal Navy, had discovered Scott at a sailing regatta in St. Kitts. He immediately took great interest in Scott and was rumoured to be instrumental in his unusually rapid rise through his navy ranks, culminating in his command of *Discovery*.

At the Royal Geographical Society, Scott's lack of experience in a masted ship became an issue, and RGS director Mostyn Field was deeply suspicious of Markham's enthusiastic support of Scott. He pointed out Scott's lack of naval experience afloat.

To be fair to Scott, he hadn't sunk a vessel, but his service record was decidedly strange. He had been in the service of the Royal Navy for years, but there were periods where Scott's name would mysteriously disappear off the list of active officers. Scott did make a voyage up the Pacific Coast on HMS *Amphion* in 1889 and was a big hit in the social scene in Victoria, British Columbia. Only twenty-one years old, dark-haired and handsome, he was the most sought-after of the ship's officers. However, the only re-cord of *Amphion*'s stay in Victoria was of its ignominious departure:

> The close proximity of Haro Point was not observed, owing to the fog, and the first intimation of danger was the loud, crashing sound as the warship's side was pierced by the saw-like rocks, followed by the rushing noise of the water pouring into her forward compartments. *(Victoria Daily Colonist,* November, 1889)

Scott was just a lieutenant aboard *Amphion*, but it was not the sort of action that gets one's portrait hanging in the National Gallery, nor did it entitle one to command a brand-new and, by now, rather expensive vessel.

Clements Markham prevailed however and Scott was appointed master of HMS *Discovery*.

Provisioning the ship was left to Scott, who intended to rely on canned meat and vegetables. The subject of scurvy was always an issue for any trip of that length and prior polar expeditions had been able to avoid it by using seal meat, but Scott had a soft spot for animals and didn't want to rely solely on the local wildlife for food. Under pressure, he grudgingly allowed that seal meat would be made available a few times a week, but only for those who wanted it. As a guard against scurvy, Scott took on board 100 gallons of lime juice, although lemon juice had already been proven to be far more effective as an antiscorbutic than lime juice. When scurvy inevitably hit the party, Scott and Wilson came up with their own remedy, which involved whitewashing *Discovery*'s holds, airing out the hammocks and regular outdoor exercise. (This was thirty years after James Cook had exposed the mysteries of scurvy.)

Symptoms of scurvy:
Although one is more likely to suffer from the Norwalk virus on ships nowadays, next time you're on a cruise, keep an eye out for the following:

> Tiredness, weakness, irritability, aches and pains,* poor healing, bleeding in fingertips or old scars, bruising easily, bleeding gums, swollen purple spongy gums and a sudden fondness for Céline Dion CDs.

* Not to be confused with a bad hangover.

Upon launching, it was clear that *Discovery* had serious shortcomings. Besides a sickening roll, she was undermasted and her engines had the same horsepower as a sewing machine. C.R. Ford, seaman on *Discovery*, recalled the first time he saw *Discovery*: "I got to Dundee and couldn't find the ship, then I saw a barrel at the edge of the wharf. I went along and saw this ship below the wharf. I was quite horrified."[1]

Regardless, Scott accepted *Discovery* from the shipyard and sailed her down to London for provisioning. While Scott was standing on deck with a group of other men, a heavy block fell from aloft, missing him by inches and putting a large dent in the deck. Scott reportedly went white with rage, startling the crew, as it was the first they had seen of Scott's temper. It wouldn't be the last. He once dressed down a man who had the temerity to complain about burned hot cross buns at Easter and punished the offender by having his grog cut off for two days. When the sailor protested, Scott ordered the man to be removed from his sight before he struck him.

> He [Scott] was a strict disciplinarian, anything not up to the naval standard he was used to would cause his quick temper to flare up. He would fly at us, but we never minded much as it would be over in a minute. On one occasion, he went for me, which I thought was most unfair but a few hours later, he met me on deck and with a sweet smile offered me plum pudding.
>
> —C.H. Hare, seaman, HMS Discovery[2]

Prior to sailing, *Discovery* was visited by a steady procession of cranks and wackos. The Flat Earth Society turned up armed with charts showing the Antarctic ice barrier was actually a safety ring around the Earth, and if the men sailed through it they would disappear into outer space. Another group turned up on deck and cursed the voyage. It took everything Scott had to prevent the sailors from tossing that group into the Thames. They finally shooed the last of the zealots off the ship and, on August 6, *Discovery* sailed south.

Almost immediately things began to go wrong, starting with their food:

> We found out before we left, our food supply was bad. We had to sail with what we'd got, it was too late to change it. It didn't strike anyone that we didn't need to take what we'd got; we could have got fresh food in New Zealand.
>
> —C.H. Hare seaman, HMS *Discovery*[3]

The ship leaked badly, wormholes were discovered, planks turned out to be unseasoned and defective bolts were letting in water. Blame was immediately put on shoddy workmanship at the Dundee yard. The yard countered that plans for the ship were constantly being altered during construction and that they were only trying to stay within an impossible budget. *Discovery* did reach New Zealand without sinking and the crew were able to effect repairs while in Lyttelton. The remainder of the voyage to the ice was uneventful, except for Seaman Charles Bonner, who fell from a mast and died from his injuries. They made their way through the pack ice in a record five days, reaching Ross Island in January 1902, where they erected a hut on Hut Point.

> The *Discovery* hut was actually a prefabricated Australian sheep drover's hut and had no insulation and a roof more suited to the dry Australian outback than the Antarctic. Ignoring the lessons of de Gomery's expedition some years earlier, Scott anchored *Discovery* in McMurdo Sound, where he planned to use the ship, instead of the hut, for accommodation. *Discovery* ended up firmly trapped in thick fast ice for two years.

Scott, Ernest Shackleton and Scott's close friend Edward Wilson headed for the South Pole on November 2, 1902, planning a route over the Great Ice Barrier and up the Beardmore Glacier to the Polar Plateau at 9,000 feet elevation. Wilson probably should never have gone on the journey. The medical department of the Royal Navy had twice rejected him for the expedition, as he was still recovering from a long illness related to tuberculosis. It was Markham who stepped in and over-rode the medical doctors.

Weather conditions on the Barrier were ideal and they made good time, but things began to unravel fifty days into the march. The dogs were getting sick from tainted dog food, and Scott and the party were incompetent at handling the dog teams: the three men ending up dragging the sledges themselves. They kept going until December 30, 1902, when at 82°17' S they gave up and turned back. Shackleton had started exhibiting symptoms of scurvy, which was not surprising, for they had

Shackleton, Scott and Wilson prior to the start of their Southern Journey, November 2, 1902.

long since exhausted their meagre supply of seal meat and were reduced to living on canned pemmican and dog biscuits. On January 14, 1903, on their return journey, Scott described Shackleton's condition:

> Shackleton has very angry-looking gums—swollen and dark; he is also suffering greatly from shortness of breath; his throat seems to be congested and he gets fits of coughing, when he is obliged to spit and once or twice a day he has spat blood. I myself have distinctly red gums. And a very slight swelling in the ankles. Wilson's gums are affecting one spot, where there is a large plum-coloured lump; otherwise he seems free from symptoms.[4]

Shackleton's condition deteriorated alarmingly, to the point where Scott and Wilson had a discussion outside Shackleton's tent about his chances for survival.

Scott: "Do you think he'll last?"
Wilson: "I don't think so."

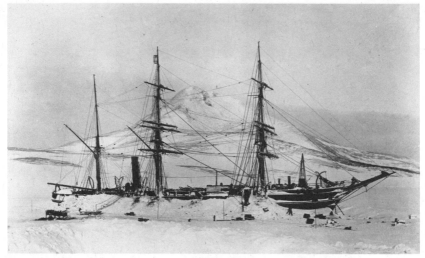

Discovery locked in the ice in McMurdo Sound. Observation Hill in the background.

A strong voice bellowed from within the tent: "I'm not going to die. I tell you this, I shall be alive when both of you fellows are dead!"[5]

Rather prophetic of Shackleton ...

They made it back to the coast alive, on February 3, 1903, to find *Discovery* still locked in the ice, but the relief ship *Morning* had arrived in their absence. Scott sent eight men, including Shackleton, home on *Morning*, while he and the remaining men would stay on the ice-bound *Discovery* for another season.

Scott and Wilson spent the following summer exploring and doing extensive mapping of the surrounding area, with Scott, Petty Officer Edgar "Taff" Evans and William Lashly spending some weeks poking about on the Great Ice Barrier. They returned to find the ship was still locked in ice and winter approaching fast. This time it was serious. They didn't have enough supplies to last another winter, and in fact what few supplies they did have were turning rancid, with Dr. Wilson having to personally examine each food tin when it was opened. They tried using saws to cut a channel in the ice, but after two weeks of sawing, all they had been able to do was cut 450 feet of channel—with another 20 miles of ice to go.

Back at the Royal Geographical Society in London, the directors were getting nervous. *Discovery* was overdue in New Zealand and the RGS feared the worst. Reluctantly, and after much snivelling and grovelling from Markham, the British Admiralty sent two relief ships. *Morning* and the sealing vessel *Terra Nova* were dispatched with orders to pick up the stranded crew (if they were still alive) and abandon *Discovery*.

Royal Navy ships towed *Terra Nova* and *Morning* across the Mediterranean Sea and through the Suez Canal to the Indian Ocean, in order to save burning coal.

On January 5, 1904, Scott was shocked to look out of his cabin on *Discovery* and see the two relief ships hove-to in McMurdo Sound, and even more shocked by the orders he was given from the Admiralty: upon arrival of the relief vessels, *Discovery* was to be abandoned and the crew and officers transferred to the relief vessels.

Scott was livid. He was convinced he had an enemy in the Admiralty who wanted to scuttle his career, and he was determined *Discovery* should not be abandoned. The relief ships stood patiently by as the *Discovery*'s crew frantically dynamited a passage for their ship through the ice, much to the annoyance of any sea life that happened to be living directly underneath. Eventually, after freeing their vessel on February 14, they prevailed and headed for home, but not before *Discovery* struck a reef, where the ship stayed for eight hours until the tide floated her off. *Discovery* arrived back in England in September 1904, where Markham immediately put her on the auction block. Factoring in the Admiralty's bill for the rescue attempt, the final cost of the expedition had ballooned to a colossal £200,000—roughly £4 million today. *Discovery* leaving the RGS with an embarrassing deficit of £190,000. Regardless of the pickle the RGS found itself in, Scott was anxious to return to the Antarctic and this time reach the South Pole.

But Ernest Shackleton, who had arrived back in London a year earlier on *Morning*, had a head start on fundraising for his own expedition to the South Pole.

Scott had barely got his oilskins back from the cleaners when Shackleton announced he'd raised £30,000, got the backing of the Royal Geographical Society and purchased *Nimrod*, a clapped-out whaler, to transport him back to the Ross Sea. To Scott's fury, Shackleton was heading back to Antarctica before him.

Ernest Shackleton

Shackleton was born to Yorkshire parents in County Kildare, Ireland, on February 15, 1874. He went to sea at the age of sixteen and was a competent ship's master by the time he joined the 1901 Discovery Expedition about eight years later. Relations between Scott and Shackleton soured after their return from the aborted trip to the South Pole.

Ernest H. Shackleton, Explorer. Resumé:

Discovery, 1901:   Got to within 297 miles of South Pole, returned with scurvy. Ship almost crushed in ice.

Nimrod, 1907:   Got within 97 miles of South Pole. Ran out of supplies. Got scurvy.

Endurance, 1914:   Ship crushed by ice. Sailed 4,000 miles to South Georgia in an open boat. Ross Sea party stranded without supplies for two years. Two men died.

Without social connections or money, Scott had no choice but to sit on the sidelines as the Royal Geographical Society paraded Shackleton as the man to claim the Pole for England. Scott was mollified by the title of "backup explorer" should anything go wrong with Shackleton's expedition. Scott was convinced Shackleton would fail, and to make things difficult for him, he extracted from Shackleton a written promise he would stay away from Ross Island, specifically the hut they'd erected on Scott's previous 1901 Discovery Expedition, as he already had plans to use the hut as a base for his own upcoming expedition.

The strange case of the Dublin Crown jewels: On July 6, 1907, Ernest Shackleton's brother Francis was implicated in the heist of the Dublin Crown Jewels* but avoided prison time by threatening to expose a homosexual ring operating out of Dublin Castle—the site of the safe containing the jewels. Sir Arthur Vickers, the keeper of the keys to the safe, was charged with "failing to exercise due vigilance or proper care of the regalia." Despite his protests, he lost his job and was murdered by the Irish Republican Army in 1921. Francis Shackleton eventually went to prison for defrauding a widow of her savings.

*Actually a set of diamond-encrusted beer mugs.

Although Shackleton's expedition was not billed as "scientific," Shackleton did take along a token collection of scientists, including my great-uncle Raymond Priestley, who later recalled that upon applying for the position of geologist on the expedition, Shackleton interviewed him personally, posing only two questions:

1. "Can you identify gold?"
2. "Can you play a musical instrument?"[6]

Priestley presumably answered both questions correctly, as he was hired. Years later, my other great-uncle, Griffith Taylor, the Australian geologist on, put it bluntly: "Shackleton had not the slightest interest in science."[7]

On July 30, 1907, promising to send Scott a postcard from the South Pole (no doubt postage-due), Shackleton sailed for New Zealand on *Nimrod*, along with twenty-nine expedition members, a collection of sledge dogs, a motorcar and old *Discovery* shipmates Frank Wild and Ernest Joyce. To conserve their coal reserves, *Nimrod* was towed by *Koonya* from New Zealand as far as the pack ice, then made the rest of the trip under her own steam. Like *Discovery* a few years earlier, *Nimrod* sailed into McMurdo Sound, but due to heavy sea ice was forced to anchor miles away from the site of their camp on Cape Royds. The delay in unloading meant the

Raymond Priestley in the Western Mountains, 1907.

Austral summer was fading and by the time they got their hut erected, average temperatures had plunged to minus 20°F.

The group waited out the winter until the return of the sun, when Shackleton, Jameson Adams, Eric Marshall and Frank Wild, would head for the Pole, while a second party, made up of Edgeworth David, Dr. Alistair Mackay and Douglas Mawson, would set out on a 1,200-mile journey to reach the estimated location of the Magnetic South Pole.

The position of the Magnetic South Pole varies from year to year due to the drift in Earth's magnetic field. Edgeworth David and Douglas Mawson put the location of the Magnetic Pole in the middle of Wilkes Land at 72° 25′ S 155° 16′ E in 1909. Geographers later found that to be incorrect. The likely location of the Magnetic South Pole in 1909 was actually at 71° 36′ S 152° 0′ E. (But that was just being pedantic.)

At time of writing, the Magnetic South Pole is in the Southern Ocean.

The Magnetic Pole Party immediately ran into difficulties; their motorcar overheated constantly, requiring frequent stops for long periods in order to allow the vehicle to cool down, which slowed their progress. They eventually abandoned the motorcar and continued on foot, dragging their sledges, running out of food, suffering from severe frostbite and snow blindness. Finally, on January 15, 1908, they raised the Union flag at what they calculated was the Magnetic South Pole.

Their return journey was tight, as they had set a prearranged time and place to meet *Nimrod*, making it to the ship with only hours to spare.

The Geographic Polar Party was having an even worse time. The ponies were sick and weak and being shot at regular intervals, Adams' leg was injured from being kicked by a pony (score one for the ponies) and Shackleton had badly miscalculated the amount of rations they'd need. By November 26, 1908, they passed the point where Shackleton, Scott and Wilson had turned back six years earlier. They celebrated this milestone by shooting another pony. This not only meant fresh pony meat; they could also eat the deceased pony's fodder.

By Christmas Day, Shackleton's party had struggled up the Beardmore Glacier and was on the Polar Plateau, being brutalised by constant blizzards and plunging temperatures.

On January 9, at 88° 23' S, they were only 97 miles from the South Pole, but their rations were so depleted that if they carried on any farther, they would not make it back alive. They planted a flag, took some photos and headed home, leaving behind a trail of dog and pony carcasses, along with a few hundred cigarette butts (Shackleton had a fondness for cigarettes). The return journey was made a little easier due to their rigging a sail on the sledge. By the time they reached the coast, they had walked 1,700 miles for nothing. The South Pole was still up for grabs.

Frank Wild, a member of Shackleton's expedition, became close friends with both Raymond Priestley and Silas Wright, spending much time at the Priestley family home in Tewkesbury.

Wild, Shackleton, Marshall, Adams, and dogs after failing to reach the Pole. Credit: Alexander Turnbull Library.

Back in London, Scott had returned to active duty in the Royal Navy and married sculptor Kathleen Bruce. Like everyone else, he was waiting to hear the news of Shackleton's expedition. However, he was also worried that Shackleton might have learned from the mistakes of the Discovery Expedition and had actually reached the South Pole. To his delight, Shackleton returned with the news that he had failed. Captain Robert Scott would be going back to the Antarctic.

2. CHARLES SEYMOUR "SILAS" WRIGHT

Most people say that it is intellect which makes a great scientist. They are wrong: it is character.

—Albert Einstein

Charles Seymour "Silas" Wright.

Charles Seymour Wright was born on April 7, 1887, in Toronto, Ontario. His father, Alfred Wright, was the son of a doctor who had emigrated from England and settled the family in Woodstock, Ontario. Alfred was employed by the Toronto branch of the London and Lancashire Insurance Company and retired many years later as head of the Canadian branches. Silas's mother, Katherine Kennedy, was a Lowland Scot and died when Silas was quite young, while giving birth to his second brother, Adrian.

The house where my grandfather and his two brothers spent much of their childhood still stands on Crescent Road, Toronto, and is probably now worth more than my grandfather earned in his entire lifetime. Apart from the expensive automobiles parked in the driveways, not much has changed in the past hundred years. Rosedale

Silas's older brother, Alfred.

is a quaint, genteel part of Toronto, so it's easy to see why Silas spent most of his childhood roaming the backwoods of Ontario. He always felt trapped by concrete and lace curtains.

Silas had a rough start in life. Hit by scarlet fever in 1888, he survived and recovered in time for both himself and his older brother, Alfred, to be circumcised. (Their grandfather was a doctor and their father had been similarly treated, so the brothers didn't have much say in the matter.) The operation was performed by the family doctor, who was a little overzealous on bandaging the area, leaving Silas in great pain as night came on, clutching the bars of his crib and yelling blue murder. As a result, the doctor had to pay a return visit to relieve the situation for Silas, who later recalled that he got some satisfaction from the incident, claiming, "I got my own back" but felt he was unjustly blamed for not being able to "hold on" any longer.

His education was initially at a school run by two Gibson Girls whose brother was suffering from tuberculosis. Both Silas and Alfred were subjected to hours of instruction in arithmetic (this was before math), and Silas found his studies laborious—but they became much easier when he discovered the answers to the questions were at the back of the arithmetic book. As a result, he left the care of the Gibson Girls under a slight cloud.

Due to the absence of a mother and with their father working long hours, Silas and his brothers were brought up by their Aunt Louie, who was a stern taskmistress and fanatically religious. Any lapse from perfect behaviour was followed by a session on their knees and prayers to the Almighty for forgiveness. As Silas put it, he "would rather have had a modest beating."

The only diversion from their dreary studies in the clutches of Aunt Louie was in the empty field across the street, where the local boys would play some form of football. The matches ended, so far as Silas was concerned, with a broken arm, after which Aunt Louie forbade the Wright boys to take part in what she considered frivolous activities.

To their relief, they outgrew Aunt Louie's basic instruction on hell-fire and damnation and ended up at the more liberal Toronto Church School, which initially was reached by horse but later by the brand-new electric tram.

By the time Silas was eight, he was as tall as his older brother, Alfred, and the two were almost inseparable, while their younger brother, Adrian (or "Brownie," as he eventually came to be known), tended to be excluded from Alfred and Silas's wild outdoor games. Adrian was of smaller build than his older brothers and had red hair, a throwback to his mother's Scottish Kennedy clan. Later, Silas came to feel that the neglect of their younger brother had been rather unkind—Adrian was "of much finer character than we two older ones." Silas was skinnier than Alfred and had long legs that were disproportionate to his body, but his long legs helped him win numerous athletic events. His athletic career came to an end when his father, who was on the school sports committee, had him pulled from the field because he felt his son looked ridiculous among his shorter and tubbier school chums.

Silas and Alfred left the Toronto Church School in 1899 without any regrets. Silas was glad to be rid of what he considered the most useless of classes: Latin. As he put it, "Who on Earth would ever address a table as 'Oh table?'"

Together, Alfred and Silas entered Upper Canada College (UCC) and for the first time, they felt truly independent. From the earliest times, Silas and Alfred had been called by their middle names, Seymour and Esten respectively, which they both considered "sissy and namby-pamby." They managed to have their names changed to Charles and Alfred at UCC, but it took a lot longer to have such a liberality accepted at home.

"Charles" only lasted until 1910, when Silas was aboard the *Terra Nova*, headed for the Antarctic:

> "Silas" struck me one day on the ship as a typical Yankee name and in a happy moment I called him Mister Silas P. Wright of the Philadelphia Educational Seminary. Since then he has never been called anything but "Cousin Silas," or "Silas." He is a charming fellow—one of the best—and should have been an athlete, not a scientist.
>
> —Henry "Birdie" Bowers[1]

In 1898, Silas's father married again. His bride, a widower named Emily Nichol, brought along her own brood—Benson, Edward and Helen—who were all younger than Silas and Alfred, so the pair carried on with their own outdoor pursuits as if nothing had changed domestically.

Silas loved his time at Upper Canada College, and it wasn't until much later that he realised what a financial strain it must have been on his father to put three boys through college. But as the Wright family had been attending Upper Canada College since it had opened, to go anywhere else would have been unthinkable.

The Wrights were what was known as "day boys" and rode an electric tram to college. On their return home, though, they got off the tram at the terminus of Bloor Street and Avenue Road and walked the two miles back to their house, which was then on Dovercourt Road. Not for the exercise, but to save the onward car fare, enlarging their allowances by a few precious cents a week. To the boys's chagrin, the family moved to Rosedale—within walking distance of Upper Canada College—and their alternative source of income came to an untimely end.

When Silas was twelve, he and Alfred came into possession of an ancient 16-foot sailboat. Although she was long past her prime and needed hours of patching to keep her afloat, she was their pride and joy. Kept at the Argonaut Pier in Toronto Bay, she was grossly overmasted and carried just one large lug sail, meaning anything more than a stiff breeze and they had to be ready to let the sail out before she capsized. This led to an unfortunate incident with Silas's uncle outside the Royal Muskoka Hotel on Lake Rousseau. The uncle insisted on taking charge of the sailboat, despite his nephew's protestations that the boat was tricky to sail. This of course led to predictable results, made all the more humiliating for his uncle, as the entire episode was played out in full view of his new lady friend, who was staying with him at the hotel.

I often feel sorry for the youngsters nowadays growing up so close to their families in high rise apartments in big cities and who have not taken or will not take the opportunities for getting away from doting or disapproving parents and of not seeing something of a more natural life in the bush.

—Wright memoirs

The long summers were the happiest for Silas and Alfred. As soon as college was out, he and Alfred would pool their modest resources, pack

their canoe with supplies and disappear on long journeys up to, and beyond, what was called "the head of steel" of the Temiskaming Northern
Ontario Railway. Their ultimate goal was to find gold and stake a claim
in a gold mine. They lived on sowbelly (required for frying fish), porridge,
rice, beans, tea, sugar and dried apples and apricots. They never had a set
plan; they'd just go as far north as they could before their supplies ran out
and hunger forced them to return.

One summer they predictably ran out of food but didn't want to return because they felt they were close to the motherlode. As luck would
have it, they came upon a moose (bad luck for the moose), which allowed
them to get so far north that they ran out of unfrozen ground.

*These journeys used to take us up over the height of land separating the rivers
flowing into Hudson Bay and into the Gulf of St. Lawrence, far into black fly
country where, together with mosquitos and sand flies, life in midsummer hardly
seemed worth living. I know we used to swear on our return we wouldn't go again,
but next winter always found us making plans, poring over such maps as were
available and discussing how best to reach the places where no maps had yet been
drawn or even surveyed. On one occasion, we got the canoe up so narrow a stream
that further progress was impossible and we decided we must back track only to find
a note, printed on the bark of a birch tree, that two people (named) had reached the
place by dog team the previous winter.*

—Wright memoirs

It was Silas's first encounter with the value of dog teams.

As their summer trips to the wilderness had failed to turn up any
gold, they reluctantly lowered their expectations and agreed to settle for
a silver mine. According to Silas's memoirs, "It was interesting to note
that any samples later sent to the metallurgist for analysis of gold *always*
yielded $5 worth per ton in gold. It happened too frequently and we just
didn't believe the figure."

They weren't the only prospectors in the area with dreams of striking
it rich. Once, while camped on the shore of an unnamed lake (actually,
the lake was named rather colourfully, by Alfred, when Silas neglected
to hold on to the bow of the canoe as Alfred was disembarking, depositing him into the frigid water), they were visited by a prospector who had
just bought six claims in the area and was having a hard time finding the
claim stakes, which, according to Silas, were non-existent. The prospector

was not at all dismayed at the news, saying cheerfully that he would just "sell the claims on to some other idiot."

In later years, Silas felt that the reason they picked the blank spaces on the provincial maps was more to explore uncharted areas rather than look for gold claims to stake. Regardless of why they were there, the local winged inhabitants of Northern Ontario were always pleased to see them turn up.

To examine a rock, one had to strip off about a foot of wet moss: as one did, clouds of these pests flew up into one's face and the black flies started to search for ways to get inside one's clothing. The only real relief from these pests is afforded by a camp on a small island in a large lake with a half a gale of wind blowing.

—Wright memoirs

By 1904, Silas had left Upper Canada College, with fond memories of his masters: "Gussie" Parkin, the principal; "Stoney" Jackson, the classics master; "Duke" Somerville, physics and chemistry; "Guts" Sparling, mathematics; and "Choppie" Grant, in charge of creating nicknames for fellow masters.

Silas entered the University of Toronto for the four-year honours course in mathematics and physics and immediately began working towards the coveted 1851 Scholarship.

The 1851 Scholarship was set up at the completion of the 1851 World Exhibition in London, which was such a financial success, the land it occupied, including the Crystal Palace, was purchased and rents from it were used to set up and support scholarships in the natural sciences as well as the British School of Art in Rome. What is most unusual about this scholarship is that there was no limit on which university or in which country the research could be carried out. Today, with capital assets of more than £40 million, annual charitable disbursements exceed £1.6 million.

Silas was determined to take a shot at the scholarship. An all-expenses-paid position at one of the best universities in the world was something his father could have never afforded.

Summer holidays at university were longer than at college and even though Silas and Alfred had abandoned their search for gold, Silas still

Silas on a surveying party in Northern Ontario.

preferred to spend his summers in the wilderness, taking a job as a chain-man in Northern Ontario for one dollar a day.

In the surveying hierarchy, the position of chainman rated at the bottom of the heap. A chainman would, by means of an axe or machete, cut thousands of feet of line in the bush, wide enough to drag a 200-foot steel tape and sight a transit. A chainman's life is much easier these days, as distances are measured electronically, eliminating the laborious and often dangerous task of cutting line and dragging tape.

During his time at university, Silas became absorbed with the study of penetrating radiation: radiation that ionized the Earth's atmosphere and whose origins at the time were unknown. Silas proved that the intensity of radiation varied from day to day but almost always gave the same figures whether the measurements were made high up on the university tower, the university basement, or even deep in the rock tunnels below Niagara Falls.

There appeared to be much penetrating radiation deposited from the atmosphere that could not be accounted for, and it was known that even a simple bucket of water could absorb large amounts of radiation.

An experiment was set up on a frozen pond that had solidified enough to support one hundred lead cell batteries, a table, a chair and Silas. It proved there was an appreciative decrease in radiation under the ice, but the experiment was hastily abandoned when the ice was about to give way under the weight of Silas and the equipment.

The question was: At what altitude was penetrating radiation the strongest and from where did it originate? Silas's experiments were incomplete, but with the deadline for competition for the 1851 Scholarship coming up, he hastily wrote up his report and sent it off.

While waiting to hear the results of his application for the 1851, Silas found to his surprise that he had won the Edward Blake Scholarship for general proficiency, which came with a stipend of £100 a year plus tuition fees! He was surprised because he had nearly failed his physics paper: "I lost my head and panicked."

Besides radiation, Silas was experimenting with magnetism and the properties of metal alloys (studies that would end up saving thousands of lives during the Second World War). He thoroughly enjoyed the research but found writing and illustrating the resulting reports rather stressful. Years later, he met Dr. Gordon Shrum, then chancellor of the University of British Columbia, who took great delight in letting Silas know that his illustrated reports were used in subsequent university physics lectures as perfect examples of bad reporting.

With university out for the summer, Silas and Alfred set off on a canoe trip on Lake Temagami, unaware it would be the last wilderness canoe journey they would take together. Stopping at the local post office to mail some letters, Silas found a letter from home with the news that he'd been accepted by the 1851 Scholarship Commission. What's more, Gonville and Caius (pronounced "keys") College had awarded him the Wollaston Studentship of £100 a year for two years. This, along with £150 from the 1851 Scholarship and the £100 Edward Blake Scholarship, made Silas a reasonably wealthy young man.

Returning to Toronto, Silas was eager to get going, but his father and stepmother were determined their son would not embarrass them during his time at Cambridge:

Prior to departure for England, I was given a wealth of advice on how to conduct myself in the old country, including a few relations I must visit, most of whom were

scattered about near Worcestershire and the Midlands. I remember being told I must
have not only a Tuxedo (with one stripe down the trouser) but also a dinner suit with
two stripes on the outside of each leg. Then there was a black morning coat and grey
top hat and grey striped trousers. The morning coat and dinner suit had long tails of
course, but the frock coat had none. These cost a lot of money and the last of these I
never found any use for and I doubt if the morning coat and grey top hat were used
more than two or three times.

—Wright memoirs

Armed with his new suits, Silas set off for England late in the summer of 1908—first by steamer across Lake Ontario and then by train to New York, where he was to board ss *Umbria* for the voyage across the Atlantic. But the sailing was delayed a couple of days, meaning he had to spend a portion of his precious scholarship money in New York. He spent his time sightseeing, but for someone who preferred spending his days in the wilderness. In his memoirs, Silas said he found New York boring—in contrast to some time he had once spent in Amsterdam, where, as he delicately put it, "There really was something of interest to see."

After a rough Atlantic crossing—"*Umbria* rolled like a bitch"—Silas arrived in Liverpool and took the boat train to London, where he immediately reported to the office of the 1851 Scholarship Commissioners on Queen Victoria Street at 8:30 AM, only to be met by a woman with a mop and broom. The offices didn't open until 10 AM. This was England, after all.

After turning up in Cambridge, he was immediately initiated into the old university town's quaint peculiarities. It was customary for students to arrive at the last minute on the first day of the term, and Silas was a few days too early, which meant he had to find a hotel in Cambridge, spending more of his precious scholarship money. He congratulated himself on finding the cheapest lodging available but was later admonished by his houseman for stopping at what was considered a "commercial hotel." However, he soon integrated into campus life and was actually allowed to eat with senior students at the "high table" and even allotted a room in St. Michael's Court, along with his own "bedder." He was lucky; in the Cambridge caste system, the general rule was for the new boys to sod off and fend for themselves in outside digs during their first years, but they were required to come in for dinner at the college hall each night in order to be counted present and correct. (And presumably to be tortured by the senior lads.)

Silas tried to carry on with his experiments in penetrating radiation at Cambridge's Cavendish Laboratories, but the facilities were minimal and somewhat bereft of equipment. Fortunately, due to his scholarship money, he was able to pop around the corner to the Cambridge Instrument Company and purchase the equipment needed to continue with his research.

By 1910, Silas was close to perfecting a device to accurately measure radiation through magnifying the effect of single particles by high-speed collision with gas molecules. All that was needed was to devise a suitable container for the electrode and generate a stable voltage. But it was 1910; his two-year 1851 Scholarship and his money were rapidly coming to an end.

Silas was faced with returning to Canada, when fellow student Thomas Griffith "Griff" Taylor, an Australian and also an 1851 Scholar, met Douglas Mawson at the Philosophical Society dinner. Mawson, an old chum of Taylor's from their university days in Sydney, had just returned from the 1907 Shackleton Expedition to the Antarctic and was now on the lecture circuit to pay off some bills. To save money, Mawson stayed in Taylor's rooms at Cambridge, where he met Silas, who, along with Taylor, would sit around the tiny coal fire in Taylor's room, enthralled with Mawson's accounts of exciting Antarctic exploration. Mawson may have skipped over the more horrific incidents of his trip, as it is doubtful Silas or Taylor would have gone anywhere near the place if they suspected they would be subjected to the same miseries.

By coincidence, Robert Scott had just announced he was putting together his second expedition to the Antarctic, and Mawson encouraged Taylor and Silas to apply for positions on Scott's expedition:

> Later that evening, he [Mawson] regaled us with his accounts of
> his many escapes. He suggested that, as the expedition was to be so
> much a naval occasion, we scientists learn how to box, just in case
> we had to hold our own against the naval stalwarts.
>
> —Griff Taylor[2]

Thomas Griffith "Griff" Taylor

Born on December 1, 1880, in Walthamstow, Essex, Rhomas Griffith Taylor emigrated with his family in 1893 to Australia, where he studied sciences at the University of Sydney. In 1907 he went back to England, where he met Silas Wright at Cambridge. He was a teetotaller who would draw attention to his foible by firmly turning his glass upside down so that all should see how teetotal he was. Taylor was the older of the expedition's scientists, with a passion for the job and an equal passion for passing on his considerable knowledge of geology. In the Antarctic, Cecil Meares gave Taylor the name "Ram-Jatass," which in a Lolo Tibetan dialect means "verbally flowing eternally."

Silas casually remarked that he'd apply for a position on Scott's expedition if Taylor would too. Taylor immediately wrote to Scott and was accepted as the expedition's geologist. Silas also wrote to Scott, applying for the position of physicist on the 1910 British Antarctic Expedition. A few days later, Silas received a letter from Scott politely turning him down. Silas was devastated. His 1851 Scholarship was almost at an end and what little money he had left would have to go to pay for passage back to Canada.

3. THE 1910 BRITISH ANTARCTIC EXPEDITION

All you need is ignorance and confidence and the success is sure.

—Mark Twain

Back in London, Scott could scarcely conceal his delight at Shackleton's spectacular failure to reach the South Pole. With a superior "I told you so" attitude, and urged on by his new wife, artist and sculptor Kathleen Scott, who rather fancied herself married to a famous polar explorer, he lobbied the Royal Geographical Society, demanding that it finance his expedition.

But the Royal Geographical Society wasn't in a position to finance anything more enterprising than a bus trip to Bournemouth. It was still mired in debt from both Scott's 1901–04 Discovery Expedition and Shackleton's 1907–09 Nimrod Expedition. Another fiasco like that and the society would be reduced to serving a cheaper sherry in the dining room.

Besides, all of London was talking about the North Pole, because United States Naval Officer Robert Peary claimed to have reached it on April 6, 1909. (His claim is still disputed.) The RGS was embarrassed that an American had reached the North Pole first. To complicate matters, perennial American explorer Dr. Frederick Cook claimed that it was actually he who had been first to reach the North Pole—one year earlier. (His claim is also disputed.) Polar exploration was getting messy and was now temporarily out of fashion in the London salons.

Those who had been busy planning their own expeditions to the North Pole tossed out their charts of the Arctic and scrambled to get their hands on charts of Antarctica. German explorer Wilhelm Filchner announced an expedition to not only reach the South Pole but to march across the entire continent, capturing it for Germany and presumably enslaving the local population. A French expedition under Jean-Baptiste Charcot was already in Graham Land on the Antarctic Peninsula, surrendering to a flock of penguins, and Japanese naval lieutenant Nobu Shirase was packing his whale sashimi recipes in preparation for a Japanese expedition to the South Pole.

Scott was frantic. The thought of the Pole being claimed by anyone other than an Englishman was too much to bear. And on top of it all, Shackleton had just got himself a knighthood!

Scott figured he'd need at least £40,000 to put together his expedition, but to date his attempts at fundraising had been met with crashing indifference. Undeterred, he lowered his expectations (and his standards) and plunged into the rubber-chicken circuit to raise cash. He criss-crossed England, speaking at rummage sales and town halls, staying at musty hotels with no hot water and toilets located down the hall—or in the next building. At one point in 1910, he noted: "Lecture in aid of boys' home—cleared £150 to £200."[1] (There was no indication as to what the boys cleared.)

Raising pennies when he needed pounds, Scott hit on the idea of promoting the expedition as one of "scientific discovery." It worked. He was able to persuade various universities and government agencies to come up with money. Not all of it was in the form of gifts, however. Something was expected in return: a few quid for some rocks from the Antarctic, twenty quid for a stuffed penguin to mount over the bar in the faculty lounge ...

Although Scott touted his 1910 upcoming expedition as the first "scientific expedition," there had in fact been numerous scientific reports from previous expeditions, most notably the German, Swedish, French and Belgian expeditions.

Meanwhile, Silas was still in Cambridge, wrapping up his experiments in penetrating radiation before his scholarships expired. His dwindling savings meant that continuing at Cambridge without a scholarship was out of the question. He had pinned his hopes on being able to carry out his radiation experiments on terrestrial magnetism and atmospheric electricity in the Antarctic and wasn't looking forward to going back to Canada.

Early Antarctic expeditions had reported massive magnetic storms that regularly swept the continent. Silas was convinced they were extraterrestrial in origin and was keen to prove his theory. Magnetic storms were a serious matter, as compasses on ships would be affected by these severe magnetic phenomena.

Silas was instrumental in calculating accurately the variations in magnetic pull on compasses. His pendulum observations at Cape Evans during the first winter confirmed that gravitational pull at the North and South Poles was identical, confirming the Earth was the same shape at both ends. The gravitational pull is less in summer than in winter, presumably because of the large icebergs that calve off from the poles's respective land mass. Silas theorised that the Antarctic had been shaking off its ice over the millennia and slowly rising out of the ocean.

Griff Taylor suggested to Silas that he shouldn't accept Scott's rejection letter and instead go to Scott's office in London and reapply in person. As the pair were both short of funds, they cooked a dozen boiled eggs over the coal fire in Silas's room and the following morning set out on foot for London, 50 miles south of Cambridge.*

We forgot to remember how dry hard boiled eggs were and that a little liquid is required to help them down. In our desire to walk down to London at 5 miles an hour, we did not stop even for a mug of beer and most of the eggs did the whole journey intact.
                                        —Wright memoirs

Griff Taylor remembered it this way:

Wright came through "smiling" but my feet were so sore I could hardly stand the next day. My chief recollection is one of loathing

---

*In 1910, their journey on foot took them more than ten hours. If you did the same trip today on the British rail system, it would probably take fifteen hours …

for hard-boiled eggs, and of the relief with which I dropped three-quarters of our provisions in a secluded corner of King's Cross.[3]

Silas turned up in Scott's cluttered office on Victoria Street the next morning and was able to meet with Scott personally. After a brief interview, Scott changed his mind and accepted Silas in the position of physicist for the sum of £200 a year. (On the crew manifest he was listed as "Chemist.")

Ecstatic, Silas and Taylor returned to Cambridge to wrap up their studies in preparation for the trip. Silas's last activity before leaving Cavendish Laboratory was to write up his final results on penetrating radiation, and the device he had come up with to detect it, turning the paper over to his physics master, who would submit it for publication.

> Silas hoped his radiation-measuring device had commercial applications and would make him a small income. On returning to England in 1913, he was dismayed to discover that a German by the name of Hans Geiger had filed patent for a similar device while he was in the Antarctic. Silas's paper was still sitting in his physics master's desk drawer ...

To legitimise the scientific angle, Scott persuaded Dr. Edward Wilson, a close friend of Scott's and doctor on the 1901 Discovery Expedition, to join him once more on this latest expedition as head of scientific staff. The closest Scott had got to anything scientific was when he was fiddling with torpedoes as a midshipman in the navy. It was vital he put someone he trusted between himself and a demanding and very un-naval scientific staff. Wilson was perfect for the job.

Edward Adrian "Uncle Bill" Wilson

Born on July 23, 1872, in Cheltenham, Gloucestershire, Wilson, a naval doctor, never had much time to practise his profession. He was stricken by tuberculosis after graduating from medical school and spent many months recuperating, sinking into a deep depression during that period. He eventually recovered and was picked by Scott to be the doctor aboard *Discovery* for the 1901 expedition. His diaries from both the 1901 and 1910 expeditions show very little, if any, connection to medicine, as he was far more interested in the study of ornithology. He became close to Scott and got along with him when many didn't. His gentle demeanour meant he was not the type to argue with the more moody and volatile Scott—which probably helped keep the friendship together.

Silas liked Wilson and appreciated the value of "Uncle Bill" (as he was fondly referred to), writing in his diary: "Wilson was a great friend of Scott's and Scott was a friend of his. If you wanted to get anything across to Scott, we learned the wise way was to pass it through Wilson."

Wilson was an accomplished watercolourist and produced stacks of paintings and sketches of the landscape and local wildlife. But his main role in 1910 appeared to be keeping the crew from tossing Scott overboard.

Silas remembered him as being key to the expedition:

"I've never met anyone like him. He was the reason, I think, that the expedition was a very happy group and if it hadn't been for him, there might have been difficulties between the naval and the scientific people. He was a remarkable man."

Bill Wilson with his pony, Nobby. "Edward Wilson was the closest to a perfect man any of us have ever known." —Silas Wright

Scott was still desperately short of funds and everyone was expected to pitch in for fundraising. Silas doing his part, hitting up his Alma mater, the University of Toronto:

May 1, 1910
My Dear Wright.
I will keep the copy of the letter you enclosed from Toronto, and will show it to Capt. Scott tomorrow and then let you have an answer.

One would like to know how much they propose to grant, for unless it is a substantial sum it might not be worth while hampering oneself with undertakings to collect for them—there is always the prospect of dissatisfaction with what one brings home, though I don't think there would be any difficulty at all in collecting them a sample lot of Antarctic rock specimens. You yourself could undertake to do that, the only thing that would be necessary is that the geologists should be allowed to look them over and sanction the lot going to Toronto. I see no other difficulty, and there is good reason to collect for as many people & nations as we can, only if they can help us with a grant beforehand.

But don't do anything further til I have seen Scott and written to you again—tomorrow.

Yours ever, EA Wilson

Scott was basically selling off the Antarctic, one rock at a time. Which may explain why he decided to jettison equipment, like camera and theodolite on the return journey from the South Pole, but kept more than 30 pounds of rock samples on the sledge.

Scott preferred to surround himself with people he knew and felt comfortable with, regardless of their competence. Petty Officer Edgar Evans, who had been with him on the 1901 Discovery Expedition, was high on his list of trusted naval personnel, although he was the exact opposite to Scott's effete and reserved persona.

PO Edgar "Taff" Evans

Born on March 9, 1876, in Swansea, Wales, "Taff" Evans joined the Royal Navy at fifteen and served a few years as an ordinary seaman before getting his commission and serving on *Trafalgar*.

It was a petty officer 2nd Class on *Majestic* that he first met Scott. Scott requested his services for the 1901 Discovery Expedition, and Evans spent the next three and a half years in Scott's company, leaving as a petty officer 1st class, on Scott's recommendation. After his discharge from *Discovery*, Evans drifted, drinking and whoring (not that there's anything wrong with that).

PO Edgar "Taff" Evans. Taylor described him as "always eager for more work" on the Western Journey, a statement that was echoed by Scott's remark about Taff always roving about adjusting and adding improvements to equipment on the Southern Journey.

On November 26, 1910, in Lyttelton, New Zealand, the day *Terra Nova* sailed for the Antarctic, Scott wrote: "Evans, PO. Drunk, disgraced ship. Later saw him at the British hotel and spoke straight."

Silas was very fond of Taff Evans and grateful to him for sharing his previous knowledge of the Antarctic and handy tips on sledging and polar survival. During their first expedition to the Western Mountains, across McMurdo Sound from Cape Evans, Evans's experience saved them from serious frostbite on more than one occasion. Not only was Evans invaluable when it came to polar survival, he was a raconteur of some note and kept Silas and his companions enthralled with tales of his exploits.

Scott's wife, Kathleen, was heavily involved in picking the crew and scientists and was present at all the interviews. It's not known whether she was the person who initially rejected Silas for the expedition, but she was a forceful woman with strong opinions and Scott usually respected her wishes. Henry "Birdie" Bowers was initially rejected by Scott, but was overruled by Kathleen, who felt that someone with such obvious physical deformities and who was so unprepossessing would be ideal for the job. Scott relented and hired Bowers, which, as it turned out, was a an excellent decision—though not so for Bowers.

Henry Robert "Birdie" Bowers

Henry "Birdie" Bowers. Caricature by Dennis Lillie.

Born on July 29, 1883, at Greenock, Scotland, "Birdie" Bowers was an only son, raised from the age of three by his mother after his father died in Rangoon, Burma. Bowers entered the British Merchant service at an early age, joining the Royal Indian Marines in 1905. He commanded a riverboat and eventually ended up in the Persian Gulf, aboard HMS *Fox*.

Bowers was five foot, four inches, and had a distinctive beak-like nose that earned him the nickname "Birdie," although he was good-natured about all the ribbing he got from the others over his appearance. After reading accounts of the 1901 and 1907 expeditions, he applied for and was at first turned down for a position on Scott's 1910 expedition. However, Scott listened to his wife and hired Bowers.

Bowers was initially just to take the ship down to the Antarctic and return to New Zealand, but he turned out to be such a resourceful jack-of-all-trades that Scott persuaded him to stay on with the Shore Party, where Bowers proved expert at altering boots, harnesses and other related items, most of which had proved woefully inadequate for the Antarctic climate. He was also given the task of managing the expedition's stores and diligently measured out daily sledging rations to the last ounce.

Said Frank Debenham: "Bowers would have been a bigger man than Scott if he had lived. He was the best and most gifted polar explorer I can think of. He was perfect in every way."[3]

Kathleen Scott took a much dimmer view of Apsley Cherry-Garrard, "an ugly youth of 23 who was only accepted because his family advanced £1,000 towards the expedition."[4]

Apsley George Benet "Cherry" Cherry-Garrard

Born on January 2, 1886, to a family of wealthy landowners, Apsley Cherry-Garrard was educated at Oxford. In 1909 he applied, but was turned down, for a position on Scott's 1910 expedition. He reapplied with £1,000 as a sweetener and was accepted, becoming an invaluable member of the expedition.

Apsley Cherry-Garrard with his pony Michael. *"An Oxford man and very well educated, well read and much better educated than the rest of the scientific staff. He endeared himself to all by his readiness to help even with the most unsavoury jobs. I admired him from afar especially after the way he stuck with the job of the great winter journey with Wilson and Bowers."*—Silas Wright

In a financial bind, Scott was resigned to putting together the expedition on the cheap, resorting to the "few quid down, the rest when we get back" plan, hoping that the sale of his future book and a lucrative lecture circuit would pay off the mountain of IOUs that would be waiting for him upon his return.

He approached Douglas Mawson, who had been with Shackleton in 1907, offering him a position on the expedition, but Mawson turned him down as he was planning his own expedition—the Australian Antarctic Expedition, which would revisit the Magnetic South Pole—and was himself out beating the bushes for funding.

The Australian Antarctic Expedition: In 1912, Douglas Mawson and his party sailed *Aurora* to Cape Denison, roughly 1,000 miles northeast of Scott's base at Cape Evans. The expedition was a complete shambles. A dog team and sledge disappeared down a crevasse, taking with them most of the supplies. The remaining dogs were driven to exhaustion, at which point Mawson and his party ate the dogs, which almost proved fatal: the dog livers were toxic, causing the men to hallucinate.

Mawson left his party behind and wandered off on his own, eventually returning to the main base at Cape Denison only hours after *Aurora* had left for home. Mawson and six others were stranded for the winter until the ship could return for them in the spring.

Scott still needed a ship and would have preferred *Discovery*, but she was serving as a supply ship to the Hudson Bay trading stations in Canada. He considered *Aurora*, but Mawson had already laid claim to her. He looked at *Morning*, and the smaller *Bjorn* and *Nimrod* (Shackleton's ship on his previous failed expedition)—in fact he looked at everything except the *Good Ship Lollipop* before settling on *Terra Nova*, which he bought for £12,500 from the Canadian sealing company Bowrings, for £5,000 down, the remainder due when he got back, with the owners reserving the right to buy back what was left of the vessel after the expedition.

Ex-whaling vessel *Terra Nova* sitting higher in the water than she was on her voyage south in 1910.

Terra Nova was built by Alexander Stephens & Sons of Dundee and launched in September 1884. She was 744 tons, 187 feet long, 31 feet wide and had three masts and one 65-hp steam-driven engine. It was purchased a month later by sealing company C.T. Bowring of Newfoundland. Bowrings still exists in Canada today as a chain of high-end gift shops, with *Terra Nova* as its company emblem.

Silas and his companions on the scientific staff were forced to scrounge around for the equipment required for their respective experiments in the Antarctic, and thanks to the generosity of various instrument manufacturers and universities, they were more or less able to find what they needed. Scott, meanwhile, was busy making deals with manufacturers, such as Fry's Cocoa, Coleman's Cornflour and Woolsey underwear, with the proviso that Herbert Ponting, the expedition's official photographer, would send back photographs of the expedition members enjoying their products. They were, in effect, the world's first product endorsements.

> Perhaps you have seen a photo of three people sitting on a sledge drinking Fry's Cocoa, you may also see the same three outside a tent eating Colman's Cornflour & again sitting on sleeping bags in Woolsey underclothes. They were all taken last year as soon as we got down here for advertisements, so you must not think they are real.
> —F.J. Hooper, in a letter to his fiancée, February 5, 1911

Scott had written off sledge dogs as useless and instead commissioned three motorised tracked sledges, planning to rely on these and ponies to drag their supply sledges, with a few Siberian dogs as backup.

Scott had a dim view of sledge dogs, as he thought dogs performed poorly on his 1901 Discovery Expedition—conveniently ignoring the fact that they were fed a substandard diet and no one on the party had a clue how to properly handle a dog team.

Members of the expedition modelling Woolsey underwear.

The Wolseley Motor Company in Finchley undertook to build the motor sledges and shipped them, and Scott, to Fefor, Norway, for testing on a frozen lake. Scott pronounced them a smashing success, even though they were tested in temperatures and conditions far more benign than those in the Antarctic. While in Norway, Scott met Tryggve Gran, who was also contemplating putting together a Norwegian expedition to the South Pole.

Tryggve Gran

Born in Bergen, Norway, in 1889, educated in Switzerland, a graduate of naval college and expert on skis, Tryggve Gran was introduced to Scott by Norwegian polar explorer Fridtjof Nansen while Scott was testing his motor sledges on a frozen Norwegian lake.

Gran obligingly set up a meeting between Scott and Arctic explorer Roald Amundsen, whom Scott most admired. Inexplicably, Amundsen failed to show up at the meeting. Unbeknownst to anyone except his own brother, Amundsen was already well ahead on his secret plans to go to the South Pole and was most anxious to avoid Scott at all costs. If the slightest hint of what he was up to were to get out, there was no question he would be stopped by the king of Norway, who was pals with the British Royal Family. Unaware of Amundsen's skulduggery, Scott persuaded Gran to abandon his own Antarctic expedition and throw his lot in with Scott. He had observed Gran's prowess on skis and considered his expertise would be invaluable on the trek to the Pole.

Publicly, Roald Amundsen had assured everyone he was going to the North Pole, which should have raised some suspicions, as both Peary and Cook had already claimed to have reached it first. Why would Amundsen bother going over old ground?

Scott was completely absorbed in planning and equipping his expedition, however, and had no reason to assume he wouldn't be the only one making the trek to the South Pole.

Despite Scott's animosity, Shackleton offered much helpful advice on how to prepare for the trip, but was ignored by Scott, who considered himself an old polar hand.

Scott's plan was to set up base at Cape Evans and by means of motor sledges, ponies and manhauling, haul supply sledges the 900 miles to the South Pole—and back (the equivalent to walking from Montreal to Winnipeg and back, in minus 30° F at an elevation of 9,000 feet, dragging your dining-room set behind you on a wooden pallet). With the exception of the motorised sledges, this was no different from his plan in 1901 and Shackleton's plan in 1907. That those two attempts were colossal failures was conveniently forgotten.

At this point, Scott's fortunes turned for the better. Still smarting from an American reaching the North Pole first, and faced with the real possibility that Germans, or even the French, might claim the South Pole first, the Royal Geographical Society changed its mind and was now solidly behind Scott, coming up with a modest amount of cash.

Even with the RSG's support, the expedition was still being put together on the cheap. Edward Wilson was very aware of the financial squeeze Scott had got himself into and was scrutinising every request from the scientific staff for equipment. Every item was being looked at, right down to the number of reference books they could take with them. Scott, meanwhile, had gone out and blown a wad on a pianola and 500 rolls of songs.

The British and Foreign Sailors' Society stepped in, providing reading material for the crew. A couple of their books are still in the family library. (I would return them to the BFSS, but I'm not sure I can afford the fine that will have accrued over the last one hundred years.)

Silas had accepted the post as expedition physicist but was concerned he'd be stuck at Cape Evans while everyone else was swanning around on glaciers and legging it to the South Pole. He reasoned that if he was also the expedition's glaciologist, he'd have an excuse to be out and about. Silas approached Wilson with the idea, who spoke to Scott, who was more than happy to take up Silas's offer; either because he felt a Canadian would have an excellent knowledge of ice or, as was more likely, because he was getting two scientists for the price of one.

> Everyone was issued £50 for sundries like sea boots, nautical caps and oilskins, which came just in time for Silas, his scholarship money having been almost completely drained.

For Silas the downside to being official glaciologist was that he was now required to expound at great length about a subject he knew little about. In order to legitimise the scientific side to the expedition, Scott was inserting as much science into his fundraising lectures as he could, and Silas was called upon to provide "popular accounts" of proposed scientific activities. In a reply to Scott, dated November 22, 1910, Silas wrote:

Dear Sir,

Many thanks for your note of yesterday. I have tried to make the account as popular as possible, but am rather doubtful as to the "popularity" of the first sentence.

But perhaps the most interesting investigation to be undertaken in the Antarctic is the study of ice. There, where icebergs are daily being formed, where ice sheets are to be found thousands of square miles in area & glaciers whose width is measured in tens of miles, where saltwater ice and freshwater ice, ice moving ice at rest; freshly formed ice & ice whose age can be measured in centuries, are all to be found within a few miles of one another; surely no more suitable spot than this can be found for the study of ice in its various forms.

The two problems whose solution is most pressingly needed are:

1. The origin of the great ice barrier & time of its formation.
2. Its previous extent.

The most powerful method of attacking these problems is furnished by the polariscope. Thus from the size and shape of the ice crystals as seen in the polariscope, information must be given regarding the past history of the ice and its rate of formation, in exactly the same manner as an examination through the microscope of the crystal structure of a solid metal gives information regarding the previous treatment of the metal and its rate of change from the molten into the solid state.

The information thus given must be most valuable as throwing light on the conditions which obtained on the earth during the glacial period.

Charles Wright

Silas was making it up as he went along, but it seemed to work and no one questioned how much he actually knew about glaciers—which at that time was pretty much zero.

As the equipment piled up on *Terra Nova*'s decks, it became obvious the vessel was far too small for what was required of her and that she was so badly overloaded it was doubtful the harbourmaster would let *Terra Nova* leave port. Scott managed to get around this predicament by re-registering *Terra Nova* with the Royal Yacht Squadron (RYS) as a pleasure craft, immune from annoying commercial shipping regulations.

If anyone from the RYS had bothered to visit the ship, they would have been hard-pressed to see any pleasure in the impending cruise. Scott had paid the dues, however, and since they would be out of the country for a couple of years, there was little likelihood the stoker and his mates would be dipping their grubby fingers into the punch bowl at the RYS annual ball.

And just to be absolutely sure nobody interfered with their sailing plans, Scott sent PO Taff Evans over the side to repaint the Plimsoll line a few inches higher ...

Plimsoll line: Loading mark painted on the hull of merchant ships, first suggested by the nineteenth-century English politician Samuel Plimsoll. It indicates the depth to which a vessel may be safely (and legally) loaded.

After all Scott had been through, a piddling strip of white paint wasn't going to come between him and the South Pole.

Unfortunately the new Plimsoll line did nothing to solve overcrowding aboard *Terra Nova*. George Simpson, the expedition's meteorologist, had been able to scrounge some sacks of special coke, which would be burned in a non-magnetic copper stove in the so-called "absolute" magnetic hut at Cape Evans, where they'd be keeping the sensitive magnetic variation recorders. When the barge carrying the coke came alongside *Terra Nova*, Scott sent it away, as there was just no room for the coke. On this "scientific" expedition, science was having a hard time finding a spot on board the ship.

4. VOYAGE TO NEW ZEALAND

"Scott was working on rather a narrow margin"
—Raymond Priestley.

On June 1, 1910, *Terra Nova* sailed from London bound for Cardiff, where she would take on coal. By coincidence, as they sailed down the Thames, they passed Scott's old ship, *Discovery*, now sailing under the flag of the Hudson's Bay Company. Arriving at Spithead on June 3, they anchored near HMS *Invincible*, where they were entertained by her officers while a few choice items from *Invincible*'s stores were transferred to the more poorly fitted-out *Terra Nova*.

Arriving in Cardiff, they were welcomed by the city with free docking, free coal and free beer. They were also joined by more of the scientific staff, including Silas Wright.

On June 15, 1910, *Terra Nova*, under the command of Lieutenant Edward R.G.R. "Teddy" Evans,* steamed out of Cardiff, accompanied by a flotilla of small boats. Even though Scott had the Plimsoll line painted higher on the hull in London, the ship had sunk another two inches below the waterline, which was nothing compared to how far under water it would be when *Terra Nova* left Dunedin, New Zealand.

---

*Lt. Teddy Evans and PO Taff Evans were not related.

We left Cardiff amid great excitement; boats packed with people accompanied us about ten miles on our way. All that day we steamed down the Bristol Channel, shedding literature as we went. This literature consisted of tracts and periodicals left on board by well-meaning people.

—Wright memoirs

Silas always had a suspicion of religion, due probably to his austere aunt and lessons from the pious Gibson Girls. Robert and Kathleen Scott, along with Wilson's wife, Oriana, and Hilda (Mrs. Teddy) Evans, left *Terra Nova* on the pilot boat and headed back to shore. Scott was staying behind to do some last-minute fundraising and along with the three women would travel by the more luxurious Union Line steamer RMS *Saxon* to rendezvous with *Terra Nova* at Cape Town, South Africa.

RMS *Saxon* was built by Harland and Wolff in 1899—the same shipyard that built *Titanic* a few years later. *Titanic* sank on April 14, 1912, sixteen days after Scott perished on the Great Ice Barrier.

Terra Nova could steam at 5 knots and could maybe make 7 knots, with a following wind and the tide with the ship. But at that speed, *Terra Nova* burned too much precious coal and there was always the possibility her aging boiler would explode under the pressure. Under sail, she could make 5 knots in a stiff breeze, 7 in a screaming gale. *Kapitan Khlebnikov* could do 15 knots in a calm sea—neither ship would be classed as a greyhound of the sea.

With so much heavy gear piled onto her decks, *Terra Nova* wallowed in the swells, the only relief coming when the engine was shut off and the sails were set. Unfortunately, while under sail the ship leaked like a sieve due to the masts twisting a hull that was long past its "best before" date—meaning the crew had to spend up to an hour during every watch manning the antiquated and unreliable hand pump, to prevent the ship from going to the bottom.

Perhaps they should have hung on to that "literature" back in Cardiff. If the Lord turned a deaf ear to their prayers for the ship to stay afloat, they could have used the tracts to plug numerous leaking seams. *Terra Nova* was a tough old scow, but too many miles had slipped under her keel, and by the time Scott got his hands on the ship, she was more suited to duty as a floating dance hall in Brighton than plowing through another South Atlantic gale.

Lawrence Oates, who was in charge of the ponies, was most dismayed at the state of *Terra Nova* and wrote in a letter home: "This is a frightfully dirty ship, as we have had no rain since we left Cardiff and all the gear ropes, etc., are still all smothered with coal dust."[1]

Silas's cabin was nicknamed "the nursery," due to the tender age of those who inhabited it. Built for four people, it would eventually be occupied by six, along with the pianola and the ship's library. Dragging a pianola 10,000 miles to the Antarctic may sound as useful as a Zamboni in the Sahara Desert, but when you consider they expected to spend at least two years cut off from civilisation, Scott probably felt a cheery evening singalong might be the only thing that would stop his crew from beating him to death with ski poles in the middle of winter.

Within a few days of leaving Cardiff, a shipboard routine settled in. The scientific staff were expected to join the ship's crew in their regular tasks. Coal trimming, pumping out the ship, stoking, pumping out the ship, washing, pumping out the ship … it was hard work for those unaccustomed to getting their hands dirty, but the weather was improving the farther south they sailed and everyone was getting along well together, due to the decidedly un-naval discipline of Lt. Teddy Evans.

Lt. Edward R.G.R. "Teddy" Evans

Born in 1881 in London, Teddy Evans received a spotty early education and like so many boys of his age joined the Merchant Marine, which led to a naval cadetship. In 1900 he was promoted to sub-lieutenant and was second officer on *Morning*, one of the relief ships for *Discovery*.

In 1910, Scott got wind that Evans was planning his own expedition to the South Pole, which, to Scott, was out of the question. Scott persuaded Evans to join his own British Antarctic Expedition, promising him command of *Terra Nova* and the motor sledging party. Evans's wife, Hilda, was furious when she heard Teddy had thrown his lot in with Scott, convinced that Kathleen Scott was behind the dirty deed. The animosity between the two women lasted long after *Terra Nova* left New Zealand.

Evans, unlike Scott, had an easy manner about him, which must have irritated the moody and distant Scott, who could never make the same personal connection with his men.

Lt. Teddy Evans and Cooke theodolite.

Life on *Terra Nova* was relaxed in the absence of Captain Scott. Silas recalled wild games of "pirate," where the occupants of one cabin would attack those of another cabin with buckets of water and mops. They had with them four dogs—two Eskimo dogs named Cook and Peary (descended from dogs Peary used on his North Pole expedition) and two white English Samoyeds, one of whom had given birth to two pups during the voyage. One of the pups, Oussa, died before they reached Cape Town, with the remaining three Samoyeds given away as pets upon their arrival in Christchurch.

On July 5, 1910, Frederick Hooper opened a hatch to discover smoke. Wilson grabbed a fire extinguisher and put the fire out before it did any serious damage. The cause was traced to a lamp, which had been placed on a table and fallen over. A hat belonging to Francis Davies, the ship's carpenter, was found at the scene, which earned him a write-up in the ship's log. Not something one would want Scott to see when he came aboard in Cape Town.

Frederick J. Hooper

Born in 1891, Frederic Hooper joined the Royal Navy and was appointed to *Terra Nova* as a steward, but was transferred to the Shore Party, where he became part of the ill-fated Motor Party.

Terra Nova's first landfall was Madeira, where Cherry-Garrard thoughtfully purchased a cask of Madeira, which proved a welcome change from the tepid water that was slopping around the ship's rusty water tanks.

Nicknames

Everyone had his own nickname, usually referring to position, character or physical abnormality:

Atkinson—"Atch"

Bowers—"Birdie"

Bruce—"Jumbo"

Campbell—"The Wicked Mate"

Cherry-Garrard—"Cherry" or "Chewwy"

Day—"Frog Face"

Debenham—"Deb"

Drake—"Franky"

Evans (Lt. Teddy)—"Skipper"

Gran—"Willie"

Levick—"Old Sport" or "Tofferino"

Lillie—"Lithley"

Nelson—"Marie"

Oates—"Titus" or "Soldier"

Pennell—"Penelope"

Ponting—"Ponto"

Priestley—"Ray"

Rennick—"Parny"

Scott—"The Owner"

Simpson—"Sunny Jim"

Taylor, Griffith—"Griff," "Skuagull," "Ram-Jatass" or "Keir Hardie"

Wilson—"Uncle Bill"

Wright—"Silas"

The high point of the voyage was the customary crossing-the-equator ceremony, which involved liberal quantities of vinegar, cayenne pepper, flour, soot, a pool made from sailcloth and cross-dressing. The ceremony was cut short by a fire in the lazarette, due to an overturned lantern, which was enthusiastically put out by the assembled Neptune inductees. This time it wasn't the carpenter's fault.

Back in London, Scott and Kathleen, along with Oriana Wilson and Lt. Evans's wife, Hilda, set sail from London on *Saxon*. As the voyage progressed, the chilly relations between Mrs. Scott and Mrs. Evans became glacial. Hilda Evans was still brooding over the fact that Robert Scott was in charge of an expedition that by rights should have been commanded by her husband, Teddy. Kathleen Scott, of course, felt the exact opposite and the two women made a point of avoiding each other, which wasn't easy on board a small ship.

Things were considerably jollier on *Terra Nova*, when on July 31, 1910, they made landfall on South Trinidad Island, a barren, volcanic rock with 200-foot-high cliffs, but a welcome diversion after their painfully slow plod through the equatorial doldrums. The island was rumoured to have been where pirates hid their treasure, and the crew was itching to get ashore to start the treasure hunt. Wilson was most anxious to get ashore. On his previous visit to the island on *Discovery*, he had been forced to leave all his specimens behind (read: dead wildlife), due to deteriorating weather conditions, and he was keen to get back to resume the slaughter.

Terra Nova anchored a mile offshore, with the scientists and crew—along with a sick seaman in need of some fresh air—landing on the island by whaleboat. Birdie Bowers and Silas were appointed bug hunters, even though they both loathed spiders.

After a day of picking flora and clubbing fauna, everyone gathered at the shore to compare the day's catch. Tryggve Gran marched down from the top of the island proudly carrying in his arms a large gannet. Fortunately for the bird, they already had enough gannets, so Gran's was reprieved and released to rejoin its now-depleted family.

I and Bowers first sneaked up to one of the sleeping beauties [gannets] and slipped a butterfly net over him which he promptly tore to pieces before we got him tight. After an animated discussion on ways and means we decided to stick a knife into his head as the best means of doing away with him. I then tied him on my back and was recounting the tale of his capture and death to the ornithologist and artist [Dr. Edward Wilson] when he came to life and had to be dispatched again.

—Wright, August 1910

The *Terra Nova* in West Bay seen from the crumbling hillside of South Trinidad Island.

So preoccupied were they with depopulating the island that no one noticed conditions had taken a turn for the worse and a vicious swell was now pounding the shore. *Terra Nova* sent up a rocket signalling the Shore Party to return to the ship post-haste, sending the whaleboat and two Norwegian "prams" [dinghies] to retrieve them.

The first two men swam out to the pram carrying a light line tied to a life buoy from which a thicker line was paid out from the whaleboat. The buoy was then pulled to shore by the light line so that we had the thick hawser (floating grass rope) with one end ashore and the other in the whaleboat. Unfortunately a series of heavy swells fouled the hawser on the rocks and it took the better part of an hour to disengage it. After that, it all went swimmingly: all one had to do was seize the proper moment, say once every two or more minutes and swim out to the whaleboat. The grass rope was for those that could not swim. Dr. [Edward] Atkinson and his patient were left ashore and all the cameras and scientific gear. The patient should not have been brought ashore, of course. The swell had not subsided overnight and it took half the crew and four hours before the two men and the gear were safely aboard. I think we were all very lucky. One could see at one time three shark fins cruising along the shore between the short stretch we had to swim to reach the whaleboat. Why is it that one's toes curl down (not up) when there are sharks about?

—Wright memoirs

The sick seaman and Dr. Atkinson were left on shore overnight. The seaman was rescued the next day, but the boat was tossed onto the rocks while going back for Atkinson. He ended up swimming for the boat, carrying Wilson's equipment—aneroid, watch, glasses, gun, and etc., all of which were much damaged.

Terra Nova sailed into Simons Bay, near Cape Town, at the tail end of a gale on August 17, 1910, where the ship was careened to fix the

Dr. Edward "Atch" Atkinson

Born in 1882, Dr. Edward Atkinson studied medicine at St Thomas's Hospital, London. After graduation, he joined the Royal Naval Hospital. He was appointed parasitologist and bacteriologist to the 1910 Scott Expedition.

numerous leaks. It was here that Scott joined the ship, with Wilson and the three women carrying on ahead by steamer for Melbourne, Australia, where Wilson would recruit the last of the scientific staff. Herbert Ponting also joined them in Cape Town with all his photographic equipment. Silas and the rest of the crew didn't see much of Ponting during the voyage from Cape Town to Melbourne, as Ponting suffered from seasickness and spent most of the time in his cabin.

After they left Cape Town on September 2, 1910, both the weather and the atmosphere aboard *Terra Nova* changed for the worse. To Lt. Evans's chagrin and despite his promise back in London, Scott had relieved him and assumed command of *Terra Nova* at Cape Town.

As captain, Scott enforced rigid naval discipline; games of "pirate" and rags in the mess deck were immediately stopped—Scott considered them to be dangerous to life and limb. That Evans had brought the ship this far without a single incident and had turned an eclectic group of scientists, officers and crew into a working vessel was ignored by Scott.

Herbert "Ponco" Ponting

Born in Salisbury, England, in 1870, Herbert Ponting's fascination with the American West drew him to California, where for a short period he was a miner. After taking up photography, he travelled to Japan and China, returning to sell his photographs to various publications. Ponting was the first person to take a cine camera to the Antarctic, releasing his cine footage in cinemas as "The Great White Silence."

Ponting had the reputation among the crew as a "Jonah," as things would always happen when he was around.

They had planned on landing at St. Paul Island, halfway between Cape Town and Tasmania, but heavy seas made the approach too risky, so they passed by—much to the relief of the local wildlife. Silas was the most disappointed, because he had hoped to test the island's hot springs for radioactivity.

Besides recruiting scientific staff, Wilson was sent ahead to Melbourne to try to change the Australian government's mind about the offer of £5,000 it had initially promised Scott and had since withdrawn. Wilson begged Prime Minister Andrew Fisher to honour his word, reminding him the Australian government had given money to Shackleton when he stopped in Australia on his way to Antarctica. Fisher replied that Shackleton "had come out there insufficiently equipped and unable to proceed further" and that they only helped him because he was stuck.

Scott eventually wrung £2,500 from the federal government and the other £2,500 from Samuel Horden, a department store mogul.

So they wallowed on, the ship leaking worse than ever before. Silas wrote on October 5, 1910:

The dry-docking of the ship [in Cape Town] seems to have started all the seams in the deck so that water simply pours in on the bunks below. As far as can be ascertained there are only three reasonably dry top bunks and of these, two were protected by a waterproof covering. Most of the lower bunks are wet as well and the weirdest places are now used as sleeping apartments.

The dogs were beginning to feel the cold, so Scott ordered them moved off the deck and into Silas's chemical lab where, to Silas's chagrin, they promptly smashed some of his delicate chemical apparatus.

Terra Nova reached Melbourne on October 12, where they were met by Wilson and the remaining scientific staff, including geologists Griffith Taylor and Frank Debenham. Geologist Raymond Priestley was recruited by Wilson in Australia, but joined the ship in New Zealand.

Raymond "Ray" Priestley

Born in Tewkesbury, England, on July 20, 1886, to Quaker parents, Raymond Priestley was educated at Tewkesbury Grammar School (where his father was headmaster) and Bristol University. He was a geologist on the

1907 Shackleton Expedition and a relative of writer Hilaire Belloc (1870–1953), who, among numerous other books, wrote *Cautionary Tales for Children*.

Priestley took the place of geologist Alan Thomson, who was to join the ship at Melbourne but came down with a lung condition at the last minute. As the more senior man and a member of Shackleton's previous expedition, Priestley took on the role of old Antarctic hand—sometimes to the irritation of his colleagues, who felt Priestley was coming along more for the ride than to actually do any geologising.

Frank "Deb" Debenham

Frank Debenham conducting a plane table survey, 1911.

Born in December 1883, in Bowral, New South Wales, Australia, Frank Debenham studied geology at Sydney University, under polar explorer Edgeworth David. Upon graduation, he was selected by Wilson to be one of the three geologists on the expedition. The only member born in Australia, Debenham often felt the others were down on those from the colonies.

Dr. Wilson met the ship with the news of his cool reception in Australia. Undeterred, Scott hustled off the ship to plunge into a series of cocktail parties and fundraising lectures, and it was while tossing shrimps on the barbie for a penny a plate that Scott got more bad news. A telegram arrived from Fridtjof Nansen, in London, with the news that Roald Amundsen had turned left instead of right when he sailed out of Norway and instead of hopping about on ice floes in the Arctic was now in Madeira, on his way to the Antarctic.

For the next few days, the local Melbourne telegraph office did booming business as cables flew back and forth, with Scott trying to get more details of Amundsen's plans. Even though it was known that Amundsen had requested copies of British Admiralty charts of the Ross Sea, Scott felt that if Amundsen was indeed going to make a run for the South Pole, it would be from the Weddell Sea, at the other side of the Antarctic continent. For now Scott's plans would remain unchanged.

Roald Amundsen

Born on July 16, 1872, in Norway, Roald Amundsen was inspired from an early age by polar explorers like Fridtjof Nansen and John Franklin. He spent his early years on sealing ships, eventually managing to secure a position on de Gerlache's 1897 *Belgica* Expedition that ended up being trapped in the ice and spending the first winter on the Antarctic continent.

In 1903 he led an expedition that successfully traversed the Northwest Passage in the tiny ship *Gjoa*, and it was during his time in the Arctic that Amundsen went "native," adopting the Inuit style of dress and becoming an expert in the use of dog teams.

Amundsen returned to Norway and immediately set about mounting an expedition to reach the North Pole. He even acquired a suitable vessel: the sturdy *Fram*, lent to him by his pal, fellow polar explorer Nansen. His plans were dashed in 1909 when Peary claimed to have reached the North Pole.

All pumped up and with nowhere to go, Amundsen turned his attention to the South Pole. But he dared not tell anyone of his plans, as Nansen surely would have taken his ship away from him and his patrons might have pulled their financial backing. Even his own crew didn't know about his change of plan until they were far down the English Channel and there was no turning back.

Back in London, the elite club of polar explorers who had agreed that Scott was next up to try for the South Pole were outraged. Amundsen's actions were considered underhanded, and definitely "not cricket." That Amundsen was a seasoned veteran of polar exploration raised the distinct possibility that what was rightfully British was going to be Norwegian. This latest development was most uncomfortable for Norwegian Tryggve Gran, who was already disliked by some of the more xenophobic of *Terra Nova*'s crew, and news of Amundsen's subterfuge didn't do anything to lift the chill around the wardroom table.

The ship buzzed with the news of Amundsen, and conspiracy theories: Was Nansen actually a traitor acting for Amundsen? Who was funding Amundsen?

Amundsen's *Fram*, Nansen's specially constructed, diesel-powered polar ship—127 feet long, 408 tons, it had more cargo-carrying capacity as it was not required to allocate space to carrying coal, as *Terra Nova* had to. The Fram sits in the *Fram* Museum in Norway.

This was the first information we had that his [Amundsen] plans for reaching the North Pole in Nansen's specially constructed ship, the Fram, had been abandoned, presumably because Peary had returned from his journey to the Pole. I think that we all felt that this change of plan was a bit offside; especially because it was not sent before he had reached Madeira.

For my part, my chief regret was that the great man [Amundsen] who first made the complete Northwest Passage of Canada should send such a curt message, apparently not followed by a letter, or any explanation. I wondered if he was not afraid that his Norwegian sovereign and the subscribing Norwegians might take steps to stop him and therefore he set off for Madeira before this happened. Not in the best of taste!

—Wright, November 7, 1910

Leaving the residents of Melbourne a few quid poorer, Scott set out across the Tasman Sea to New Zealand. Prior to departure, the crew had spent some time spiffing up *Terra Nova*—there was a fleet of Royal Navy ships in harbour, along with an admiral, who was due to inspect *Terra Nova*. Strangely it was the ship's cat that got the most attention.

"Nigger," the ship's cat, lived with the seamen in the ship's fo'c'sle and had her own personal hammock with blanket and even a tiny pillow for her head. The cat was solemnly inspected by the admiral and went through her paces to the satisfaction of the inspection party.

On departing the harbour, Lt. Evans decided to show the navy lads what experienced sailors they had become, which, according to Silas, was only courting disaster. The afterguard walked away with the halyards smartly—too smartly, causing the crew on the tail of the halyards to trip and leaving everyone piled in a heap and the sail only halfway up. All in full view of a fleet of dressed ships of the Royal Navy. This unfortunate display did nothing to improve Scott's gloomy demeanour.

With the exception of several albatrosses that had the misfortune to cross paths with the ship, the voyage across the Tasman Sea was uneventful.

In Lyttelton, the ship was dry-docked yet again to fix more leaks, leaving the scientists and crew to amuse themselves in Christchurch. (The leaks were located and fixed so that in future only fifteen minutes of pumping was necessary in each watch, instead of the usual one hour.)

The main Shore Party hut, which had been prefabricated back in London and stored in pieces aboard the ship, was erected ashore as both a dry run for when they landed in the Antarctic and as a way to bolster their funds, due to members of the public being charged a small fee to tour the hut.

As Scott had planned to ascend to the Polar Plateau by way of the Beardmore Glacier, which flowed to the ice barrier from a height of 10,000 feet, he felt it would be good to give some of the scientists experience on a real glacier. Scott dispatched Silas, Frank Debenham and Griff Taylor to the Tasman Glacier below Mount Cook, where they spent the night at the Malte Brun hut and, with a guide and an assortment of skis, climbed to the head of the glacier the next morning. Silas later wrote about the experience:

I don't remember who had the other ski, but I had one pair on the strength of my announcement that there could be no difference in operation of skis to a man used to skates and to Canadian snowshoes. Griff was brave enough to accept my offer to take him down standing behind me on the two "planks." We had no difficulty as it was a straight run down the top part of the glacier and no crevasses worthy of the name. So ended my first experience with ski.

Back in Lyttelton, the ship was out of drydock and settling deeper in the water. The Plimsoll line, which had been so carefully repainted higher on the hull before they left England, was by now out of sight below the waterline—probably due to the three motor sledges that had been loaded aboard, along with numerous drums of petrol. The ship was lightened by a few pounds when Scott removed chief engineer Edgar Riley from the vessel and sent him home to England. Scott was upset that Riley had the audacity to eat at the officers's table in the wardroom, even though, as an officer, that was technically his right.

George Simpson, whose non-ferrous coal was refused loading by Scott in Cardiff, was further aggrieved when Scott ordered Simpson's specially constructed meteorological hut unceremoniously dumped on the dock to make room for more fuel for the motor sledges. Birdie Bowers, who was in charge of stowing cargo below decks, was marking with a green band of paint the stores destined for Lt. Campbell's Eastern Party and those for the Main Shore Party. Silas and his companions on the Main Party, as well as those of Campbell's group, kept a close eye on this operation to ensure there was a fair division of stores, as everyone was well aware how severely limited their provisions were.

Bowers was also keeping an eye on the other members of the party, specifically the two Russians: Demetri Gerof, the dog driver, and Anton Omelchenko, who would look after the Siberian ponies. Bowers felt that foreigners had no place on what was a British expedition, and that the dog driver and groom should have been supplied from the British Empire— "even two Kasmiris would not have been out of place."[2]

Scott had dispatched Cecil Meares to Siberia to purchase both dogs and ponies, with the stipulation that he only purchase white ponies. From Shackleton's account of his 1907 expedition, it appeared the white-coated ponies had a better survival rate over those with darker coats. There is of course no scientific basis to this, and the majority of the ponies on Shackleton's expedition ended up being shot anyway.

Cecil H. Meares

Cecil Meares was born on Valentine's Day 1877, in Inistioge, Ireland. When he was one year old, his mother died and he went to live with his grand-

father. By the age of four, he had taught himself to read, and he advanced rapidly academically until he ended up in Cambridge, where he finished his education in preparation for entering the British Army. To his disappointment, he was rejected on medical grounds.

After failing in his chosen career, Meares knocked about the world: Spain, Italy, Ceylon (coffee planting), Vladivostock and Peking (now Beijing).

When the Boer War broke out, the army reconsidered, and

Meares making dog harnesses

accepted Meares into the Scottish Horse Regiment. Meares's battalion saw plenty of action, serving from 1901 to 1902. He was assigned many posts after South Africa, including Burma; Ceylon; Manchuria, Asia; and

Kamchatka, Russia, where he acquired a decent knowledge of Russian.

While in Siberia, Meares befriended Russians Demetri Gerof and Anton Omelchenko, hiring them on Scott's behalf to assist in the care of the dogs and ponies during the expedition.

Anton Lukich Omelchenko

Born on a farm in 1883 at Bat'ki, Ukraine, Anton Omelchenko learned how to handle horses as a boy; his short stature made him an ideal jockey. In 1909, while racing in Vladivostok, he met Cecil Meares and assisted him in purchasing the infamous Manchurian ponies. Although more reserved than fellow Russian Demetri Gerof, Anton was learning English from the other men, but not the English spoken in polite society.

Demetri Semenovich Gerof

Born in 1888 in Sakhalin, eastern Siberia, Demetri Gerof met Cecil Meares in Niko-layevsk, on the shores of the Volga River, when Meares he was there to purchase dogs for the expedition. Demetri was a great help to Meares when collecting dogs in the Amur River region .

Twenty-two- year-old Demetri Gerof (Dmitriy Girev) at Hut Point. When Glennynos, one of his dogs, lost his coat, Demetri made a rug for him and let him sleep in his tent every night.

William Bruce was to assist Meares in shipping the animals to New Zealand, and to rendezvous with *Terra Nova* in New Zealand. By coincidence, the ponies began their sea voyage in Vladivostok, the home port of *Kapitan Khlebnikov*. In a letter to his father on August 22, 1910, from Vladivostok, Meares wrote:

Lawrence Edward Grace Oates

Born on March 17, 1880, in London, England, and educated at Eton, Lawrence Oates, joined the 6th (Inniskilling) Dragoons and saw action during the Second Boer War, where he was badly wounded in the thigh, which left his left leg shorter than his right. He applied for a position on the 1910 expedition and was accepted by Scott, due to his knowledge of horses—and a £1,000 donation to the expedition.

I had a job shipping them at Vladivostok as it was pouring with rain and the mud was two feet deep ... at Kobe I had to transship the whole bunch and the German steamer was 24 hours late so I had to keep them in open lighters in a blazing sun which was very hard on them. Captain Scott's brother in law (W.M. Bruce) came out to help me. He is chief officer on a P&O steamer. Quite "one of the boys" but too "kid glovey" for this job.[3]

The ponies, along with the dogs, had been quarantined on Quail Island, in Lyttelton Harbour, waiting for *Terra Nova*'s arrival. Lawrence Oates, who had extensive experience with horses in the army, was appalled when he saw the state of the ponies, describing them: "with narrow chests," "knock-kneed" and a "bunch of old crocks." Scott, though, was pleased with the animals; they were all white-coated, as specified. Scott had reasoned that as it was mostly the white ponies that had survived Shackleton's 1907 expedition, surely they must be able to stand the cold climate better than the darker-haired ponies. Meares didn't have much to choose from when it came to white-haired ponies—the only white-coated ponies being basically on their last legs. Anton Omelchenko, who was present at their purchase in Mukden, Manchuria, said the seller of the ponies went away "with a 'plenty big smile' on his face."[4]

Oates and Francis Davies, the ship's carpenter, set about building stalls for nineteen ponies, which proved to be almost impossible due to the diminutive size of *Terra Nova* and the clutter they already had on board. But they persevered and eventually were able to shoe-horn fifteen ponies into tiny stalls in the ship's fo'c'sle, located over the seamen's quarters—most unfortunate for the seamen lodged below, as the decks leaked like a sieve. The remaining four ponies were housed in stalls on the main deck. Space was so tight that the only way to get to the ponies in the fo'c'sle was to climb through a skylight. Oates was most concerned about the suitability of these arrangements and wrote to his mother: "I only pray we won't have heavy weather going south, or there is bound to be trouble."

On taking stock of the pony fodder stowed aboard the ship, Oates informed Scott that it was substandard (cut too late, not enough seeds) and insufficient for their needs. It could have been Bowers who underestimated the amount and quality of hay ordered for the ponies. Regardless of whose fault it was, Scott refused to allocate money for more fodder, as he felt what they had was more than adequate. Oates couldn't bear the thought of the animals starving and paid for more fodder out of his own pocket. This was the first falling-out between Oates and Scott, but it would not be the last.

They were running out of space on *Terra Nova*. Drums of petrol were lashed to the deck, sacks of coal were squeezed into every crevice, and everyone was tripping over squabbling Siberian sledge dogs chained to the deck. Above the dogs, mutton carcasses dangled tantalisingly from the ratlines, with the delicious smell of butter and cheese wafting from the nearby lazarette.

There were no Greenland dogs available when Scott was provisioning *Terra Nova*. The argument has been made that Scott had no choice but to take Siberian dogs because Amundsen had made a deal with the Danish government to allocate him all available Greenland dogs for his trip to the North Pole (read: South Pole), although the Danish government has always denied this. Dr. A.P. Low, a director of the Geological Survey of Canada, apparently offered Scott Canadian sledge dogs, as well as his services as dog driver, but Scott turned him down.

While in Christchurch, Robert Scott, Bill Wilson, Teddy Evans and their respective wives spent time sightseeing and fundraising. During this time, relations between Kathleen Scott and Hilda Evans deteriorated further, coming to a head at a fundraising ball in a local hotel with a shouting match between the two, and according to Lawrence Oates, punches were thrown.

PO Taff Evans was also making good use of his time, enriching the local taverns and ladies of the evening, all of which came to an ignominious end when he staggered off the end of the dock and into the water prior to *Terra Nova* sailing for Port Chalmers, Dunedin, to take on coal. Scott was furious and formally removed Evans from the ship, threatening to send him home, but when Scott joined the ship a few days later in Port Chalmers, Taff Evans was at his side as though nothing had happened.

Having finally filled every possible square inch of space with coal, and before they sank at the dock, they sailed out of Port Chalmers on November 29, 1910, with sixty-two officers, crew and scientific staff, nineteen Manchurian ponies, thirty-one Siberian sledge dogs, two Canadian huskies, one cat, a guinea pig and a few rabbits.

The wives of Scott, Evans and Wilson left *Terra Nova* at the harbour heads and were ferried back to the dock on a steam tug. It was the last time Kathleen Scott and Oriana Wilson would see their husbands.

Dogs and cargo competing for space on *Terra Nova's* deck.

5. TO THE ICE

Every man is a damn fool for at least five minutes every day; wisdom consists in not exceeding the limit.
—Elbert Hubbard

December 14, 2008, Lyttelton, New Zealand

I'm standing on the dock, looking up at the icebreaker *Kapitan Khlebnikov*. She has all the appeal of a downtown parkade: streaks of rust are showing through the mustard yellow paint on her superstructure, and she appears tired. But she looks solid and presumably has made this trip dozens of times before.

A couple of Russian crewmen are dangling from a scaffold, unenthusiastically applying blotches of blue paint to the lower hull of the ship in places that make me wonder if a few large slabs of ice were hurled against the hull in a recent gale.

Negotiating the rickety gangplank and stepping onto Khlebnikov's deck, I'm careful where I put my feet. This is a working icebreaker after all, and an unfamiliar ship can be a treacherous place, especially at night and in a heavy sea, but not half as treacherous as it was on *Terra Nova* …

Have just finished setting sail for a slight breeze which can hardly last, and it was by no means an easy job to dodge about between motor sledges and ponies and coal bags and dogs—chiefly the latter as the price for stepping on a dog is a bite, besides the fact they are not the tidiest animals at any time.
—Wright, south of Port Chalmers, New Zealand,
November 29, 1910

Kapitan Khlebnikov 122.5 metres long, 12,2288 tons. Six diesels producing 24, 120 hp.

* * *

On *Terra Nova*, by November 30, New Zealand was well over the horizon, with a fresh breeze kicking up waves that were drenching the unfortunate seasick ponies and dogs on deck. The forecast was for gale-force winds, which didn't concern any of the crew, as they'd already weathered a few gales on the trip. But in the early hours of the morning of December 1, 1910, at 50 degrees south, they sailed into a ferocious gale.

Silas was "snotty of the watch" when the wind picked up and the seas began to build. He noticed the water level rising below the engine room. Figuring it was just water leaking through from the decks above, as it invariably did during even a light drizzle, he wasn't too concerned. Just to be sure, Silas checked that the fastenings on the deck hatches and the canvas on the wooden grid over the main hatch were secure, but the water in the engine room was still rising. It wasn't a good sign, and he let the officer of the watch know the ship appeared to have sprung a rather serious leak.

By now winds had built to hurricane force and huge seas were by now sweeping right over the ship, her bulwarks trapping the water, weighing the already overloaded ship down to the point where less of her was above the water than below. The crew set to chopping away the bulwarks, assisted by subsequent pounding seas, which conveniently removed the remaining bulwarks and anything else that wasn't securely lashed down, like drums of petrol, sending them careening across the deck, smashing everything in their path. Scott ordered them jettisoned, rather than risk

Osman, who survived near-drowning on the voyage south and went on to save his dog team when they fell down a crevasse on a depot-laying party.

life and limb in an attempt to restow them. Fortunately, they were able to save a few drums, for without petrol, Scott's precious motor sledges would be useless. (As it turned out, they were about as useful in the Antarctic as riding lawn mowers.)

Besides the crew, the sledge dogs were having a terrible time, chained to the open decks, soaked and shivering. Osman, the toughest, orneriest dog of the pack, was hit by a massive wave that snapped his chain and washed him overboard. He would have surely drowned but was grabbed by a sailor and hauled back aboard as he floated past on the next wave. This chastening experience led to his miraculous conversion to friendliness towards the crew for the rest of the trip.

Conditions were far worse for the Siberian ponies, who were being flung about their cramped stables in the fo'c'sle and, unlike the dogs, didn't have the luxury of taking shelter below decks. Lawrence Oates and Dr. Atkinson attempted to calm them, as the ponies were vital to the success of the expedition and they needed to keep them alive at all costs. However, if the ponies had even the slightest idea of what was waiting for them at their destination, they would have chewed through their stalls and leapt overboard, joining various other animals at the bottom of the ocean who had had the misfortune to sign on as crew aboard *Terra Nova*. The ship's rabbit had been squashed under a pony hoof, and the ship's guinea pig, who had set up house in an empty cigar box, met an unfortunate end when a seaman on cleaning detail tossed the box overboard.

Herbert Ponting had fallen and injured his leg, but that was the least of his problems. His photo lab was flooded by sea water pouring through a mushroom ventilator on the ceiling and he was floundering about his lab, desperately trying to bail out water that was trapped in the cabin by the sill on the threshold. Wrote Silas: "It was too bad Ponting was out of action, as cinematic footage of the crew hanging off the pumps in a full gale would have made most splendid viewing."

All hands were on deck manning the hand pump, as the engine-driven pump was fighting a losing battle against the rising water inside the ship. By dawn, after working intermittently through the night, the hand pump finally clogged for the last time.

The hand pump had been in constant use since the ship left England, but the pump's intake clogged constantly, leaving them with their only backup—the decrepit steam pump attached to the propeller driveshaft, which could only be used when the boilers were fired and the engines were engaged.

In her previous life as a whaler, *Terra Nova*'s holds contained whale oil and blubber. On passing into Captain Scott's hands, the holds were supposedly scrubbed clean, but now sea water was pouring into them, creating a thick soup of coal dust and congealed blubber, clogging the pump's intake. Although this had been a constant issue, nothing was done to rectify the problem when *Terra Nova* was dry-docked in South Africa or New Zealand.

The water had by now risen to the level of the stoke holds, and the boiler was shut down to prevent the ship from being blown to smithereens. This meant the backup steam pump was out of service and *Terra Nova* was helpless, battered by 30-foot-high waves and taking on water from sprung planks in her hull and water streaming in from the gaping holes in her decking. The wind was logged as "force 10 rising to force 12." (Force 10 is a gale blowing 60 miles per hour. Force 12 is a hurricane blowing 90 mph.)

The hand pump being manned during the gale.

Captain Scott had, of course, much the worst time, but never showed it so far as I am aware. He had to face up to the possibility that his expedition and all his hopes were in jeopardy and this when we had only left New Zealand.

—Wright memoirs

Teddy Evans called for all hands to form a bucket brigade, involving a lift of more than 30 feet from the hold to the deck. Silas commented that those on deck were the luckiest. Anyone at the lower end of the chain down in the engine room was soaked in sweat, fetid bilge water, congealed coal dust, rancid blubber and, occasionally, vomit from those above them. Raymond Priestley, who would get seasick in a bathtub, thoughtfully took the end of the chain closest to the lee rail so he wasn't too much of an inconvenience to others when he had to throw up.

> It was a weird night's work with the howling gale and the darkness
> and the immense sea running over the ship every few minutes, and
> no engines and no sail, and we all in the engine room as black as
> ink with engine room oil and bilge water, singing shanties as we
> passed up slopping buckets full of bilge, each man above slopping
> a little over the heads of all of us below him wet through the skin,
> so much so that some of the party worked altogether naked like a
> Chinese coolie—and the rush of the wave backwards and forwards
> at the bottom grew hourly less in the dim light of a couple of
> engine room oil lamps whose light just made the darkness visible.
> The ship all the time rolling like a sodden, lifeless log, her lee
> gunwale under water every time.
> —Edward Wilson, December 3, 1910

Attention was briefly diverted from the rising water in the bilges when smoke was seen rising from the after hold, where coal was stored. It was immediately assumed the coal had caught fire and the ship was truly done for. Thankfully, it turned out it was just steam from water having risen to the level of the hot coal and they could turn their attention back to bailing out the ship.

The bucket brigade had slowed the rise of water in the hold, but the men on the chain were getting exhausted. They had to find a way to re-start the hand pump. But the hand pump's inlet was in the one spot in the hold that was only accessible through a hatch on deck, which they didn't dare open as it would have only taken one large wave down the hatch to finish off the ship. The only other way to get at the inlet was by cutting a hole in the engine room's steel bulkhead. The odds of them getting through the solid steel plate before the ship sank were poor, but—submerged to their necks in sea water—Lt. Teddy Evans and chief stoker

William Lashly began pounding on the bulkhead with hammers and wood chisels. (Being a wooden ship, there was little in their tool chest in the way of metal-cutting devices.)

While Evans and Lashly attacked the bulkhead, the bucket brigade carried on, although they had barely made a dent in the level of the water and every roll brought more water pouring through the decks. Each team had two hours on the chain and two hours off. Silas stayed on deck during his off time as the cabins were a mess—water pouring in from the decks above had left everything either soaked or floating.

The gale finally eased to the point where they gained on the water in the hold, bringing it below the stoke hatches to the extent the furnaces could be relit. By the time they got the boilers up to steam and the engine restarted, Teddy Evans was able to wriggle through the small hole they'd punched in the bulkhead and clear the hand-pump intake. Twenty-two hours after the bucket brigade was formed, both the hand pump and engine pumps were restarted and the holds were pumped dry. *Terra Nova* and her crew, although a bit soggy, had survived.

Looking back over this event, I must confess that I enjoyed this period. Quite literally, we were all in the same boat. The two-hour stints did not seem a long one and if the ship sank, well that was that. We would go down with good friends together and we were all doing our best to stay alive. I was interested, not for the first time, to note we were always cheerful and passed the buckets up and down to sea shanties and any scraps of doggerel known to more than a single member of the team.

—Wright memoirs

It is really rather fun at times going aloft in the blackness at 2 AM to reef sails or furl the same. If there is a big swell on and one is perched in the t'galant yards, every roll moves one through a distance of 70 feet or more. With a dark night, one can see big patches of phosphorescence two or three hundred yards away from the ship, appearing and disappearing as a wave intervenes and hides them from sight.

Then there are other times when we are scudding along almost under bare poles and the air is filled with spray or rain or hail driven along by the force of a 70 mile per hour wind, when one can't see the man four feet away on the yard, or hear the orders for the flapping of the sails and the screeching of the wind and when every few minutes one has to warm one's fingers again by banging them on the sails.

—Wright, October 25, 1910

Furling the mainsail in the pack ice. Silas never completely figured out which line did what, and many times in the pitch-dark he'd have difficulty finding a "particular rope in response to a particular order."

Hunting on *Terra Nova* was a way the crew would pass the time when they weren't on watch. As they progressed south, the ornithological body count was mounting: gannets, petrels, frigate birds, terns, albatrosses, everything but budgies were cheerfully shot out of the sky by the crew.

"If it moves, shoot it; if it doesn't, stuff it," was on the family crest of most British explorers of the time. The planet is littered with the bones of local wildlife butchered either for dinner, curiosity, to further science or a desire to hang something large and hairy on the blank wall space next to the portrait of great-uncle Ponce in the drawing-room of the family estate in Little-Puddle-on-Marsh.

Terra Nova left New Zealand with very little fresh water, as many of the water tanks were used to stow pony fodder. This meant no water for washing and after a few days out, everyone began to smell a bit ripe. Wrote Silas:

Another result of the shortage of water is the lack of something decent to drink. One does pall of champagne, beer and ginger ale in the course of time. Indeed I can think of nothing more calculated to turn a man a rabid T.T. [teetotaller] than a voyage on the Terra Nova R.Y.S.

Infrequent baths were taken "Fijian style" in the engine room, with hot water supplied by the engineer dropping a red-hot fire bar in a bucket of water.

When *Terra Nova* reached the pack ice, everyone eagerly awaited Silas's sage pronouncement as to its condition. His surveying background had taken him to Canada's Far North, but he had never seen polar ice, let alone an iceberg, nor had he even attended a single lecture on glaciers, for that matter. But, being the master of improvisation, he became an instant expert and supervised the process of extracting fresh water from icebergs.

When the temperature of the salty ice rises to a certain point, a salty solution is formed that slowly drips away, leaving fresh ice behind (that is purged of salt content). The longer the block of ice is exposed to this higher temperature (but still below the freezing point), the fresher the water obtained.

Everyone crowded the deck as *Terra Nova* entered the pack ice

The novelty of navigating the pack ice soon wore off for the crew, who turned their attention to more interesting pursuits, like shooting crabeater seals—which were sitting ducks as they were naturally curious and had no fear of humans.

Terra Nova carried enough weapons and ammunition to equip a small army, and anything that was unlucky enough to be in her path was met with a hail of bullets.

After they crossed the Antarctic Circle on December 10, 1912, the crew of *Terra Nova* encountered their first penguins, and, naturally, immediately tried to kill them, but the penguins were some distance away and the crew gave up after expending more than twenty cartridges. The next day, *Terra Nova* was tied up to an ice floe and the crew were able to get out on the ice and close in on the wildlife. Ponting took the opportunity to roam the ice with his camera, dressed in a long fur coat and white hat, which, according to Debenham, made him look exactly like an old woman. Fortunately, the crew weren't shooting old women...

We sighted four crabeater seals and a lot of other ones and steered towards them. At about 200 yards off, the battery (two rifles, my Mauser pistol and a revolver) opened fire and secured the whole four for an expenditure of fifty cartridges. They were got to the ship by hauling with a cable the whole floe up to the ship. While Evans and some of the others were securing the cable to the floe, an Adélie penguin came up to say good day, and on being knocked down with an oar, got up and wanted to fight Evans, but on being knocked down again dived into the sea, turning up later to give a derisive squawk.

—Wright, December 11, 1910

As *Terra Nova* ventured deeper into the ice pack, their progress slowed and in many cases stopped completely. Numerous times they'd have to backtrack to get out of an open-water lead that ended up in a dead end of impenetrable ice.

We have just made it through a piece of open water and will soon strike more heavy pack—in fact, have just struck a floe. It is wonderful how the old tub stands the butting into the floes. If anything, she leaks less than on leaving New Zealand. The heavy floes we break by climbing on top and crushing pieces off. The smaller by cracking

across; most floes however we shove out of the way and that is why even in thin pack
to make any headway the pack must be reasonably open.

—Wright, December 20, 1910

During the times when the ship was stopped, the crew piled off the ship in search of sport. However, vast amounts of ammunition were expended on penguins to little or no effect. A penguin could easily take a dozen bullets and still be able to waddle into the water, whereupon the bird no doubt sank quickly due to a high lead content. Before they exhausted their ammunition supplies, Dr. Wilson devised an efficient killing method called "pithing," which involved running after the penguin, grabbing it, pushing a long needle through the back of the penguin's head and spinning it around in the bird's brain, killing it in twenty to thirty seconds.

With *Terra Nova* at a virtual standstill in the pack ice, Silas and those who weren't required to pump out the ship took the opportunity to wander about on the ice floes, stretching their legs and practising their skiing and seal-shooting skills. It was common knowledge among the crew that Scott was compiling a list of who would be assigned what task once they made landfall, and accordingly everyone was keen to show off their prowess on skis because it was assumed (erroneously, as it turned out) those with the best Nordic skills would be picked for a coveted spot on the party that would make the final push to the South Pole.

While men and dogs could wander around on the ice floes, the ponies on *Terra Nova* were still confined to their stables. The lack of activity was causing them serious harm, and Oates was anxious they reach land as soon as possible. They'd already lost two ponies, and if they were delayed any further, they would surely lose more. As Scott's plans for reaching the Pole relied on the ponies, to lose two was bad. To lose a dozen would be a disaster.

It was in the pack ice where the sledge dogs first encountered penguins and vice versa. The normally docile penguins took exception to their incessant barking, and the dogs naturally took exception to the penguins. On occasions when *Terra Nova* was stuck in the pack ice and the dogs were allowed out for a bit of exercise, they would invariably take off after a flock of penguins, who would stand there, daring the dogs to take them on, then diving off the ice floe at the last possible second. Fortunately, the dogs were always stopped before they plunged into the ocean

Oates with ponies on *Terra Nova*. Notice the chewed wood on the stable door.

after the penguins. Silas thought that the penguins were fascinated by the dogs because they had never seen an animal with four legs before.

Christmas Day was celebrated in *Terra Nova*'s cramped wardroom, with the crew tucking into traditional Christmas fare such as roast frigate bird, barbecued seal steaks and sautéed penguin lips, while the diners toasted their toes on Atkinson's newly invented seal-blubber stove.

Finally, on December 30, they cleared the pack ice and entered the open water of the Ross Sea. It was now daylight twenty-four hours a day and for those on lookout, snow blindness was becoming a problem. As enough dark glasses for the entire crew had inexplicably been left off the supply list, Silas drew on his experience improvising in Northern Canada and put together sets of cardboard glasses with small slits cut into them, which proved remarkably effective.

Due to their proximity to the Magnetic South Pole, the binnacle compass was worse than useless. Not only were they unsure of their precise position, but another gale blew up and the ship was back to rolling in steep, choppy seas, requiring the crew to spend the last day of 1910 manning the pumps. Scott eventually ordered the ship to heave to in the lee of the ice pack, although more for conserving coal than for making conditions easier for the crew, as they would need every lump of coal for the planned survey of the coastline.

Silas's homemade snow goggles were crude, but proved remarkably effective.

That evening, they sighted the Antarctic continent:

At 10:30 PM, yesterday, everyone arose to take a look at the Admiralty Range. Mount Sabine (10,000 feet) shows up magnificently with the sun shining on it. The higher peaks stick out in jagged points too steep to hold the snow and the lower slopes are totally covered in an ice or snowcap. In places, too, one can see where the ice cap drops sheer over a cliff face thousands of feet high and apparently straight into the sea.

—Wright, January 1, 1911

On *Terra Nova*, Wilson also had whales on his mind, having borrowed a small whale gun from a Scottish whaling company, in the hopes of harpooning some whales for their meat and blubber. Upon finally sighting a couple of whales, Wilson brought out his whale gun, and he and Atkinson took a couple of shots with it. The first was for sighting purposes and the gun performed well, except for a rather nasty recoil. The second shot was a disaster, with the recoil slamming into Atkinson's jaw and the harpoon disappearing, because they had forgotten to tie a line to it. Thus ended Wilson's whaling venture.

The smoke from *Terra Nova*'s funnel was really foul. The crew were still burning New Zealand Westport coal, and as they had been using the engine almost constantly since entering the pack ice, the rigging was coated in a greasy black soot.

Now that they were in calmer seas and close to their destination, everyone got busy writing letters home. Special "Victoria Land" stamps were issued to the crew, but most people preferred to put the stamps inside an envelope, rather than on them, where they would be—be as Griffith Taylor put it—"exposed to the tender mercies of the post offices of the world."

January 3, 1911: *Terra Nova* arrived off Cape Crozier, which fortunately was free of fast ice. Scott's plan was to set up their base at Cape Crozier, on the recommendation of Wilson, who had been in the area on the 1901 Discovery Expedition. Cape Crozier had easy access to the Great Ice Barrier, which would be a distinct advantage when it came to the polar journey the following spring. Wilson, Scott, Victor Campbell, Cherry-Garrard, Oates and Griffith Taylor set out on the whaleboat to scout landing places. Cruising past the towering basalt column cliffs, they were chuckling over what would happen to their little boat if the cliff gave way when a section of cliff promptly did just that, almost swamping the whaleboat. They beat a hasty retreat back to *Terra Nova*, which was now being pushed close to the cliffs by pack ice. They barely made it out of the area before the swells dashed the ship against the rocks. To effect a landing here was impossible, and Cape Crozier was abandoned as a potential campsite.

   Terra Nova steamed back around Ross Island, towards Cape Evans, passing the spot where Ernest Shackleton's 1907 expedition hut still stands—Cape Royds.

December 23, 2008, off Cape Royds

At Cape Royds, I get my first close-up view of Ross Island, which has all the charm of the moon's backside. The island is made up of black volcanic basalt rock outcroppings and gravel moraines left behind by the numerous glaciers methodically grinding the island into dust. What few snow-free areas exist are only snow-free because hurricane-force winds have scoured them bare.

   Shackleton's hut looks remarkably well restored from the outside. Numerous empty packing crates and dog houses are stacked up against the wall, giving it the air of a place that has seen a lot of use over the years. Entering the hut from a tiny door and passing through an annex, inhaling the musty smell of grease and leather. Bunks are lined up against walls and old worn socks hang from clotheslines strung from the ceiling. At the far wall is a stove, which obviously was the central gathering place. Jars and tins of canned plums, peaches, sultanas, are neatly stacked up on the walls—supplies Silas and Griffith Taylor never got around to nicking, no doubt. I recognise some of the products they helped themselves to: canned peaches, cocoa, canned plums, apricots … If there weren't others around, I'd open a can of peaches to see if what's inside is still edible. It must be genetic.

Dog houses outside Shackleton's hut at Cape Royds.

Terra Nova crept back along the coast of Ross Island, and on January 4, 1911, they arrived at the ice shelf off Cape Evans. Overlooked by the very active Mount Erebus volcano, Cape Evans (originally named The Skuary, but renamed by Scott, after Lt. Taff, as a thank you for being with him on the 1901–04 Discovery Expedition) was a barren place. Nothing grows here, except for some lichen desperately clinging to rocks far above the beach, which was just a thin strip of pebbles competing with patches of snow that stubbornly refused to melt. This was to be their home for the next two winters.

Leftover provisions at the Shackelton corner store.

PART II

1911 – 1912

THE FIRST INLAND EXPEDITIONS AND THE JOURNEY TO THE SOUTH POLE

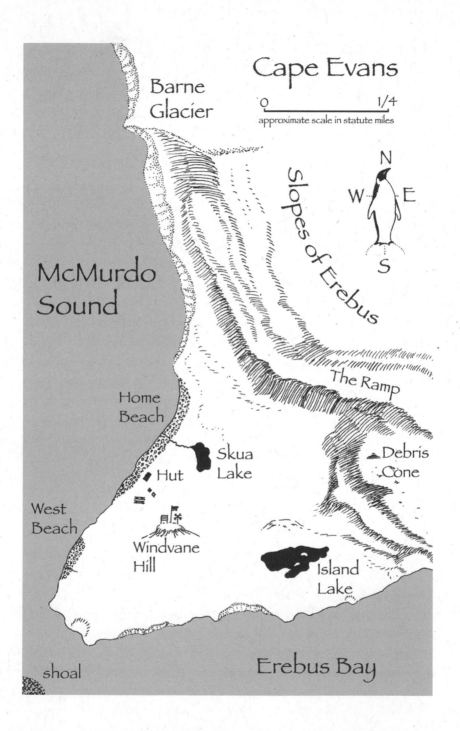

Cape Evans

Barne Glacier

0   1/4
approximate scale in statute miles

N
W   E
S

Slopes of Erebus

McMurdo Sound

The Ramp

Home Beach

Skua Lake

Debris Cone

Hut

West Beach

Windvane Hill

Island Lake

shoal

Erebus Bay

6. ARRIVAL, 1911

Can't say I've had a good night on this trip yet.

—Frank Debenham

December 24, 2008, Cape Evans

It's a short walk from the beach to the hut. Pretty much all the external clutter I remember from photographs has gone—the exception being the latrines, which are still standing, probably because they face the ocean and the hut shelters them from the destructive southerly winds.

The wind has picked up and I'm anxious to get inside. Once I finally get the door open, I step inside the Bowers annex, which both protects the main entrance and connects to the stables located at the ocean side of the hut. I pause. The first thing I notice is the smell. It's unlike anything I've encountered before—a mixture of leather, grease, saddle soap, soot and sweat. Griffith Taylor's bicycle, which looks as though it's been trampled by an elephant seal, hangs just inside the door. The smell of oats and pony shit wafting up the passage indicates the stables are still in one piece.

I pull the rope latch on the battered wooden door leading to the main hut. Opening the door feels as though I'm opening a tomb. It's dark and silent beyond the door. Stepping inside, I pause again, letting my eyes become accustomed to the gloom. It's so quiet that even the sound of the wind outside is muted to a muffled whisper and my footsteps on the wooden floor sound deadened. It's bigger than I had imagined, with a dim light filtering in from two small windows that allow me to just make out objects in the room. The mess table, the cookstove, heating stove, clothing piled up on bunks, dog and pony harnesses hung up on hooks ... everything gives the hut the feel of still being lived in. I'm not one who believes in ghosts, but I can feel more than one presence in the room with me. I didn't expect that, but The *Terra Nova* hut at Cape Evans. Latrines on the right, Windva whoever they are, I don't feel any malevolence; if anything, I feel they're happy to see someone. Are they the ghosts of Robert Scott, Birdie Bowers, Taff Evans, Edward Wilson and Lawrence Oates, trapped for eternity in this tiny hut? For some reason I don't feel there are five spirits in the hut and I don't think Silas is among them. There would be no reason for him to want to be here. I move past the well-worn mess table, made famous by Ponting's photograph of the midwinter day celebration. On my left are "the tenements," the bunks where Cherry-Garrard, Bowers, Oates and Atkinson slept, and they look like they were slept in just last night.

On my right is the cubicle occupied by great-uncle Griffith Taylor and Frank Debenham. The cubicle is dark and seems somehow detached from the rest of the room. Perhaps that explains why Debenham felt a bit ostracized by the others that first winter. Griff wouldn't have cared less and probably preferred his solitude. Finally, what I've travelled halfway around the world to see: I reach the far corner where Silas and George Simpson had their bunks—next to Simpson's meteorological lab. Silas slept on the top bunk and Simpson on the bottom. A greasy caribou-hide sleeping bag sits on Silas's bunk, with a grease-impregnated pair of pants draped over the post. The bunk appears short and Granddad was anything but short; he must have had to curl up in the fetal position to sleep. I notice his bunk is right next to the coal fire, so Silas must have been the warmest in the cabin.

Ponting's darkroom is at the end of the hut and, appropriately, is pitch-dark inside. By flashlight you can still see bottles of chemicals, developing trays and the pegboard he used when assembling the rough cut of his cine film. In the other corner and next to the darkroom is Scott's cubicle. The chart table is still there, but instead of charts and his journals, a stuffed emperor penguin lies on the table. For the first time I am able to put into context all the old photos I grew up with. I had no idea Silas's bunk was so close to Scott's cubicle. I had no idea the galley was so big, and I certainly didn't expect the hut to feel so welcoming and cozy. I'd like to stay longer, but I want to go outside to walk up Windvane Hill, where Silas and Simpson kept a lot of their meteorological instruments. It takes just a few minutes to climb the hill, but with each step, the wind gets stronger. My fingers are freezing inside my gloves, and I wish I'd brought my hat because my ears are already frozen. This was after only a few minutes on the hill. Imagine being here three years ... The remains of various meteorological stations dot the hill, and it's incredible they've survived almost a century of being sandblasted from the constant wind off the Barrier.

The occasional dog skeleton can be seen around the hut, two of them still chained to the hut with collars around their necks. Presumably they were abandoned by Shackleton's Ross Sea Party, who were stranded in the hut in the winter of 1917, during Shackleton's disastrous *Endurance* Expedition—but then what Shackleton expedition wasn't disastrous?

* * *

Stepping back almost a century in time. Photo by Peter McCarthy, grandson of Mortimer McCarthy, crew member aboard Terra Nova.

In January 1911, *Terra Nova* had tied up to the edge of the fast ice, which that year extended out from shore only a quarter-mile, making it an excellent deep-water dock. If the ice had been out 12 miles from shore or more, the way it was in 2008, the crew would never have been able to get all their stores and provisions to land before winter set in. As it was, emergency rations, tents and assorted scientific instruments were unloaded first, as there was always the threat of a sudden gale blowing the pack ice into the bay, forcing the ship to leave at a moment's notice.

Next off were the dogs, squabbling among themselves and anxious to continue their feud with the penguins. The Adélie penguins quickly obliged, parading up and down in front of a pack of dogs who couldn't be restrained any longer and broke loose from the wire they were tethered to, pouncing on the one penguin who couldn't scuttle out of the way fast enough and disappeared under a snarling mass of teeth and fur. No matter

The *Terra Nova* hut at Cape Evans. Latrines on the right, Windvane Hill in the background.

how much they yelled, beat and cursed the dogs, the men couldn't pull them off their prize until there was nothing left of the miserable bird except feathers—an event that was to repeat itself as more penguins turned up to see what the commotion was all about.

Silas complained that time which should have been directed to unloading the ship was taken up with trying to prevent the penguins from committing "suicide by dog"—with the enthusiastic assistance of the dogs.

The penguins are fool birds, some thirty or so to date have been killed by the dogs for wanting to fight them. The death of one seems to have no deterrent effect on the others. [Cecil] Meares got mixed up with his dog team yesterday when they rushed after the penguins.

—Wright, January 5, 1911

It wasn't just penguins that would drive the dogs wild. Seals had a terrible sense of timing and would pop up from a blowhole in the ice directly in front of a dog team. In the ensuing melee, it would be all the dog driver could do to prevent the dogs from disappearing down the blowhole after the seal.

After the dogs were separated from what was left of the penguins, they were bullied into their harnesses and hooked up to sledges for hauling supplies from the ship to the beach. As hardly anyone had any experience with dog teams, all were instructed by Meares and Demetri Gerof, the Russian dog driver. "Ki Ki" meant "go right," "Chui" meant "go left," and "Eshte" meant "lie down"—the rest were Russian swear words.

Wilson became quite fond of the dogs, with Mukaka being his favourite. Mukaka was paired with Nugis, a fat little dog who had a reputation of being greedy and lazy. On a march, whenever Mukaka saw that Nugis wasn't pulling his weight, he leapt over his traces, bit him and jumped back to his own position before Nugis knew who'd bitten him.

Next off the ship came the ponies, whom Oates would coax into a box on the deck that was lowered over the side and onto the ice by means of ropes and pulleys attached to the boom. After six weeks jammed into their tiny stalls, the ponies were delighted to be free of their prisons, kicking up their heels and rolling about in the snow.

Four hours after they had arrived, they had all the dogs and ponies off the ship, along with tents and emergency rations, and by midnight most of the lumber for hut construction was also ashore. Everyone was putting in long hours because there was the distinct possibility the condition of the ice between the ship and the beach could deteriorate in the warm summer conditions. It was light 24 hours of the day, which made it easy to work round the clock, but already Atkinson, Henry Rennick and William Bruce were down with snow blindness.

By 6 PM the next day, the frames for the hut were up and two of the motor sledges had been unloaded and were performing well, pulling to shore sledges loaded with more than 3,000 pounds of supplies. Although Bernard Day had pointed out to Scott that the wooden rollers the tracks ran on would probably not last long and would require constant repair, there was no reason to think the tractors wouldn't be perfect for the Antarctic—although the loss of so many petrol containers overboard during the New Zealand gale meant the sledges would have a limited range.

Terra Nova tied up to the ice sheet at Cape Evans.

January 8, 1911: Debenham and Silas were sent to the hut to get ponies and, on the way, noticed cracks in the ice in several places, indicating the ice had become unstable. They hurried back to warn Scott, but he was confident the ice was sound, just a little thin in small patches.

Shortly after, Day was in the process of unloading the third and final motor sledge. Attached to lines held by men on the ice and suspended from a boom, it was swung out from the ship and gently lowered to the ice surface. As its back end landed, the ice cracked ominously. The tractor lurched and broke through the ice, with those that were hanging on to the lines barely able to detach themselves from the tractor before it sank in 60 fathoms. Within minutes of the tractor's disappearance, Raymond Priestley fell through the ice and sank out of sight. Fortunately he surfaced at the hole and was hauled out, soggy and freezing—to the secret satisfaction of Debenham, whose nose was out of joint over Priestley's attitude towards the other members, and who went on to write that Priestley was "rather hectoring to the minor members and just a shade toadying to the major members."[1]

Forced to admit the ice was rotten, Scott ordered the ice anchors hauled in and prepared to move the ship a short distance north, where the ice was thicker, but not before Silas, returning to the ship pulling an empty sledge, was met by an agitated Ponting, who was racing for the shore dragging a sledge loaded with camera gear. "You're wanted at the

Bernard Day

Born in 1884, in Wymondham, England, Bernard Day was a mechanic with the Arrol-Johnston Motor Car Company before joining the 1907 Shackleton Expedition. He was in charge of the motor sledges on Scott's expedition, but with the demise of the motor sledges, he went home after the first year.

ship!" he gasped as he galloped past. Silas arrived at the ship to hear of an attack on Ponting and the dogs by a pod of nine killer whales.

The whales had been cruising off the ice, diving and raising their heads out of the water. No one noticed that they had taken an unhealthy interest in two sledge dogs tied to a wire. Anxious to capture the whales on film, Ponting arrived with his camera gear at the moment a whale heaved up beneath the floe, shattering it into pieces, and climbed up on the ice, all teeth and appetite. Ponting and the dogs barely made it back to solid ice with their hides intact.

Whales, having never encountered humans or dogs, naturally assumed things wandering about on the ice were just large penguins.

Silas and George "Sunny Jim" Simpson, the meteorologist, began constructing an ice cave, where they could carry out their observations on magnetic variations.

As the hut that was supposed to be used for that purpose had been jettisoned on the dock in Dunedin, New Zealand, by Scott, they had to chip away at the ice for four days with nothing more than ice axes to hollow out a space large enough to hold two people and the required instruments. The idea was to have a place free from sudden temperature variations. It worked for the first year, but a year of salt spray soon took its toll on the wires and instruments. (Later, a small wooden hut was constructed and the equipment moved inside out of the elements.)

George "Sunny Jim" Simpson

Born in 1878 and educated at Owens College, Manchester, George Simpson joined the British Meteorological Office after graduation, and he eventually joined the Indian Meteorological Service. In 1909, Scott hired him as the expedition's meteorologist. He loved an argument and would often start a sentence with: "You are completely wrong in all you say." As Silas recalled, he was an expert on a number of subjects and would usually win the argument.

Sunny Jim on the phone to Silas, who was outside measuring occultations, and cursing the stars when they refused to line up.

Unloading a motor sledge. It's unknown if this was the sledge that disappeared through the ice.

Scott advised Silas he felt he was spending too much time assisting Sunny Jim with his "troubles." Silas wasn't sure if that was Scott's opinion, or that of Wilson (the chief of the scientific staff), because the order came from Wilson. But Silas was happy to comply, as he didn't like "hanging around meteorological work."

Ponting had been enthusiastically photographing activities in the area surrounding the hut—careful to avoid ice floes—and was always recruiting members to pose in his pictures, to give scale to his landscapes. This became known by the reluctant models as to "go Ponting" or "to Pont."

Ponting spent a lot of time at the Cape Evans Adélie penguin rookery a few miles along the coast, photographing the antics of the penguins. The emperor penguin rookery was situated across the island at Cape Crozier, with the emperors more reserved than the gossipy, curious Adélie.

The emperor penguin lays a single egg in the middle of winter when temperatures can dip below minus 60°F. Huddled together, the birds keep their eggs on their feet to keep them from freezing to the ice.

The Adélie lay their eggs in the summer and incubate their egg in nests made from pebbles. Considering there is nothing softer than lichens in the Antarctic, a rock nest makes sense. The Adélie mating ritual has the male offering the female choice pebbles in order to get her attention (the penguin version of jewellery).

There is a story that an Adélie penguin once offered Priestley such a stone, but he didn't accept it. Which was a pity, as Silas said, "thereby losing the opportunity of an interesting scientific discovery."

Silas had hoped to have Ponting photograph what were known as "ice feet," a phenomenon where icicles formed on low cliffs that faced the prevailing wind and were subjected to brine spray. Ice feet started life as icicles, but through a combination of warmer weather and the buildup of snow, they became ice feet. Ponting obliged Silas, but was more interested in dramatic images—like the famous photograph of the ice cave, which was formed from a stranded tabular iceberg that had blown ashore and tilted, sliding down to form the triangular ice cave. By a stroke of luck, the ice cave faced the *Terra Nova* tied to the ice sheet. Ponting spent hours pottering about the cave, with Griffith Taylor and Silas as models.

Then it came to Ponting that he had not used his cine camera, so he had us climb the tilted iceberg up to the top which overhung a pool in which a couple of killer whales were disporting themselves. To our objection that we would have to rope up and cut our footing with ice axes—a slowish job which would waste a lot of film, his reply was cut the steps first and then ascend again quickly pretending to do so this second time. We thought this was somewhat dishonest and said so. In reply he said this would come out all right in the cine film so we roped up and off we went. I was in front slashing away with my ice axe and feeling a perfect fool. At the very top, an unguarded swipe brought down a sizeable chunk of ice, which fell down vertically into the pool below. Said Ponting, "That's Wonderful, do it again." I didn't. I did not at all like the look of those killer whales below.

—Wright memoirs

When he arrived back in England, Ponting released the footage he'd taken in the Antarctic as *The Great White Silence*. When talking movies arrived in the 1930s, Ponting reissued his cine film, with sound added, as *90° South*. In the introduction to the film he claimed it was "all shot as he saw it and nothing was created for the camera …"

Silas and Taylor, who had gained reputations as the expedition's official scroungers, had been dying to check out Shackleton's 1907 hut down the coast at Cape Royds, not for scientific reasons, but to see if anything had been left behind that might be useful—specifically food.

Using a practice run on skis as an excuse, they took off in the direction of Cape Royds. Tryggve Gran, Victor Campbell and Edward Nelson prepared to follow them, but Scott, on finding out that Silas and Taylor had left Cape Evans without his permission, flew into a rage and ordered Gran to send the errant pair back when he caught up with them. Fortunately, Silas and Taylor were going at a fast clip—they had already crossed the Barne Glacier and were out of sight.

Shackleton's hut was perfectly sealed up and had not a grain of snow inside it (unlike Scott's old *Discovery* hut). Silas was amazed. "It contained all sorts of fancy stuff," he wrote. "It was astonishing. Condensed milk, biscuits, jam, gingerbread, even a tray with freshly baked scones along with a freshly baked loaf of bread."

The *1907* expedition left in a hurry, I believe, which accounts for the somewhat unkempt appearance of the hut. Boots were scattered on the floor, books over the bunks, socks drying on lines. In one corner a roulette machine, in another a packet of paper used in their printing press. I fear I was most interested in the tinned fruits, and searched through a huge store of unused food in one corner of the hut. Tea, pickles, jams, milk, onions, sausages, hams, cocoa, delicatessen, everything but canned fruit. Finally we saw that the darkroom was built of cases of bottled fruit, and in honour of the first crossing of the Barne Glacier we broached a case and extracted a bottle of gooseberries and another of currants. It was a queer meal. I had brought bacon and ship's biscuit. Wright selected plum pudding, sardines and Nestle's milk. I found preserved ginger, raisins, and corned beef. We drank alternately of currant and gooseberry vinegar and ate through the above menu. Antarctica is immune from dyspepsia, for we felt none the worse.

—Griffith Taylor[2]

They also came across the thermometer inside the hut, which had recorded minus 72° F as the coldest temperature since Shackleton's party had left the hut.

January 16, 1911: *Terra Nova* had been completely unloaded of stores and was preparing to leave with the Eastern Party. The crew was hard at work ballasting the ship, dragging 25 tons of rock a mile over the ice and loading it into the ship's hold. They had been chopping ice off a nearby glacier foot and dragging it over the ice to the ship to replenish the water tanks when a 20-foot-high iceberg drifted past *Terra Nova*. The sudden proximity of this iceberg was too much to resist. They quickly lassoed it and drew it next to the ship. But no sooner were they on the berg and chipping at the ice than it disintegrated, with pieces bouncing off both ship and crew. The remains of the berg easily broke the ropes holding it to the ship and it drifted away, carrying with it various picks and shovels.

That same day, Scott returned from Hut Point in a foul mood. Not only had Shackleton broken his word to him and used his old *Discovery* hut, they'd left a window open when they abandoned it, and the hut was now choked with snow, ice and debris. If that wasn't bad enough, some of the *Nimrod* the sailors had had the effrontery to carve their names on the planks outside the hut.

The condition of the *Discovery* hut, which figured prominently in Scott's plans for depot laying and the eventual trip to the Pole, paled in comparison to what nearly happened to *Terra Nova*.

Now under the command of Captain Harry Pennell, *Terra Nova* had boarded the Eastern Party and was about to set sail for the eastern corner of the Ross Ice Shelf where it meets King Edward VII Peninsula. On board the ship was Lt. Victor Campbell, who was to lead the small exploration party, which included Raymond Priestley, Dr. George Murray Levick and petty officers George Abbott, Frank Browning and Harry Dickason.

Victor "the Wicked Mate" Campbell
Born on August 20, 1875, in Brighton, England, Victor Campbell joined the Royal Navy at an early age. He was appointed first officer of *Terra Nova*.

Dr. George Murray Levick
Born in 1877, George Levick studied medicine at St. Bartholomew's Hospital, London, later joining the Royal Navy as a surgeon. He was an amateur zoologist and photographer.

Frank Browning
Born in Devonshire, England, Frank Browning joined *Terra Nova* from HMS *Talbot*.

Harry Dickason
Born in London, Harry Dickason joined *Terra Nova* from HMS *Defiance*.

George Abbott
George Abbott joined *Terra Nova* from HMS *Talbot*.

Within minutes of *Terra Nova* casting off from the ice sheet, the ship ran aground between Inaccessible Island and Cape Evans.

The interior of Ponting's ice cave with *Terra Nova* in the background. Griffith Taylor left, Silas Wright, right.

Packing a sledge at the top of the moraine, for a trip to Shackleton's hut. Over the next three years, they would make as many forays to Shackleton's hut as they could—especially Silas and Taylor—armed with a shopping list of things needed by other members. Tubing for Day, ginger for Atch ...

It happened that Captain Scott and I (and I think one or two others) were watching the ship when she ran aground facing south apparently with a strong current from the north. She tried to go astern, even launching the whaleboat and crew to assist the ship's engines to back off but even this failed to budge the ship. Pennell then set the rest of the crew to running back and forth to roll the ship while the ship's engines were still trying to back her off the rock. This [sallying the ship] did the trick and the crew gave a lusty cheer and I may even have done the same. But all Captain Scott had to say was "Yes, they may well cheer." I mention this because it was the first time I had actually seen him meeting suddenly a catastrophe which might have wrecked completely his plans for the expedition.

—Wright memoirs

This was the closest the expedition had come to a complete disaster. There were no plans for a relief ship (i.e., no money) and to lose *Terra Nova* would have pretty much finished the expedition and could very well have meant that Silas and his companions would have been marooned on Ross Island for years to come.

Freed from the reef, *Terra Nova* carried on to the Bay of Whales, at the edge of the Great Ice Barrier, where Campbell's Eastern Party was to camp.

In 1911, it was about to turn ugly at Cape Evans. Unaware that the Eastern Party had stumbled upon Amundsen, Scott set off with ponies and dogs on the first depot-laying party on the Barrier. The party consisted of Scott, Evans, Wilson, Bowers, Atkinson, Oates, Cherry-Garrard, Gran, Meares, Robert Forde, Thomas Crean and Patrick Keohane, along with eight ponies, two dog teams and a ton of supplies to be taken as far south on the Barrier as they could get before the weather turned on them.

A few days after the depot-laying party had left, *Terra Nova* returned to Cape Evans with news of Amundsen and his party having set up house on the Barrier.

At the Bay of Whales, Pennell had moored *Terra Nova* next to *Fram*, and Campbell (who spoke Norwegian) along with Tryggve Gran met with Amundsen, who was most hospitable and pleased to show them around his camp. Priestley wrote an account of the meeting:

> I think no incident was so suggestive of the possibilities latent in these terms as the arrival of Amundsen at the side of the *Terra Nova*. His dogs were running well and he did not check them until he was right alongside the ship. He then gave a whistle and the whole team stopped as one dog. With a word of command he inverted the empty sledge and came on board, leaving the animals to

The edge of the Great Ice Barrier, or the Ross Ice Shelf as it is now known.

themselves; and there they remained until their master had finished his visit. They were all exceptionally strong-looking brutes and completely under control; and when dogs are good, they have no compeers as draught animals under Polar conditions.[3]

When he left Madeira, Roald Amundsen had 90 tough, squabbling dogs, all wanting to fight one another. There was every chance they'd be either dead or too torn up to be of any use by the time they reached the Antarctic. He had a brainwave: muzzle them and let them loose. It worked splendidly; they fought all day until they were exhausted. He tied them up, fed them, let them loose muzzled again, where they fought some more. But they could do one another no damage and eventually got along with one another. So much so that the 90 dogs he started with ended up as 116 dogs.

Amundsen was most curious to see *Terra Nova* and couldn't resist getting a dig in. On looking up at *Terra Nova*'s masts, he asked Campbell, "What, no radio?" He then asked about the motor sledges he'd heard so much about. Campbell airily said that they were most likely on their way south by now, carrying Scott and his Polar Party to the South Pole, which gave Amundsen pause.

After Amundsen's departure from the ship, Campbell ordered Pennell to turn around and head back to Cape Evans. It wasn't an enviable task for Campbell to write a note to Scott letting him know he'd found Amundsen at the Bay of Whales. There is a story of how he put the note in an instrument box for someone to give to Scott at the appropriate moment. Then presumably, run for the hills.

With the Bay of Whales out, Campbell decided to explore the Northern Coast up to Cape Adare. The two ponies they had on board the ship would be useless on the rocky northern coast and would have to be unloaded at Cape Evans. As the ice sheet had broken off, they anchored as close to shore as they could, put a sling under each of the ponies and dropped them over the side off the ship, where they were guided to shore by crew members in a whaleboat. Once ashore they got a brisk rubdown by the Russian groom, Anton Omelchenko—and a half-bottle of brandy each.

Out on the Barrier, it was probably just as well that Scott was unaware Amundsen was in the area. He was in a bad mood due to Oates criticising the handling of the ponies and decisions on placement of depots.

Scott and Evans boss the show pretty well and their ignorance about marching with animals is colossal. On several points Scott is going on lines contrary to what I have suggested. However, if I can only persuade him to take a pony himself he will learn a lot this autumn, Scott having spent too much time of his life in an office, he would fifty times soon stay in the hut seeing how a pair of Fons spiral puttees suited him than come out and look at a ponies [sic] legs or a dogs [sic] feet. I suppose I think too much of this having come strate [sic] from a regiment where horses were the first and only real consideration.

Scott thinks he [Amundsen] has gone to the Weddell Sea to try for the Pole from there. If it comes to a race he will have a great chance of getting there as he is a man who has been at this kind of game all his life and he has a hard crowd behind him while we are very young.

—Lawrence Oates, January 22, 1911

The farther south they went on their depot-laying expedition, the more prescient Oates appeared to be.

Fram moored at Framhelm in the Bay of Whales.

7. THE WESTERN PARTY

Nothing helps a man to understand the mentality of
animals more clearly than a long spell of pulling a sledge.
—Frank Debenham

By January 24, 1911, only four officers and five men remained at Cape
Evans, assigned to lay in enough provisions for the coming winter—which
would involve the slaughter of 1,000 unfortunate penguins and skuas. Silas
and his Western Party had boarded *Terra Nova* and, along with Campbell's
Northern Party (née Eastern Party), sailed the few miles across Erebus
Bay to Hut Point, where they helped move supplies from the ship to a
cache outside the old *Discovery* hut. With the dogs still unruly and Silas
and Frank Debenham unfamiliar with handling dogs, there were anxious
moments when the dogs would bolt for a seal, with Silas and Debenham
hanging on to the sledge, desperately trying to steer it away from the open
water the seal would invariably head for.

January 27, 1911: *Terra Nova* was anchored to the sea ice off the Ferrar
Glacier as the Western Party's sledges were unloaded. Priestley took
Debenham and Campbell off to find Edgeworth David's depot camp, set
up when Priestley was on Ernest Shackleton's 1907 expedition. (Because
Priestley had been on Shackleton's expedition, he considered it his duty to
commandeer any of the gear that was worth having, including ski boots,
sledging thermometers and a belt.)

Construction of the hut, complete except for the Bowers annex, which would be built later.

The Western Party deposited fourteen cases of provisions for their party, with Priestley and Campbell leaving just a few of their stores, as they didn't plan on spending much time in the area. *Terra Nova* continued north, across McMurdo Sound and into the Ross Sea, carrying Campbell's Northern Party and the Western Party, which was made up of Silas, Griffith Taylor, Frank Debenham and PO Evans. The aim of the Western Party was to explore the coast, Dry Valleys and Ferrar Glacier, mapping and naming landmarks as they went. Upon landing at Butter Point, where *Terra Nova* was able to tie up to the ice sheet, the crew unloaded sledges and supplies. Campbell's men wished them farewell, and *Terra Nova* carried on up the coast with the Northern Party.

From Butter Point, Silas and his companions harnessed themselves to the sledge and made for the Ferrar Glacier, where they came across a number of emperor penguins that had come up to moult. One of them was unfortunate enough to come into range of Silas's Mauser, and was soon being unceremoniously dragged behind a sledge as a future dinner entree.

By January 30, they were still on the glacier and struggling to pull the sledges through deep snow. Regardless of how much they cursed the conditions, things did not improve. Debenham was the first to notice how differences in height between the men pulling the sledge affected control-

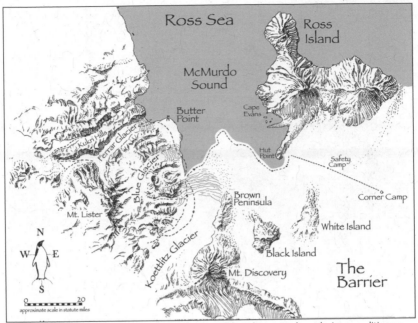

Map showing the route of the first Western Party and the subsequent depot-laying expedition on the Ice Barrier.

ling its direction. Long-legged Silas pulling next to shorter-legged Debenham meant one was either pulling too hard or jerking—or not pulling hard enough. Either way, the disparity would soon tire them both out.

Only days into their expedition, Silas complained that their daily sledging rations were inadequate—something that Campbell's party farther along the coast had already found out, switching over to the more robust Shackleton sledging diet.

Silas would have dearly loved to have the rations increased, but Griffith Taylor, whom Scott had appointed leader, was a light eater and capable of going twenty-four hours or more without food. As far as he was concerned, their rations were more than adequate—much to the disgust of Silas, who noted: "Had lunch at 2:15 PM and stopped at 8:45 PM. A horribly long interval between lunch and dinner. I must hold back a half biscuit in future from lunch in order to gnaw at in the early evening."

On Scott's depot-laying expedition out on the Barrier, it wasn't just empty stomachs causing tension. Dr. Atkinson was stricken with an abscess on his foot and Lawrence Oates decided he hated Tryggve Gran. In a letter to his mother, dated January 31, 1911, Oates wrote: "I can't stand this Norwegian chap he is both dirty & cagy. I have had one row with

Silas in summer gear. "One of the greatest successes is Wright. He is very thorough and absolutely ready for anything. Like Bowers he has taken to sledging like a duck to water, and although he hasn't had such a severe testing, I believe he would stand it pretty nearly as well. Nothing ever seems to worry him, and I can't imagine he ever complained of anything in his life." —Scott

him and I should think it won't be long before we have another."

The ponies were being battered by the Barrier winds and feeling the cold, especially as they were wearing their summer coats. The dogs were disinclined to pull the loads that were asked of them, and relations between Scott and Oates had deteriorated further.

On the Ferrar Glacier, everyone in the party was getting along, and Silas was discovering camping on glacial ice was rather different than camping in the Ontario wilderness. Sleeping bags would warm the ice, creating pools of water under whoever was sleeping at the lowest point in the tent. Silas always seemed to bear the brunt of the melt, writing: "I woke up in a puddle of water and could not understand at first why my underside was cold. Of course, instead of warming the water, I was merely melting more ice."

It didn't help that the equipment they were stuck with was substandard. Sleeping bags were made from half-tanned reindeer skin and could be used with the hair outside or inside, but either way, they shed hair faster than a sheepdog in a vet clinic, and were all a few sizes too small. Their ski boots were coming apart, with Taylor's boots being in the worst shape:

> Already my boots began to give trouble. The soft leather sole would not hold the short nails, which only were available on the *Terra Nova*, so that I attempted to mend matters by driving in some Canadian lumber spikes supplied by Wright.[1]

Ski boots were totally unsuitable for scrambling over rocks, as they had soft soles, which were designed to bend while skiing. Nails for mending boots had been left off the supply list, and those nails they did have wore through the leather transferring the cold to the wearer, sometimes causing spot frostbite. The only other footwear they had were finnesko, made from supple reindeer hide, which were warmer but useless on anything except soft snow.

From Silas's experience in Canada's North, he knew footwear was of paramount importance and prior to leaving with the Western Party had taken the precaution of cadging some nails from Ponting. They were able to effect makeshift repairs to get their boots to last until they got back to the coast but were now somewhat restricted in the type of terrain they could traverse with the state of their footwear. PO Taff Evans kept asking them how their feet were feeling, getting replies like "Killing me" or "Hurting like blazes." "Good," he would say, and they would carry on. One time, Debenham replied that his feet were feeling fine, with no pain. Evans quickly removed Debenham's boots, revealing that his toes were white and frozen. He had Debenham lie on his back in the snow, tucking his feet under his jacket and against his stomach, until the circulation returned. Debenham later recalled: "The more it hurt the more pleased Taff was."[2]

The design of their helmets was also an issue, as the opening was too small. Cecil Meares called it a "wind catcher" because when they marched into the wind, it funnelled the wind into your face. Breath would condense inside the helmet and freeze when it was taken off, turning it into a helmet of ice. Their summer windbreakers didn't break any wind, with some of the party taking to wearing their thick pyjama coats underneath their jackets, which not only cut the wind but provided lots of handy pockets.

From the Ferrar Glacier they approached the Dry Valleys. They cached their sledge before entering the Valleys, as it would be useless in the rock-strewn, snowless landscape. Packing enough supplies for a few days, each member adopted his own style of carrying his gear. Evans tied everything to tent poles and carried the load over his shoulder, English-style. Griff carried everything slung from one shoulder, Swiss-style. Deb carried his stuff front and back, Australian-style, and Silas the Canadian native Indian way, with a "tump line" across his forehead, gear slung over his back.

The adjacent Taylor and Wright Dry Valleys cover an area of 4,800 square kilometres. They are ice- and snow-free year-round and are the driest deserts on Earth. Besides being a treasure trove for geologists, they are seal graveyards, with mummified carcasses of crabeater seals littering the valley floors. Due to the extreme dry conditions, it has been speculated that some of these mummified remains are more than 700 years old. NASA has used the Dry Valleys as stand-ins for the surface of Mars in preparation for Mars missions.

The Wright Dry Valley was so named in 1959.

The Dry Valleys held all sorts of interesting features. Ice-free lakes, the only river in the Antarctic, a fossilized crabeater seal. What it was doing so far from the ocean was a mystery (fleeing a sledge dog?). By February 10, 1911, they had returned from the Dry Valleys and were back

Sledging on the ice of the Ferrar Glacier.

at their depot at the base of the Ferrar Glacier. Silas was starving and dreaming of feasting on the emperor penguin he had shot and carefully cached earlier. He was devastated to find his penguin had been well picked over by skua gulls and was now just a collection of bones. It was also his turn to cook which was noted by Taylor, who wrote: "Charlie started cooking & we survived!"[3]

Debenham was having trouble eating because his teeth were causing him trouble, which they assumed was a result of his having had a tooth extracted by Dr. Wilson on January 15. Years later, Silas wondered if Debenham's sore teeth could have been an indication he was suffering from the early stages of scurvy.

They started the long journey back to Cape Evans, exploring the land to the south of them, including the Koetlitz Glacier. However, the Butter Glacier was inconveniently in the way. They couldn't travel on the coast, as the ice had blown out and the glacier foot was 50 feet high, with no way up or down. The only thing for it was to climb over the glacier, which was slow going, as they had to pick their way around numerous crevasses. One evening, after making camp, they discovered an ice axe had fallen off the sledge and, of course, no one wanted to go back to retrieve it. The matter was settled with Silas's ubiquitous pack of cards. In five deals, Evans got the highest number of points, so he had to trudge back to find the axe.

Betting on the most trivial things helped pass the time on sledging parties. Even something like how high the next mountain would be was worth a penny.

Wrote Wright: "I lost 1/3 [one shilling threepence] to Taff Evans that he couldn't tie a clove hitch with one hand. Taylor and Deb also lost." (Betting with a navy man over tying knots was asking for trouble.) Griffith Taylor kept a betting book in which he recorded his wins and losses. At one point he wrote: "I have lost two 1/3 dinners & £2 to CSW & dinner to Deb."[4]

On the Barrier, February 12, 1911: Scott and his depot-laying party were 76 miles from Hut Point, setting up a supply cache at Bluff Depot. They had been battered by numerous blizzards, the temperatures were bone-chilling, and the going was slow, with the ponies having an even tougher time of it—not surprising, as they had spent six weeks crammed into tiny stalls on *Terra Nova* and had been pressed into service immediately after landing, dragging thousands of pounds of supplies over miles of ice.

Pony wall out on the Barrier.

The constant Barrier winds were wearing the ponies down, especially when they were tethered for the night. Some evenings, the ponies were too frozen to want to eat. It was Scott who came up with the brilliant idea of building pony walls out of snow to shelter the ponies when they camped for the night.

Unfortunately, the ponies's walls had come too late. Two ponies—Blücher and Blossom—had already collapsed, and Jimmy Pigg was also in a bad way. Oates, ever practical, suggested to Scott they take the weakest ponies as far south as they could (taking into account the ponies' condition and worsening weather), shoot the ponies and cache the meat for use by the dog teams next season. Scott wouldn't hear of it. He needed all the ponies for the Southern Journey next spring. The next day, February 13, Scott sent Teddy Evans, Robert Forde, Patrick Keohane and the three weakest ponies—Blücher, Blossom and Jimmy Pigg—back to Hut Point, while Scott and the rest of the party continued south.

Blücher was the first to collapse and couldn't be made to stand. There was no way they could leave the pony to die, so, with Forde in tears, Keohane slit Blücher's throat with a knife. They built a snow cairn over Blücher (the spot named Blücher Camp) and continued north the next day, with Forde doing his best to coax along Blossom, who was weak and constantly falling. Eventually Blossom collapsed in the snow and died.

They built a snow cairn over his corpse, depositing his fodder on the cairn for next season. (This spot now named Blossom Camp.) Immortality for the ponies came at a high price.

On February 14, the depot-laying team was still plodding south. Gran and his pony, Weary Willy, were lagging behind the main party and Weary got stuck in a snowdrift. The dog team, which when nearby, spotted the trapped pony and set upon Weary Willie with the intention of tearing him to pieces. Weary, Meares and Gran fought the dogs off, with Meares breaking his stick beating the dogs. Eventually Weary Willie was able to shake off the dogs and gamely trotted on, bloodied but alive. Scott was furious that he almost lost a pony to the dogs:

> I was much annoyed and feel there is blame in many places: I ought not to have allowed a pony to get so far behind ... Meares should have kept them far out of range of a single horse especially a tired straggler ... Oates does not shine well as a judge of the animals's capacity for covering distance.[5]

The Western Party didn't have any animals to worry about, but they were about to encounter the indigenous wildlife. They had climbed over the Butter Glacier and arrived at the foot of the Ferrar Glacier. There appeared to be enough sea ice to be able to get around the ice foot this time, but when they were partway across, a crack appeared ahead of them that

Weary Willie set upon by the dogs. Silas speculated that the reason the dogs were so fierce on Barrier journeys was because they were starving.

Killer whales cruising the tide cracks.

widened as the ice heaved. The winds were calm and there was no ocean swell to speak of, so there could only be one thing causing the ice to heave like that: killer whales. They beat a hasty retreat back to the glacier before the whales broke through the ice. It was decided they'd be better off traversing the Ferrar Glacier, where Silas drove stakes into the ice at various intervals and tied them in with the theodolite—the idea being to return in the spring to measure how far the glacier had moved over the winter.

On February 16, they made their way off the Ferrar Glacier by lowering the sledge down to the sea ice on ropes. Keeping a sharp eye out for killer whales, they made good time around the peninsula to Chocolate Camp.

> Chocolate Camp was so named because on the day they arrived at the rendezvous point at Butter Point, PO Taff Evans announced it was his birthday and broke out a box of chocolates.

There was no celebration this day. The ice here was unstable, with many pools of water and rotten ice, resulting in slow and painful progress. Taylor's boots were now in tatters, and he had tied sealskin around his boots in a futile attempt to keep them together until they made it back to Hut Point.

At Cape Evans, Griff Taylor extended the life of his boots by adding an extra leather sole, but the only person who still had copper nails was Oates, who demanded that Taylor write an article on "Physiology for Soldiers" for the *South Polar Times* in exchange for the nails.

The short Austral summer of 1911 was fading fast, with temperatures dropping. Gear and sleeping bags were continuously soaked through from sweat and absorbing the melt from the ice. Socks and finnesko that would normally have dried in the sun were now wet twenty-four hours a day and frozen solid by morning—meaning late starts while everyone struggled to get into frozen gear. They learned that, before turning in for the night, it was a good idea to leave socks and finnesko in shapes they could get into the next morning. Physically, they were getting played out. Debenham's heel was giving him trouble, Griffith Taylor's feet were severely blistered and his boots were, as Taylor put it, "awful wrecks." Silas was starving, and even their cameras packed it in, as the bitter cold caused shutters to seize. The only person who seemed unaffected was PO Evans.

On the Barrier, Jimmy Pigg had survived the march to Safety Camp and was relaxing behind his pony walls while Lt. Evans, Forde and Keohane waited for Scott and Meares to return with the dog teams. When they finally arrived on February 21, Scott's dog team promptly fell down a crevasse near White Island. Scott and the sledge were saved, but with the exception of Osman, all the dogs had disappeared down the chasm and were dangling by their traces, snarling and snapping at one another. Osman dug his paws into the snow, straining on his harness, the only thing preventing his companions from dropping to the bottom of the crevasse. Using ropes, the men were able to retrieve the dogs and raise them to the surface. When they recovered from their ordeal, the dogs trotted over to Meares's dog team and started a fight. (Presumably his dogs hadn't been sympathetic enough to their plight.) The last two dogs who had slipped out of their harnesses were trapped on a snow bridge 65 feet down the crevasse and were rescued by Scott, who was lowered down on a rope, where he found them curled up and sleeping as though nothing had happened.

Despite the crevasse incident, Scott was impressed with the dogs's performance on the Barrier and announced he was thinking he'd take the dogs all the way to the Pole the following season. Lt. Evans wrote in his book *South with Scott:* "What a pity he didn't! Had he done so he might have been alive today."[6]

Silas's Watson camera. It could be used to take both acetate and glass-plate negatives.

The only casualty from that day was a dog that died on March 19, 1911, from injuries resulting either from the fall into the crevasse or the ensuing dogfight.

For the Western Party, temperatures were plunging at night. It was anything but glorious, minus 15° F not being uncommon. One night the toes on one of Debenham's feet froze. He was wearing too many socks and his boots were too small to begin with.

After 34 days in close quarters, nerves were beginning to fray, Silas complaining that Taylor insisted on getting into his sleeping bag before his cocoa was finished. "Gives me the pip." Silas's attempt to take a photograph of an unusual ice crystal formation became a trial, with Taylor commenting: "CSW made the skis curl with his language on trying to set up his camera on the ice."

The tent wasn't as cozy as it once had been. Their breath would create a frozen rime on the tent overnight, and once the camp stove was lit in the morning the ice would melt, creating an indoor "rain."

Griffith Taylor was just as miserable. His helmet was so covered in ice that he slept with his head wrapped in his windproof pants.

PO Evans insisted that instead of camping on the sea ice, they keep close to the Barrier. Silas thought this a complete waste of time, as it would mean wasting time ducking in and out of bays, but was forced to eat his words when they returned to Hut Point—and news of the depot-laying party's near disaster when the sea ice broke off, taking the ponies out to sea.

On March 13, they were near Castle Rock and were on a course for Hut Point when they spotted four large penguins heading towards them on the ice. The penguins turned out to be Edward Wilson, Birdie Bowers, Cherry-Garrard and Edward Atkinson, who helped them with the sledge back to Hut Point. The Western Party had been gone a total of forty-nine days, much longer than they had originally planned. Once in the *Discovery* hut, sleeping bags and boots were hung up to dry and Silas was finally able to eat a proper meal: "How we did gorge ourselves on seal hoosh and cocoa."

That evening, they were brought up to date on the news of the disaster of the ponies on the ice floes.

The Loss of the Ponies

February 24, 1911: The depot-laying party was back at Safety Camp, with a stretch of sea ice separating them from Hut Point. The season was rapidly coming to an end and temperatures were dropping fast, with the remaining six emaciated ponies feeling the effects of the wind and cold, especially the battle-scarred Weary Willie. The dogs hadn't had a much better time, with Scott having to admit a diet of dog biscuits was far from adequate to keep them alive on the Barrier. The dogs had been battered by constant blizzards and snowdrifts of up to four feet thick were burying them. The plan was for the dog teams to leave with Meares and Wilson for Hut Point first, blazing a trail across the sea ice, with the pony teams following in their tracks. Bowers, leading his pony Uncle Bill, left first, but before the others could follow, Weary Willie collapsed and couldn't be got back on his feet again. Scott sent Cherry-Garrard and Thomas Crean ahead with Punch, Nobby and Guts, while he, Oates and Gran stayed behind with Weary Willie to try to revive the poor animal. After surviving the trip from Vladivostok to New Zealand, the storm in the Southern Ocean, a savage dog attack and the gruelling trek on the Barrier, Weary Willie had had enough and died during the night.

Meanwhile, Cherry, Crean and their three ponies were on the ice near Cape Armitage when large cracks appeared in the ice and a thick mist descended that obscured the dog teams in the distance. Eventually they caught up with Bowers and his pony, who were waiting for them farther out on the ice. They carried on together but kept encountering more cracks in the ice. They retraced their tracks to a point where the ice appeared to be thicker and camped for the night.

At 4:30 AM they awoke to find they were adrift on an ice floe 30 yards across, with the ponies stranded on another ice floe—separated from them by a strip of black water. Long ocean swells were heaving the floes, splitting the one they were standing on in two. Guts had already fallen in the water and disappeared with the remaining ponies about to meet the same fate. Crean, Cherry and Bowers quickly harnessed the remaining ponies and jumped floe to floe with the ponies, trying to find a way to solid ice. For the next six hours, they'd leap with the ponies to another floe, leave the ponies on that floe, then jump back to the previous floe to get the sledges, jump back to the floe where the ponies were waiting, then repeat the process. That killer whales that had turned up hunting for seals made the leaps across the open water even more dangerous.

They finally got to what they thought was safe ice near the Barrier edge, where they met Scott, Oates and Gran. Scott was most relieved to see them. He'd assumed they had all drowned out on the ice floes. The question now was how to get the ponies up onto the Barrier. Oates tried to dig a path down to where the ponies were standing on the floe, and just as they got the sledges off, the floe moved out to sea again, with the men leaping to safety just before it floated out to sea. They could do nothing except watch helplessly as the ponies slowly drifted, with killer whales, sensing there was something nearby to eat, cruising all around them.

The next day, they watched through glasses as the floe carrying the ponies drifted close to the Barrier edge farther west. They raced to the spot where the floe had pushed up against a jumble of thinner brash ice. Oates, Cherry, and Bowers jumped onto the floe, where they first tried to coax Punch to jump the gap between the floe and the brash ice. Punch initially hesitated, then jumped the gap and missed, landing in the water, where he floundered as they tried unsuccessfully to haul him out. Eventually, as the frigid water weakened Punch to the point where he was about to slip under, Oates put his ice pick into Punch's head to spare him a more gruesome death by killer whale.

They attempted another route of escape, which would necessitate their going a more circuitous, but perhaps easier, route farther out in the sea ice. At first it seemed to work, with both remaining ponies making the jump from floe to floe. At the final jump, Nobby jumped at the exact moment a school of killer whales rose out of the water. Put off his stride, he landed badly, with his hindquarters ending up in the water. Scott grabbed his harness and was able to drag him out of the water and up on to the Barrier. Back on the floe, Uncle Bill had been spooked by the whales and refused to jump, so they laid him on his side and dragged him across the brash ice to the edge of the Barrier, but there Uncle Bill lay, unable to get up on his feet. The cold water and shock had done him in. It was a precarious position. The ice was thin, with killer whales prowling underneath. If just one whale had breached next to them, they'd all have been in the water. There was no option left for them, but it was Bowers's pony and he wouldn't let anyone else do it.

He picked up the ice axe and dispatched Uncle Bill with a blow to the head, then jumped off the ice to safety.

The depot-laying party had started out with eight ponies and returned with two.

The *Discovery* hut perched at the end of Hut Point.

December 27, 2008, Hut Point

Originally built as an Australian drover's hut, it's in remarkably good shape on the outside. The posts holding it up are set in holes that were blasted out in 1902, then filled with water. The water froze the posts into place, ice being an acceptable substitute for cement and in this case perhaps more durable.

As you walk inside the hut, you're greeted by a pile of frozen seal blubber. The entire hut reeks of seal blubber and the ceiling is black with soot, with the floor scarred in places where seal meat was cut up with an axe. It's basically a shrine to seal extermination.

Built by Scott in 1902, it was never permanently occupied during that expedition, serving instead as an infirmary. Although it was used as a transit point during the 1910 expedition, the main occupiers were Shackleton's men, who didn't have a reputation as good tenants. On the 1907 expedition they left garbage in the hut and a window open, and it was used a second time during his *Endurance* expedition when the men of the 1914–1917 Ross Sea Party sheltered here after *Aurora* was blown out to sea. During that time, most traces of the 1910 Scott Expedition were obliterated—or eaten. Interestingly, the men of the Ross Sea Party almost starved to death, unaware that a large cache of food had been left behind by the Scott Expedition, buried under the snow not more than a few yards from the hut.

The pots still remain and I daresay the stove could still be fired up.

Grease-stained canvas partitions the hut, and rusty pots and pans litter the cooking area. A bit of restoration work has been done on the hut in the ensuing years, but it doesn't have the same atmosphere as the Cape Evans hut. Perhaps this is because of its proximity to the 1,000 people housed at McMurdo base, or maybe it's because no one, except for the Ross Sea Party, has actually overwintered at the hut.

Demetri and Meares sitting around the same stove in 1911.

8. DEPOT LAYING, 1911

Everything, everything, is going against us.

—Tryggve Gran

The *Discovery* hut at Hut Point was damp, draughty and stank of seal blubber, but it was luxury compared to sleeping on a glacier. All traces of Shackleton's party, along with the ice, feces and debris, had been removed, but the hut hadn't been constructed as well as the one at Cape Evans because it was just a prefabricated Australian drover's hut and was never intended to be used over the winter. The snow and ice that piled up on the roof found its way through cracks in the timbers, where it melted, falling as a light rain on those sleeping below. Tins were laid on the floor and hung from the ceiling, but there was very little drip-free space, with anyone lucky enough to find a dry spot having to guard it with his life.

The dogs, of course, had to stay outside and spent their time in pits dug to shelter them from the elements. Some of the less rambunctious dogs were allowed to walk off-leash with members of the party, bringing a touch of home to the otherwise harsh landscape. But the dogs soon got bored with the sedentary pace of their human companions and would invariably sneak away from the party and scoot across the ice to hunt penguins.

Scott turned up at Hut Point looking for "volunteers" to take more supplies to the cache at Corner Camp. Silas had been looking forward to putting his feet up on the blubber stove, but sledging experience on the Barrier couldn't hurt when the time came for Scott to pick those who

At each overnight camp, the men would dig holes in the snow where the dogs could curl up in to escape the wind.

would accompany him to the South Pole, so Silas stuck his hand up. Besides, it couldn't be any worse than scrambling about on the rocks in the Western Mountains. Scott noticed Silas's willingness to go on the depot-laying journey and wrote: "It was very sporting of Wright to join in after only a day's rest. He is evidently a splendid puller."[1]

On March 16, 1911, even though his gear was still wet from the previous trip, Silas joined Birdie Bowers, Lt. Teddy Evans, Lawrence Oates, Thomas Crean, Robert Forde, Cherry-Garrard and Dr. Atkinson on a journey to Corner Camp depot, 30 miles to the south, dragging sacks of oats and four boxes of biscuits on sledges. Griffith Taylor, PO Taff Evans and Frank Debenham wisely stayed behind at Hut Point.

Thomas Crean

Born in 1877 in County Kerry, Ireland, Thomas Crean joined the Royal Navy, and was assigned to the 1901 Discovery Expedition. Scott was so impressed with how he carried out his duties that he asked him to join his 1910 expedition. Crean was a bear of a man, and it was his strength and stamina that probably saved Teddy Evans's life on their return from the Polar Plateau the following year.

Vaida and Beileglas were half-brothers who not only pulled side by side, but insisted on sharing the same hole. One would lie on top of the other, changing places every couple of hours.

Robert Forde

Born on August 29, 1875, near Cork, Ireland, Robert Forde joined the Royal Navy at sixteen and rose to the rank of petty officer, which was the title he held on the 1910 Scott Expedition. He suffered greatly from the cold and was susceptible to frostbite—a condition that invalided him home after the first year.

It was worse than scrambling about on the rocks in the Western Mountains, as Silas wrote on March 16, 1911:

With singular short-sightedness, we were sent off with only one can of oil and less than a week's grub for a trip that could not be done in less than five days (for which the oil could be made to spin out) and at this time of year, moreover, only one out of every two days can be relied upon for travelling.

Scott's apportioning of rations, especially fuel, was all based on speed. Including the container, fuel weighed roughly 10 pounds a gallon and was expected to last ten days. A quick trip required less fuel, and less weight on the sledge meant the team could move faster. However, temperature had not been factored in. At sea level, with a temperature of 0° C (32° F), it takes 1 calorie of heat to raise 1 gram of water through 1° C and 80 calories of heat to melt 1 gram of ice. At a temperature of minus 40° C (minus 40° F) at sea level it would take 22 percent more fuel to bring that same snow to boiling point. At an elevation of 9,000 feet (the Polar Plateau), it would take even more fuel. Spring journeys would require less oil to be burned than autumn journeys, as temperatures were usually warmer in the spring.

It was late in the season and temperatures at night were dropping to minus 30° F. Putting more pressure on their precious fuel oil, and getting into frozen gear made early starts more difficult, prolonging the time they'd have to spend on the Barrier.

Silas shared a tent with Lt. Teddy Evans, who was given cooking duty, which was a mistake because Evans was notoriously careless with rations. Even though he knew they were short of food and fuel, he used up the scran* for the hoosh† the second day out from Hut Point and tried to borrow more from Bowers' tent. Silas was so annoyed he spoke to Bowers, asking him to refuse Evans in future.

On March 19 they expected to raise Corner Camp, but due to a navigational error on Evans's part they passed by it and ran out of daylight, ending up making camp for the night 6 miles from the depot, prolonging the time they were on the Barrier by one more day. The temperature that night dropped to minus 42° F resulting in everything in the interior of the tents becoming encrusted with hoarfrost. Silas noted there were "many observations of the moon that night," meaning more frequent exits from the tent to relieve themselves, which nobody looked forward to: when they emerged from the tent in a clammy wet state, the instant freezing of their clothes made it feel like an electric shock.

---

* Scran would be miscellaneous foodstuffs, such as seal meat.
† Hoosh is the thick stew they made by adding canned pemmican to boiling water.

It was an-ill tempered group that broke camp that morning and re-traced their route back to Corner Camp.

After quickly unloading the supplies, they headed north and into a blizzard, which continued throughout the next day, slowing their progress to a crawl. They were now desperately short of food, with Silas restricted to one stick of chocolate and a biscuit for breakfast. They made Safety Camp on March 22, where they found fuel and could feast on cached seal meat. After resting for the night, they continued on and reached Hut Point on March 24, eight days after they had started their journey.

Silas was shaken by the whole experience and privately beginning to have doubts as to Scott's ability as a leader. He wrote:

It was of course foolish of me to dash off so soon after we got back from the Western Mountains with sleeping bag and all other gear full of ice and water, but it seemed worthwhile for the experience which was, in my opinion not a very well organised show and the worst thing was to take off with inadequate rations when blizzards were far too common and I could see no good reason for this sloppy arrangement.

Unlike the laid-back atmosphere when the group had explored the Western Mountains a few weeks earlier, the depot-laying party revealed tensions. Lt. Evans had not broken himself of his habit of, as Silas put it: "cadging matches and tobacco." Forde felt the cold more than anyone else (he was eventually invalided home on *Terra Nova* with severe frostbite), and since learning that Amundsen was parked down the coast, Scott's at-titude towards Tryggve Gran had changed, with Scott finding fault with almost anything Gran did—at one point giving him a tongue-lashing in front of the party, which Silas thought was "off-side."

It was one thing to run out of rations near the coast, as you could always knock a seal on the head or plug a penguin. On the Barrier, there was no wildlife to fall back on. Run out of fuel or supplies on the Barrier and you were finished.

Once back at Cape Evans, Silas wrote a longer account of sledging conditions on the Barrier:

In really cold weather, the hard work leads to profuse sweating during the day much of which remains trapped as ice in one's outer clothing which becomes windproof when frozen. All clothes except those actually touching one are thus frozen and this ice is carried into the sleeping bag melted or evaporated to condense in the coldest part of the bag being occupied by one's cold feet. In the morning one gets up in the dark cold tent with a quarter of an inch, or more, of rime on tent and sleeping bags, which drops on one at every casual touch or shake of the tent. After a warm but shivery breakfast comes the ordeal of changing socks and finnesko, a truly unpleasant one if they are not frozen into a shape suitable for easy entry. It is because of this that care must be taken to take such gear to bed with you, so that they won't become frozen overnight. While changing gear, smoke a pipe, roll up the sleeping bag for the sledge and plug away until lunch time which is easily the most pleasant time of the day. In really cold weather with the temperature down to −60° or lower, the sleeping bag must not be rolled up because of the time taken to enter it at night when the feet are used to warm the ice and very slowly make one's way in.

After the afternoon's toil and frozen sweat, supper is made by the cook for the week by candle light, the frozen breath of the party of four and frozen steam from the primus causes a fog in the air which makes it extremely difficult for the cook to see what he is doing. And, of course, the cold utensils stick tight to one's fingers when cold, causing

Thomas Crean (left) and Taff Evans (right) mending sleeping bags. Reindeer sleeping bags that weighed 16 pounds at the beginning of a Barrier journey would weigh more than 30 pounds at the end, due to the accumulation of ice from breath. Reindeer hair was prone to moulting and got into everything, including food.

repeated blisters on the fingers. The fog then condenses a bit on the tent walls, and the air in the tent clears somewhat while the struggle to get in the sleeping bags proceeds after changing finnesko and wet socks, which are put into the bag with you so they won't be frozen when they are put on the next morning. Of course the supply of frozen sweat in the bag is increased each night, and all this must be melted before one can get to sleep in the wet bag. With luck, the ice in the bag will be melted in an hour or two of shivering (really heavy shudders which you can feel coming also from the bags on either side) and one can at last sleep. However, if unlucky, one has to turn out of the bag and tent during the night, the outer clothing freezes at once and becomes covered in hoar frost from the tent. In the morning one's hands are as soft as putty from the continual wetness which persists all day as the process of taking the sweaty hand out of the gloves allows the mitts to freeze at once and to melt again when put on.

Silas and his party spent a few weeks at Hut Point with Scott, waiting for the sea ice to freeze thick enough for them to make it across Erebus Bay to the hut at Cape Evans. To kill time, Griffith Taylor and Silas looted the nearby old magnetic hut for sheets of asbestos, which Taylor fashioned into lids for their porridge pans, cement for the chimney and shims to level the floor. In fact, they did everything with asbestos except eat it.

The summer season was rapidly closing, however, and to be caught out at Hut Point during the winter wasn't something that Silas was looking forward to—especially if the rations ran out and they were trapped in the hut with Scott. Silas wasn't used to strict naval discipline and had difficulty understanding Scott's rigid personality. In an interview with the *Ottawa Citizen* in 1974, Silas commented:

I'd never had much experience with British naval captains, how much they were alone, how much like God Almighty they had to be. He lived in his own quarters and got in touch with his sailors through his officers—he'd give an order and it'd be done at once, no questions at all. How different from the scientific approach where you're expected to argue.

The more reserved Debenham was also having second thoughts about Scott, especially his frequent tantrums, and wrote on November 14, 1911: "In crises he acts very peculiarly ... what he decides is often enough the right thing, I expect, but he loses all control of his tongue and makes us all feel wild."

They remained stuck at Hut Point, cut off from Cape Evans by Erebus Bay, which so far had refused to freeze enough for them to travel on the sea ice. Silas went out on the ice every day testing its thickness, but apart from some patches close to shore, it was still too thin. The sun was low on the horizon, and it was now almost continuous sunset all day. Everyone was getting bored. There was little to amuse them except for a collection of well-thumbed magazines left behind by Shackleton's party (and no, they weren't those kind of magazines).

April 6, 1911: The day before Silas's birthday. In his diary, the ever-hungry Silas wistfully hoped that the cook would produce some marmalade on the strength of the fact that it was his twenty-fourth birthday. Sadly, in his April 7 diary entry he wrote: "No marmalade or chocolate doled out on this eventful day."

Silas wasn't getting much sleep at Hut Point, as they could never get the hut warm enough—and it was draughty. Everyone was anxious to get back to Cape Evans as soon as possible. Finally, Silas thought the ice was thick enough to enable them to cross to Cape Evans. Scott hesitated, however, preferring to wait another day for the ice to thicken further. That night a blizzard blew through and they woke the next morning to find all the ice blown out to sea. On April 13, even though Silas considered the ice was far from safe, Scott ordered them to make the dash across the bay. Silas's concern about the ice was well founded—it buckled as they went, with pools of water and slush forming all around them. And the wind picked up forcing them to camp halfway across.

Debenham recalled that this trip across Erebus Bay was the only time there were five people in a tent, which had been designed to accommodate only four men. It was such a tight fit, that he gave up and crawled outside to sleep but was forced back inside by the blizzard and spent a sleepless night "packed like sardines."[2]

The next day they made it the final few miles to Cape Evans so covered in soot and dirt that those back at the hut initially thought they were part of the Japanese polar expedition rumoured to be in the area.

Nobu Shirase 1861–1946

The crew of the *Kainan Maru* with dinner.

In the annals of poorly organized polar expeditions, the Japanese Antarctic Expedition is right at the top.

Japanese army officer Nobu Shirase had been part of an expedition exploring the islands north of Hokkaido, losing more than twenty men to cold and starvation in the process. Undaunted, he returned to Japan and set his sights on reaching the North Pole, but Admiral Robert Peary beat him to it. Like Amundsen, there was only one polar prize left to him—the South Pole. And, like Scott, his fundraising efforts were abysmal. However, by December 1, 1910, he had raised enough money to buy and equip a ship, the tiny *Kainan Maru*, and his expedition sailed from Japan for the Antarctic. Arriving in Wellington on February 7, 1911, he was met with xenophobic suspicion.

Kainan Maru left New Zealand and sailed south, encountering heavy ice and bad weather, and only got as far as the Ross Sea before the captain abandoned the attempt and sailed to Sydney, Australia. The crew's reception in Oz was as chilly as it had been in New Zealand, and they were forced to spend the winter in one of their crude prefabricated huts set up in a sympathetic resident's backyard. Completely broke, Shirase and his crew were reduced to living as beggars while the ship's captain and some of the crew returned to Japan to raise money for another attempt at the South Pole.

Buoyed by more funds from Japan, they returned to Antarctica the next spring, sailing into King Edward VII Land, near the Bay of Whales, to be met by Amundsen's crew, who were incredulous that a ship the size of the tiny *Kainan Maru* had actually made it all the way to the Ross Sea. With the Bay of Whales occupied by Amundsen, they anchored to the ice farther along the Barrier and climbed 150 feet up the ice foot to reach the top of the Barrier, but only made it 160 miles south before blizzards forced them to abandon the expedition and return to their ship while they could still find it.

They returned to Japan on June 20, 1912. Shirase spent much of the rest of his life paying off the debt he'd incurred on the expedition, settling the last yen when he was seventy-four years old. He died in poverty at the age of eighty-five in a rented room above a fish shop in the town of Koromo.

Outside the Cape Evans hut, Silas and his sledging companions paused to pose for Ponting's camera, then fell into the hut, thankful the sledging was over for the year.

The summer sledging parties after returning to Cape Evans. Griff Taylor (left), Silas (second from the left).

9. THE NORTHERN PARTY

The road to hell might be paved with good intentions, but it seemed probable that hell itself would be paved something after the style of Inexpressible Island.

—George Murray Levick

With Roald Amundsen occupying the spot where they had planned to base their exploration of King Edward VII Land, Victor Campbell's Northern Party was now planning to explore the rocky, glaciated northern coast. After dropping off Silas and his Western Party at Butter Point, they found the remainder of the relatively short voyage to the coast to be particularly nasty. A gale blew *Terra Nova* almost 100 miles north of Cape Adare at the tip of the northern coast, and they had to work their way back, picking their way through the pack ice, with swells from the gale slamming large chunks of ice violently into the ship, threatening to pierce her hull.

Upon reaching the relative shelter of the coast, *Terra Nova* steamed up and down the shore as they tried to find a landing place among the tumbling glaciers and steep rocky cliffs, finally picking a large section of flat ice, which appeared to be the only suitable campsite. But at the last minute Campbell changed his mind, and they steamed north, picking Cape Adare instead—which was fortunate, as a few months later that large section of flat ice would break away and float out to sea.

They landed on Cape Adare on February 18, 1911, and unloaded their stores next to the remains of the hut from Carsten Borchgrevink's 1898–1900 Southern Cross Expedition.

Robert Scott had touted his 1910 British Antarctic Expedition as the first truly scientific expedition to the Antarctic. In reality, Carsten Borchgrevink's 1898 expedition was a scientific expedition, although a bit of a disaster. The leader was often on bad terms with his staff, denying them the freedom they needed for their work. The zoologist, Nicolai Hanson, died at Cape Adare, and some of his notes and were inexplicably "lost" by Borchgrevink. J.J.H. Teall's short report on geology was well received, in light of his theories on continental drift. But Borchgrevink's accounts of tremendous gales sweeping the cape for days on end—the wind picking rocks up off the beach and hurling them at the side of their hut—were dismissed as the ravings of a madman.

As their new hut was not yet habitable, they spent the second night sheltering in the old *Southern Cross* hut, waking the next morning to a screaming gale that forced them to scramble to tie down their half-completed hut with wire hawsers before it was blown into the Ross Sea. Unfortunately, the wind didn't let up all day and they were forced to continue building their hut despite being continually blown off the roof.

Cape Adare. Borchgrevink's hut (left) and Campbell's hut (right). Cape Adare is not the most pleasant place to live. It lies roughly 120 miles east of Commonwealth Bay, the windiest spot in the world, where wind speeds can reach up to 200 mph.

Hut building in the Antarctic isn't an easy affair at the best of times, especially with limited tools and materials, but for the Northern Party, constructing the hut at Cape Adare was turning into a job for circus contortionists. As Priestley wrote in his diary:

> Most of us are quite capable of driving nails successfully under
> ordinary circumstances when we are in comfortable positions and
> with proper carpenter's hammers. I for one, however, found it is
> quite a different thing to drive a nail correctly when leaning back
> at an angle of 60 degrees from a ladder, with both hands occupied,
> one with the nail and the other with a geological hammer weighing
> two or three pounds, and with one leg on a step of the ladder and the
> other crooked between two other steps and wedged against one of
> the crossbeams of the framework of the hut for support.

Besides transforming nails into shapes that would impress a sidewalk balloon-animal artist, and fingers into ground meat, the Gibson quilting that was to be the insulation for the hut had to be cut from large panels to fit, and was made of a type of material that would dull a knife blade after only a few cuts. Those whose knife blades became too dull to work would slyly trade their knives with those who had knives with an edge— until everyone's knives became useless as cutting tools.

On March 1, 1911, the hut was finished and firmly secured to the rock by means of stout wires. To prevent a draft from getting under the floorboards, Campbell ordered a trench dug around the hut, with the excavated material piled against the bottom boards. Unfortunately the "material" consisted mostly of bird shit and ancient penguin carcasses. The stench from the disturbed soil was so foul that the air inside the hut became unbreatheable. Campbell attempted to rectify the problem by sprinkling a case of bleach powder on the debris to kill the odour, but the resulting chlorine gas was so strong that they were forced to evacuate the hut. Dr. Levick suffered the worst, with the fumes rendering him unable to speak and see for a few days until the effects of the chlorine wore off. (A harbinger of what many of them would witness in the trenches a few years later.)

They built an ice house, to store penguin and seal meat for the winter, by piling up empty *Southern Cross* wooden boxes filled with ice from a handy iceberg, and spent the next few days carrying out a penguin genocide—filling their freezer with seven hundred penguins.

When they first occupied the *Southern Cross* hut, they encountered a tatty-looking penguin who had decided the hut was a comfortable place to moult. They shooed him away, but he kept coming back. So persistent was he that they eventually let him stay and in fact they became very friendly with Percy, as they now called him. Percy didn't seem at all concerned that his newfound bunkmates were busy slaughtering his chums by the hundreds and, after a couple of weeks, Percy finished his moult and left the hut to rejoin his flock.

Unfortunately, as Percy now looked like all the other penguins, he most likely joined his companions in the freezer.

Campbell's Northern Party hut has been reduced to a collection of shattered planks sticking out of the gravel. The only structure left standing from Campbell's party is the outdoor latrine —a tribute to Edwardian-era latrine builders.

It wasn't just the Northern Party reducing the local penguin population. The incessant gales that swept the area created giant swells that would hurl large pieces of ice onto the shore, grinding up any penguin that wasn't quick enough to get out of the way. Priestley recounted walking along the beach after a gale and finding crushed and bloodied penguins that had gone through the meat grinder of wave-tossed sea ice.

Campbell's party was short of water on Cape Adare because the constant wind not only scoured the area clear of snow but also deposited a thick layer of frozen salt brine on everything—including ice. To get fresh water, those in the party had to make the journey to a nearby glacier or iceberg and chip through a thick coating of frozen brine in order to get to the freshwater core.

On the night of March 19, 1911, the first of the big gales hit. The six men huddled in their sleeping bags while their hut was shaken by hurricane-force winds. They alternated between cursing whoever's decision it was to use Cape Adare and cursing themselves for disbelieving Borchgrevink's dramatic accounts of the weather. Priestley recorded that "our chief anxiety was for our untested hut":

> This shook and quivered like a thing alive, and there was quite
> a rain of plates and dishes off the shelves ... I received a German
> dictionary on the side of my head, and this was followed by a
> deluge of ink bottles, pencils, pens and books.

At Cape Evans, 300 miles to the south, a winter routine had set in. Eating, sleeping, mending clothes and equipment, taking meteorological observations ... Although their met station was only a few yards from the hut, a trip to read the instruments in a full gale could take up to fifteen minutes there and back—even with the use of the guide rope, without which they would have got lost in the blizzard. There were also ponies and dogs that needed regular exercise, although the scientists were able to duck out of that chore, claiming they had too much "important" work to carry out, leaving that mundane task for those that couldn't come up with a decent excuse.

At Cape Adare, they had no dogs or ponies to feed and exercise—though it's doubtful whether such animals would have survived the battering of the winds, had they been there. The men did have a gramophone, which kept them reasonably sane during the dark polar winter, although when the record ran out, nobody wanted to be the one who had to get out of his warm bunk to change it or rewind the gramophone.

March 25, 1911: While taking a walk along the cliff side of a beach, Priestley discovered an emergency depot of supplies left behind by Borchgrevink's party. It was not uncommon for expeditions of that time to cache supplies some distance from their hut in case a disaster befell the main camp— fire, for instance, tidal wave or even an exceptionally strong gust of wind that blew their hut into the ocean. To their delight, among the coal and charcoal they found lime-juice–flavoured chocolate and a type of paste that tasted like greengage and malt extract. There were also innumerable cases of ball cartridges, presumably to ward off savage beasts or, perhaps more likely, savage inhabitants.

> By the turn of the century, Europeans had caught on that the local inhabit-ants of conquered, or about-to-be conquered, lands were disinclined to subject themselves to rape and pillage, and Borchgrevink was obviously expecting a cool reception from whoever called Antarctica home.

By the end of March 1911, the penguins had disappeared from the sea ice, followed by the skuas—signalling the onset of winter. The men settled down to their own winter routine, with Saturday mornings being the most unpleasant. True to Campbell's naval discipline, everyone had to pile their gear on their bunks and the three ratings—Abbott, Brown-ing and Dickason—set to scrubbing out the hut, regardless of the tem-perature outside. The officers—Priestley, Levick and Campbell—excused from performing such menial tasks by rank, would stamp around in the cold outside the hut until the cleaning inside was complete. Priestley al-ways feared that the 700 pounds of geological specimens he had piled on his bunk would collapse on whoever was unfortunate to be chasing dust bunnies under his bunk.

By now an endless series of gales was hitting Cape Adare, and any doubts they had of Borchgrevink's accounts of the weather were dispelled on May 5, with Priestley writing:

> I was waked by the noise of the wind at 4 AM. In spite of the creaking and groaning of the hut, and the rattle of our gear that was hanging on the walls, I could make out definite gusts which appeared to be of terrific force, and were accompanied by a rattling noise. My mind at once flew to Borchgrevink's account of showers of pebbles, and when I got outside the door on my way to take the eight o'clock observations, there was no doubt at all about it. I like to remember that I had the grace to register a mental apology even as I crouched with my back to the wind in the attempt to collect as much breath as possible. The little trip of a hundred yards or so was my first experience of what a Cape Adare blizzard really could do when it liked. My lesson was to be a final one, and as I got beyond the partial lee afforded by the hut I was picked up by the wind, my legs were flung from under me, and I slid a matter of twenty yards on the small of my back. By this time I was in a mood to believe anything, and if I had been told, as I hung on to the guide-rope and coughed up grit, and home-truths about the wind, that the speed of the gale was a thousand miles an hour, I think I should have considered it an understatement. I felt, indeed, that I could appreciate the feelings of a strongly glaciated and striated pebble.

Priestley made it back to the hut, and fortunately all he lost in the adventure was a fur mitt, although he was so scared his lungs would be blown inside out that he took only short breaths during a lull in the gusts. It became quite an art to navigate outside—to lean against a gust would mean you'd fall down in a lull. Stand up and an unexpected gust would throw you to the ground.

They instituted a series of two-hour night watches, with Browning inventing a novel way of constructing an "alarum" [sic] as they had neglected to bring one with them. Called the "Carusophone," it consisted of a candle with holes bored into it at two-hour intervals, with a string passed through each hole, connected to a piece of bamboo under strain that acted as a spring, which had another string attached to the gramophone's starting handle. As the wax melted, every two hours the string would go taut, pulling the starting lever of the gramophone, which would start playing "Flower Song" from Bizet's *Carmen*.

The reason they used "Flower Song" was not because they liked it, Priestley recalls, but because it was the loudest song they had, and it had to compete with the roar of a blizzard. However, as is human nature, they soon got used to the song and would all sleep soundly through it.

They made it through the winter intact and emerged from the hut in the spring to explore as much of the area as was possible, which wasn't much, as the granite cliffs that towered over the cape made accessing lands beyond rather difficult, and spring sledging, as they were also discovering at Cape Evans, was dodgy. Blizzards could strike without warning and temperatures plunged to dangerous levels in a matter of minutes.

Cape Adare was almost completely devoid of sea life. Despite dragging the bottom numerous times, the sea floor yielded nothing more than one sea urchin, one polychaete worm and a sea spider. The numerous icebergs that broke off the Barrier and drifted up McMurdo Sound ground their way past Cape Adare, squashing anything crazy enough to attempt living on the seabed.

Priestley discovered a natural ice cave and thought it would be a good idea to have everyone pose inside it, à la Ponting. His first attempts were underexposed, so he set up a magnesium powder flashpot to light the cave, but when the shutter was pressed, it didn't go off. He peered into the flashpot to see what had gone wrong, and just then it went off, burning his face and hair and temporarily blinding him.

While Priestley was geologizing among the rocks, Browning and Dickason were doing their own fossicking, finding a piece of quartzite they were convinced contained large amounts of gold. Priestley dismissed it as worthless iron pyrites, but Browning and Dickason were highly suspicious, thinking Priestley was lying to cover up the value of their find and perhaps cut them out of their claim.

Like their companions to the south, they were finding out that care of their footwear was of paramount importance. After a day's sledging, they would stuff their socks into the breasts of their shirts to dry them for the next day. Anyone who forgot would have to thaw them over the top of the cooker the next morning. They also hung their boots at the tops of the tent poles to prevent them from being sat on and frozen into odd shapes, which had far more serious consequences. Priestley recalled:

On two or three occasions this latter misfortune has happened to me, and I could imagine no torture which could surpass it. Not only is the physical agony almost unbearable, but no one's temper is at its best in the early morning, and you have the consciousness that you are keeping all your companions cold and uncomfortable for an extra half-hour, while, unless the party are exceptionally good-natured, the remarks hurled at the delinquent are the reverse of sympathetic.

It also turned out the windproof trousers they were issued were too small in the leg to fit over the finnesko boots. Priestley's thoughts turned to the manufacturer back in England: "We would have been well pleased to have sent them spring sledging in a thin suit of summer clothes and tight, patent-leather boots, and then turned on a blizzard."

December 11, 1911: Priestley, out for his morning walk, was shocked to find the nearby penguin colonies in a state of chaos. An ice dam behind their colony had collapsed during the night, the resulting avalanche of ice and rock flattening hundreds of birds, almost completely wiping out two entire penguin colonies. He wrote:

Some of the injuries were frightful. At least a dozen birds had both legs smashed or removed altogether, and these I killed without hesitation, as also three that were completely paralyzed. Some of the birds had had the front half of their bodies scraped off altogether, and these at any rate would have been grateful for the coupe de grace. When I had killed about twenty of the worst cases—and some took a good deal of catching—I had had enough of the slaughter, and returned to the hut to tell Campbell. He then turned all hands out and they finished the work off and collected such bodies as had any flesh left on them for eating.

January 3, 1912: After eight months at Cape Adare they sighted *Terra Nova*, which had been spending the winter in New Zealand. Campbell's party was packed and ready to leave, but due to ice conditions the ship had to remain out at sea overnight, coming in the next day to pick them up. Priestley and his companions boarded the ship, which steamed south along the coast to their next landing spot. On board, they luxuriated in their first baths in months, while catching up with their mail from home.

Assembling gear and supplies on *Terra Nova's* deck in preparation for disembarkation at Evans Coves.

Five days later they landed at Evans Coves, which the crew of *Nimrod* had originally discovered while looking for the magnetic South Pole on the 1907 Shackleton Expedition. *Terra Nova* unloaded Campbell's party and continued on to Cape Evans, with the arrangement they would return to pick the party up on February 18. However, if the ship didn't make it by March 15, all bets were off because winter would have set in and Campbell and his men would have to fend for themselves for the next eight months. This was not really an option, however. They had only six weeks of sledging provisions, were wearing light summer clothing and had stashed at a depot only enough supplies for six men to last four weeks.

Later, Priestley admitted they had made a colossal blunder:

In light of what afterwards happened, it may seem to have been a rash thing to have landed in such a place with equipment insufficient to meet the needs of the party if they should have to winter. At the time, however, we would have sworn that if there was one place along the coast which would be accessible in February, this would be the one.

Camped at Evans Coves, waiting for *Terra Nova* to arrive to pick them up.

Leaving their main supplies, such as they were, on the coast, they moved inland, exploring the Campbell Glacier, where Campbell, Dickason and Priestley come down with severe cases of snow blindness on the lower reaches of the glacier and were forced to lie in the tent for twenty-four hours before they were able to move again.

By February 18, 1912, they had returned to the coast and were anxiously waiting for *Terra Nova* to pick them up. The weather deteriorated at this point, and four days later, a full gale was lashing Evans Coves. They were all most anxious to be back on board *Terra Nova* and get clear of the area, but there was no sign of the ship. Although the sea was open, they were unaware that thick pack ice just over the horizon was keeping *Terra Nova* far out to sea. They kept watching until February 29, before giving up, assuming the ship had sunk in the gale. Taking advantage of a brief break in the wind, they dragged the sledge over behind Inexpressible Island and made camp on a gravel lake bottom to consider their options for the winter. Although there was still a 15-day window where *Terra Nova* might conceivably arrive to relieve them—if she was still afloat—they decided to proceed as though they were stranded.

Which, in fact, they were, 200 miles from Cape Evans.

Hurricane-force winds were becoming common, making sleep almost impossible, as they were up most nights piling stones around their ragged tents to stop them from blowing away. Not only were the tents getting torn, but their overclothes were in tatters and frostbite was common. It was only a matter of time before their tents would be shredded and they would then surely die of exposure. As there were no caves and no material to build a hut with, their only chance of survival lay in digging out a shelter in a frozen snowdrift. They set to with geological picks, laboriously chipping into the ice. Only five of the party could work on digging the ice cave at one time, because one was needed to keep watch over the tents, or at least what was left of them.

By March 18, 1912, they had carved out a 12-foot by 9-foot cave but still needed more height to the roof. It was essential they get the cave finished as quickly as possible, as their tents were in a fragile condition and at one point the tent containing Levick, Abbot and Browning collapsed, pinning them down under the weight of canvas blown by the wind. Struggling out of the flapping canvas, they tried to rescue their tent but were unable to stand against the force of the wind. Their biggest fear was that they would lose their precious sleeping bags to the hurricane. After piling snow blocks and rocks on the collapsed tent containing their sleeping bags, they crawled the half-mile across the rocks to the safety of the snow cave.

With the shelter finished, they turned their attention to laying in a food supply. It was, however, now late in the season, and most of the penguins and seals had already left. Priestley was put in charge of the rations, with the impossible task of making six weeks of food last eight months. So far they had killed and frozen only six seals. Priestley calculated that even on half-rations they would need at least 15 seals.

During the long months of the winter, beginning with the 1st of March, when our rations first dropped to one biscuit a day, there was one ceremony which marked the flight of time as did no other. When we awoke in the morning in March, April, May or June, our first thought was: "Is it a two-biscuit or a one-biscuit morning?" Later, in July, or September, when there were no two-biscuit mornings, we said to ourselves: "In half an hour I shall have my biscuit." Only the worst month of all—August—our mornings were clouded by the thought that there was no biscuit to come to us until the month was past.

Priestley's solemn handing out of the biscuit was intently watched by the others. The biscuits were in boxes that had spent six weeks being bounced over ice fissures and rocks, and most of them were reduced to pieces and crumbs. Priestley would carefully piece together six whole biscuits like a jigsaw puzzle. But as they always differed slightly in size, they had to devise a fair way of distribution. Priestley would have one man turn his back and shut his eyes. He'd then point to one biscuit in the collection and say to the man with his back turned: "Whose is this?" He'd reply, "Abbott," or "Campbell," etc. The process would be repeated until there was one biscuit left, which would be Priestley's—and it would often be the smallest.

March 10 was Abbott's birthday and everyone got an extra biscuit. Priestley had made provision in their meagre provisions for six birthdays to be celebrated with an extra biscuit, a piece of chocolate or half a dozen raisins, but noticed that during that winter, everyone mysteriously had more than one birthday ...

Abbott standing outside the entrance to the ice cave.

Everyone became a biscuit connoisseur. If it was undercooked, or overcooked, curses rained on the baker's head. In the middle of May, they opened a tin of biscuits and discovered to their horror that not only were they overbaked, they were smaller than the regular size! This caused much gloom in the cave and, according to Priestley, "did more to depress morale than all the gales combined."

On the subject of morale: Campbell decreed that, true to naval tradition, there would be a demarcation between the officers and the men. An imaginary line was drawn down the middle of their living quarters, the officers (Lt. Campbell, Dr. Levick and Priestley) on one side and the petty officers on the other. What was said by the officers (Abbott, Dickason, and Browning) would not be heard by the ratings and vice versa.

Years later, after 1914 when Priestley's sister married me, I took issue with Ray's approval of Campbell's emphasised distinction of the bar between officers and men, when they drew a line, in their six-man cave carved into the snowdrift, demarking the fo'csle from the aft quarters and saying that what was said on one side of the line was not to be heard or referred to on the other side. His, Priestley's statement to me in justification was that Petty Officers would be much happier that way, because of the great difference in their upbringing. For the purpose Priestley (later Sir Raymond) was thereupon appointed a temporary officer of the Royal Navy.

—Wright memoirs

Facing the very real possibility of starvation, scurvy, frostbite or more likely a combination of all three, the six men settled down to the business of surviving the oncoming winter. They had constructed a blubber lamp out of a tin can and had a little camp stove to cook on, but had to be careful not to raise the temperature of the cave above freezing. Priestley was alarmed at how much oil they were consuming for the lamp, but without their blubber lamp they would have spent their days in total darkness, as no light entered their living quarters in the cave. They experimented with elaborate blubber lamps made from cans and using wicks made from pieces of tarred rope. Nothing was entirely satisfactory, as they got either too little light or too much heat, which threatened to thaw the ice cave.

All this rendering of blubber and burning of oil created masses of oily black soot, which clung to everything: sleeping bags, clothes, cooking utensils and themselves. Food was now strictly rationed and becoming monotonous. One morning, while out retrieving items from their old tent camp, Browning came across a wayward seal, which he promptly killed, and to everyone's delight its stomach contained six not-quite-digested fish! Three were fried for dinner that night and three for breakfast the next day—a feast that lifted everyone's spirits.

Lack of tobacco couldn't be so easily remedied. Cravings became acute, with used tea leaves being mixed in with the meagre tobacco rations. Although Priestley didn't smoke, the others did, and they rummaged about looking for anything to smoke in a pipe. The teak sledge meter was carefully shaved down to small chips and used to augment the tobacco. The boxes used to hold supplies met the same fate, as well as their supplies of sennegrass.

> **Sennegrass** (n): A special moisture-absorbing grass used to stuff in boots when they were removed in the evening. It would dry during the day in a string bag hung from the sledge.

None of these proved a satisfactory substitute, and at one point Dickason experimented with smoking his hair socks. One by one, as they ran out of flammable material, smokers reluctantly quit their habit, leaving just Levick scrounging around for anything that would burn, but even he was eventually forced to call it quits.

At that time most men smoked pipes, because cigarettes were considered effeminate, although Shackleton was rarely seen without a cigarette in his mouth. Cigarettes didn't become popular until the Great War, when millions were handed out to the soldiers in the trenches.

As freshwater ice was hard to get from the glaciers, in the middle of winter when gales would keep them cave-bound for days, they had no choice but to use sea water to cook their hooshes, which was a reasonable substitute, but Browning developed an allergy and was constantly ill from it. Everyone else was unaffected by the salt water, although for the rest of his life Priestley never got much taste out of ordinary table salt.

Their steady diet of seal meat was causing rheumatism and joint pains. In an effort to vary their diet, someone discovered that ice saturated in frozen seal blood from a seal slaughter made an excellent addition to the hoosh—making a form of thick gravy, which was exciting for a while, but it was still seal. They tried on a few occasions to spice up their meals by introducing dried seaweed to their diet, but it never caught on. Possibly because the only seaweed they could gather had been lying around above the high tide mark for decades and had been pooped on by generations of penguins. Priestley described one attempt to make a seaweed stew:

> Indeed, it tasted like essence of must and mildew, and reminded me of what I should expect a concentrated solution of Old Masters to taste like. If one were to strip the walls of the National Gallery, throw the canvases into a huge cauldron, and boil them for seven weeks, I fancy the resulting soup would have tasted very like Evans Coves seaweed.

The isolation began to play tricks on their minds. Everyone had vivid dreams of home, as well as the *Terra Nova* and terrible disaster befalling the ship—which they had now concluded was the reason the ship never returned to pick them up. Food dreams were more common, though.

> Soon food dreams predominated over all others, and every night we sat at a banquet and saw provisions whisked away from before our eyes as we commenced to eat, or we suddenly remembered there was a shop around the corner where we could buy as much food, tobacco, or matches as we wanted. Cursing ourselves for our stupidity, we would walk round to buy, only to find that it was early closing day and that the shop was shut. One curious thing about these food dreams, which may perhaps be explained by a difference in temperament, was the fact that Levick almost invariably went through the whole of his meal before he woke up, while in my own case, and as far as I could gather in that the rest of the party, we invariably woke up before we started to eat. It may seem absurd, but as we grew hungrier we felt that the former [Levick] had a distinct and almost an unfair advantage over us, though we could always listen with relish to his description of a City dinner or even of an elaborate afternoon tea of which he had just partaken.
>
> —Raymond Priestley

Of all the things they had to endure—starvation, isolation, frostbite—it was the constant wind that almost drove them insane. It blew incessantly. In fact it blew continuously for 180 days. As their ragged clothing was no match for the elements, it was preferable to stay in the cramped cave, even though the roof was only 5 foot 6 inches high, causing them all to adopt a form of stoop.

They'd take turns reading aloud from the three books they had with them. *David Copperfield* was a favourite and lasted 60 nights, followed by *Life of Stevenson* and *Simon the Jester*. They did bring some magazines, but to everyone's regret, Priestley had used them to wrap geological specimens and they were cached some distance from the cave, buried under a layer of ice and snow. They also had a couple of Max Pemberton's novels, a King James Bible and a typed copy of Priestley's diary from Cape Adare, which Priestley would read from on Sundays, allowing everyone to drift off to those halcyon days of the good life at Cape Adare. Unfortunately, reading what few books they had was becoming more difficult, as weeks of living in what they called the "smitch" from the stove had inflamed their eyes, causing pain and watering. They did have crude-oil burning reading lamps that would regularly capsize—the heat from the lamp would melt the ice it was sitting on and slowly turn turtle, spilling its oil on clothes, sleeping bags or books.

They also started singing hymns on Sundays, but no one had a decent voice except for Abbott, who unfortunately had a bad memory for hymns. They therefore abandoned hymns for sea shanties, which everyone knew, and until his death Priestley would belt out a sea shanty at the slightest provocation—often to the annoyance of family members.

With their blubber stove still giving them grief, they attempted different solutions—such as pre-melting strips of blubber and using the resulting oil to produce a hotter fire, which worked well enough, but threw off even more smoke.

Early in the winter, there was no chimney for the soot and smoke to exit the cave. It had to escape out of the doorway, which had a height of 2 feet, meaning the interior of the cave would fill with greasy black smoke and the only way to breathe during the meal preparation was to lie flat on the floor in their sleeping bags. To rectify this, Priestley cut a 3-inch-diameter hole in the roof with his ice axe, in the process creating an ominous crack in the roof that threatened the whole structure. The new chimney worked splendidly, but keeping the chimney clear of snow in a serious blizzard became a problem. With the roof of their ice cave now already compromised, they dared not cut the hole any wider, so during blizzards, when the chimney would clog with snow, they resigned themselves to living in the usual clouds of sooty smoke.

April 27, 1912: The last day they would see the sun. Priestley and Abbott were out poking about on the sea ice when they saw a four-man relief party out on the ice, heading in their direction. They ran towards them but were disappointed to see it wasn't a relief party—but were actually four Emperor penguins on their way to the breeding grounds on Cape Crozier. Needless to say, they quickly dispatched the penguins and added them to the food stores. They would be the last penguins they'd see until the following spring.

Days would pass where they would just lie in their sleeping bags in the cave, venturing outside only to answer the call of nature or bring a frozen seal carcass inside for dinner. After retrieving a frozen carcass from their larder, they would butcher the seal or penguin inside the entrance to the main cave, with the resulting blood and grease tracked into their main living quarters, the floor of which was by now a sticky, glutinous mass. Every time someone lifted a foot, it came off the floor with a hideous sucking sound. The lid of a wooden box served as a cutting board, and hacking at the frozen meat with a geological hammer would send bits flying in all directions inside the cave, requiring the butcher of the day to pause now and then to collect bits of meat from sleeping bags, hair, the floor, etc. Priestley recalled later that he shuddered to think what kinds of foreign matter made it into their hoosh—along with tooth-chipping pebbles that had been frozen to the seal meat. Hacking at a bird carcass frozen at minus 40° F was a wasteful job, and every ounce of meat was needed. It was decided to hang the carcass near the stove to thaw out before butchering, crowding an already overcrowded cave.

Because they had to crawl on their hands and knees to enter and exit the cave, the knees in their pants had long since worn out, with the rest of their flimsy summer clothing so thin that it no longer afforded any protection against the wind. The only thing protecting them from frostbite was the thick layer of seal grease that covered their clothing. In fact, they were so encrusted in dirt and grease that on the very rare occasions that pants were removed, they would stand up on their own.

Months later, when *Terra Nova* stopped at Inexpressible Island to pick up cached geological specimens, one of the ship's crew remarked in his diary:

> Never in my life have I experienced such sensations as I did on this occasion. The visit to the igloo explained in itself a story of hardship that brought home to us what Campbell never would have told. In odd corners were discarded clothes, saturated with blubber. How Campbell's party lived through the conditions we found, I don't know. Although the igloo was once white, inside, blubber stoves had blackened it throughout. Campbell's diary was left on a table. I read it aloud to Capt. Bruce [Scott's brother-in-law]. It was a tale of grit so simply told, full of disappointment and privations of which they accepted with fortitude and never complained. I had to stop reading it as it brought tears to my eyes.

The entrance to the ice cave's main chamber.

Under intense pressure from the others, Levick finally relented and opened his medicine chest to the cook. Soon they were dropping citric acid tablets into their hoosh along with ginger and lime "tabloids." The discovery of a mustard plaster was a real treasure dropped into the hoosh. They all gathered around the boiling concoction, eagerly anticipating the resulting dish, but were disappointed that instead of a delicate mustard-flavoured soup, all they got was a rancid linseed-oil-flavoured glutinous mass. They ate it anyway.

It was the discovery of seal brains that picked up everyone's spirits. The flavour they added was so good that it became part of their staple diet and soon everyone was roaming the ice outside enthusiastically digging up discarded seal carcasses in order to chip out their frozen brains.

Campbell's men used toothbrushes made from the soft wood of Fry's chocolate boxes. The ends were chewed to soften them and used just like regular toothbrushes.

June 22, 1912, Midwinter Day: They feasted on four hard biscuits, a couple of pieces of chocolate and a few lumps of sugar, with an entree of penguin livers and hearts. For toasting the day, they had a bottle of Wincarnis wine,* which Priestley had kept carefully hidden for the occasion.

They drank the wine out of horn cups that were so caked in blubber that they had to be scraped with a knife before they could be used. Unfortunately, while chopping up seal meat, Priestley knocked his cup over and was only able to rescue a tablespoonful. To cap off the evening, Priestley produced some tobacco he'd preserved for the other men and with pipes lit, a "glow came over the cave" for the first time in months. The knowledge that the days would get longer from then on helped warm their spirits. However, the good luck and good health they had experienced up to now was about to change.

On July 7, 1912, the wind finally eased to the point where they could get outside and stretch their legs without suffering immediate frostbite. Out on the ice, they came across two seals that had the bad timing to hop up on the ice to snooze. Campbell and Abbot immediately leapt on them,

---

* Wincarnis is a sickly sweet wine made from grape juice, malt extract, herbs and spices. Besides being a beverage, it's also useful as a paint stripper.

and in the ensuing melee Abbott ended up cutting his hand, severing the tendons in three fingers. So pitiful were the condition of their supplies that when Levick rebandaged Abbott's hand, the old, bloodied bandages were carefully saved to be used for lighting the fire the next morning.

July 13, 1912: A blizzard piled the snowdrifts so high, the entrance to the cave was almost completely snowed in, and steps had to be cut for access. The heat from the smoke from their stove was enlarging their makeshift chimney and the sealskin they used to plug the hole at night was now too small, so precious heat escaped up the flue. Worse, the crack on the roof was expanding and new ones were forming. There was now a real danger the roof could collapse on them. When kicking a frozen piece of seal meat, Priestley's boots fell apart. It was not only his boots that were deteriorating: everyone's boots were rotten to the point where they were useless as footwear—and footwear was needed for the long journey back to Cape Evans. They experimented, repairing the boots with sealskin. No matter how much they scraped the sealskin, it remained greasy, but it worked after a fashion. Priestley wrote: "Cure it we could not under present circumstances, and it looked as if we should have to adopt the Esquimaux expedient of chewing the skin, with this essential difference, that we had no wife's [sic] to chew for us."

By August the sun had returned and, although their provisions were near the end, it looked as though they would have enough frozen meat to last them at least until they left for Cape Evans—if a relief party didn't reach them first. Priestley was always a bit peeved that his future brother-in-law never made the effort to mount a rescue expedition, although they were unaware that Silas was part of an attempt that had been made to reach them a few months previously. As Silas wrote:

It seemed to me, anyway, quite clear that if the Northern Party got through the winter safely, then they'd be able to make their own way back and the right thing to do was to find out what happened to Scott and his party.

Besides, Silas was promised a whole day poking about the rocks on the Beardmore Glacier—something he was looking forward to.

Browning, who had developed the mysterious allergy to seawater hooshes, was getting worse. His illness was becoming a concern, as they all had to be fit for the upcoming sledging trip back to Cape Evans. On

September 3, everyone fell ill from what was thought to be tainted hoosh, but with nothing else to eat, they had no choice but to continue eating the same concoction. Only Campbell was unscathed—he had thrown the liver out of his hoosh, whereas everyone else had eaten theirs. A switch to seal steaks brought a slight improvement, but four days later, they were down with food poisoning again.

Eventually the source of the ptomaine poisoning was tracked to the tin they were using as a thawing oven for frozen seal and penguin meat. It was not level, and in one corner was a pool of congealed penguin blood. The heat inside the tin proved a splendid breeding ground for bacteria, and each new piece of meat that went in to thaw ended up coated in the toxic soup. They tossed out the old oven and built a new one out of another empty biscuit tin. Everyone immediately felt better except Browning, whose health continued to go downhill.

For most of September, they busied themselves preparing the sledge with twenty-eight days of provisions for their trip back to Cape Evans, and on September 30, 1912, and even though Browning and now Dickason were down with chronic diarrhea, they left their cave for the last time and walked south.

The Campbell party hauled their sledges over the sea ice for days, reaching the Nordenskjold Ice Tongue on October 20, 1912. Fortunately, they arrived there at the point where a snowdrift made the ascent of the ice tongue accessible. Anywhere else the ice cliffs were 30 to 40 feet high, and they were far too weak to attempt climbing anything higher than a kitchen table.

They were all ravenous. This was the first physical work they had done in months and they were sledging on what few rations Priestley had been able to keep back for the trip. They left the bulk of their gear at a depot on the ice tongue, leaving a message on a piece of tin:

PARTY LEFT HERE 21/10/12; ALL WELL, MAKING FOR CAPE EVANS.

On October 29, 1912, at Cape Roberts, Campbell spotted a tattered flag attached to a bamboo pole. It was a depot Griffith Taylor and Harry

The members of the Northern Party on their return to Cape Evans. From left: Levick, Abbott, Dickason, Campbell, Priestley, and Browning.

Pennell had left in February 1912 on the off-chance that Campbell's party would find it if they were able to make their own way back to Cape Evans. It was the first time Priestley and his companions realised *Terra Nova* had not been lost at sea, as they had feared.

Buoyed in sprits and reprovisioned, they pressed on. Even Browning was beginning to feel better.

At Butter Point, they found the food cache that Atkinson and Silas had left on April 12, 1912, after abandoning their attempt to relieve Campbell's party. Everyone was pleased that there actually had been an attempt to relieve them. Unfortunately, their welcome change in diet, instead of improving their condition, actually worsened it. Their mouths and tongues were swollen and cracked to the point where Priestley recalled his face was so swollen he was barely able to speak, and every time he chewed, he would chew pieces of his tongue and cheeks.

They made their way over the sea ice on McMurdo Sound, and approached Hut Point, coming across numerous tracks of ponies, dogs and men heading south, which made no sense. There would be no reason to see so much activity on the Barrier this early in the spring. Scott and his party would have returned months earlier and their tracks would have been obliterated during the winter. Something must have happened.

There was nobody in the *Discovery* hut at Hut Point, but they found a letter from Atkinson, addressed to Captain Pennell on *Terra Nova*, which alluded to men who had gone missing, but it did not mention Scott's party by name. Even if they knew the details of the disaster, they were not in any condition to follow the search party's tracks, so they kept going to Cape Evans. It wasn't until they reached the hut at Cape Evans on November 7, 1912, that they heard from the two lone occupants, Debenham and Archer, that Scott's party never made it back from the Pole and were presumed dead and a search party had left a few days ago to find their remains.

Compared to what the rest of the expedition had been through to date, this probably was the worst journey in the world.

December 28, 2008, Inexpressible Island

Ninety-six years later, *Khlebnikov* drops anchor in Evans Coves, a quarter-mile off Inexpressible. The sea is calm and it is actually warm out. Few, if any, bother to visit this place, and why would they? There are no huts and no large penguin colonies, and not many people know the incredible story of the Northern Party surviving a winter in a tiny ice cave hacked out of a frozen snowdrift. Inexpressible Island isn't really an island; it's more of a glacial moraine left behind by either the Priestley or Campbell glaciers. The reduced remains of the frozen snowdrift in which the men carved their ice cave is still hugging the moraine, and it's a short hike from the beach over the boulder-strewn shoreline to a weathered wooden plaque stuck in a pile of rocks marking the spot where the entrance to the ice cave once was. It's pretty obvious this was the entrance, as the mummified remains of butchered seals litter the area. No matter where you look, there is nothing here. Just boulders and ice—the moon probably has more personality. I've been here for only half an hour but already the place depresses me. That the members of Campbell's party didn't go insane or resort to cannibalism is a tribute either to their fortitude or to naval discipline. I personally think what kept them alive and stopped them from boiling up pieces of Victor Campbell was Priestley's ability to stretch their meagre rations to last them the eight months they spent here.

I look in the direction of Cape Evans, 200 miles to the south. It isn't far, but it might as well have been on another planet as far as Campbell's men were concerned.

The faded wooden plaque marking the spot that was once the entrance to the ice cave on Inexpressible Island.

An overland trip would have been physically impossible, and to attempt a trek across the sea ice in the middle of winter in pitch-dark would have been suicide. How many times must my great-uncle have stood on this spot and looked in this direction, hoping to see a relief party or a sail.

It's a glorious, sunny evening and it doesn't seem fair. We're basking in weather the Northern Party experienced only in their dreams during their eight months of being stranded on Inexpressible Island. We've also just polished off a dinner of roast duck and Dover sole. The only sole Priestley and his companions could have eaten would have been the soles of their boots. I suddenly feel incredibly guilty.

Climbing higher, I clear the frozen snowdrift and reach the top of the island, from where I can see the Priestley and Campbell glaciers and the dry lake bed where the party pitched their tents before they were shredded in a gale. That they survived eight months in this godforsaken place is amazing. That they were able to muster the strength to make the long journey back to Cape Evans is extraordinary.

I stop one last time at the weather-beaten wooden plaque. It seems such an insignificant monument to what they accomplished. I hope the NZ AHT will divert a few dollars from their hut-restoring fund and erect a more fitting memorial to those incredible men.

But I doubt it'll happen. No one ever comes here.

10. THE FIRST WINTER, 1911

As for Amundsen's prospects of reaching the Pole,
I don't think they are very good.

—Edward Wilson

The first of the winter blizzards hit the coast in late March 1911. Fortunately by then most activities had moved inside the hut for the winter.
Silas was busy setting up the apparatus for measuring ion mobility and
experiments on the formation of ice crystals, briefly interrupted when the
pony Chinaman sat down on a nail and started kicking his stall to pieces.
Frank Debenham was grinding rock slides by hand, while grinding his
teeth—they had neglected to bring a proper rock specimen slicer with
them. Herbert Ponting was tucked away in his darkroom, which, although
he had more space than anyone else, was on the side of the hut that faced
the blizzards, so he was constantly battling invasions of icicles.

Conversation in the hut revolved around Roald Amundsen and his
chances of reaching the Pole first, with opinions split on who had the
advantage. The fact that he was 60 miles farther south as the skua flies
than they were, and was relying on fast dog teams rather than ponies and
manhauling, made everyone—including Silas—uneasy. Amundsen also
had a direct route to the Pole, whereas they had to manouvre around Hut
Point Peninsula before they could get up on the Barrier. Birdie Bowers,
dismissive of anyone who wasn't English, was convinced that Amundsen
wouldn't stand a chance, while Debenham felt he had a good shot at it.
Tryggve Gran wisely kept his thoughts to himself.

One thing everyone agreed on was that Amundsen would use the Beardmore Glacier to access the Polar Plateau. Although there was always wine and champagne flowing on special occasions like birthdays and Midwinter Day, the only hard spirits available to the party was of the medicinal kind, and Drs. Wilson and Atkinson were always under pressure from those that imbibed to broach the medicinal brandy. (Among the party, only Wilson, Bowers, Taylor and Simpson were teetotallers.)

Lawrence Oates had read somewhere that an epileptic fit could be alleviated by a liberal dose of brandy. Recalling the symptoms of a family cat that once had an epileptic seizure, he went out to where Wilson was shovelling snow and threw an epileptic fit. Silas recalled that it was a magnificent performance, complete with glazed eyes, moaning and scrabbling in the snow. Wilson paused from his shovelling long enough to prescribe a dose of snow down Oates's neck and went back to shovelling.

> Dr. Edward Wilson, the most loved of the officers, always had the men's well-being in mind, although he never spoke of his own troubles. Silas described him as "Christ-like."

A few weeks into winter, they were already instituting rationing, as it turned out that they were short of many items, including sugar and carbide candles. Even their precious jam was rationed to once a week, on a Sunday. Griffith Taylor was the only one who didn't seem to mind, pointing out that he'd lived on a more spartan diet as a student at Cambridge.

March 21, 1911, was the last day they'd see the sun until August 24. Even though it would be pitch-dark for much of the time, Silas and Sunny Jim Simpson would carry on with their usual scientific experiments and had set up a series of handy communication devices, one of which was a series of batteries and bells between the laboratory and the absolute magnetic cave outside. Even Thomas Clissold, the cook, had a bell that rang when his bread had risen sufficiently. If for some reason he didn't hear it, a red light flashed every half-hour until he did.

Wilson loved their hand-cranked gramophone, and often, when everyone else had turned into their bunks and hurled their last insults at each other before the night watch settled down, he would put on either

Chris and the gramophone.

"Night Hymn at Sea" or "Abide with Me" so that Dame Clara Butt or Kennerley Rumford, respectively, could lull everybody to sleep.

The ice finally froze thick enough on April 17, 1911, for the last of the depot-laying party still waiting at Hut Point to make it across the bay to Cape Evans. They arrived tired, dirty, hungry and just in time, as it turned out—a blizzard the next day blew out most of the sea ice, which would have trapped the party at Hut Point for another week. Silas was pleased to see Bernard Day back because it meant he could hand over charge of the temperamental acetylene plant, which he hated as it had never worked properly.

Those who weren't busy with their duties indulged in recreational activities, such as soccer games and ping-pong or, as Silas put it, "A beastly ping pong tournament." As far as he was concerned, the ping-pong table took up too much space in the cramped hut and precious lights that were required for writing and reading.

Tired of the usual soccer games and the uneven score (Silas's team always seemed to be on the losing side), Silas organised the southernmost hockey game, constructing a puck made from paraffin wax and shellac. Unfortunately, there was no chance for Silas to show off his hockey skills. The first time the frozen puck was hit, it shattered into little pieces. Debenham was usually the one who would be injured during these outdoor games, which wasn't surprising, considering they were playing on solid ice.

May 7, 1911: In order to improve the men's minds, Scott set up a series of lectures—three a week. Oates would speak on the management of horses, Bowers on sledging rations, Wilson on birds, Sunny Jim Simpson on meteorology, and Silas on the constitution of matter. Silas had a lifelong aversion to speaking in public and later admitted his talks were rather long and not that well received, and he'd dodge out of making a speech whenever he could. "My talk on ice problems was a fearful business and went on for 2½ hours," Silas wrote on May 25. Later, on August 15, Scott was to write: "Wright lectured on 'Radium' last night. He is not a good lecturer though he knows his subject."

The winter deep freeze was making things difficult for the scientific staff, especially in the Absolute Magnetic Hut. Silas's fingers would freeze to exposed metal parts and his breath would cloud up lenses.

The cold also made photography a problem. Although the film packs that Silas brought back from his trip to the Western Mountains survived the trip and were developed by Ponting, there were spots on the film where ice crystals had grown.

> The Absolute Magnetic Hut was used to collect measurements of the Earth's magnetic field. Copper nails were used in its construction because, as a non-ferrous metal, copper would not interfere with the magnetic measurements.

On May 6, 1911, while out on the sea ice with Scott, Silas witnessed the collapse of Ponting's beloved ice cave. The collapse sent small tidal waves rolling over the ice and rocked bergs farther out to sea. Silas and Griffith Taylor were secretly pleased to see the demise of the ice cave. They had spent many chilly hours trying to keep their balance on the sheer ice inside the cave while Ponting fiddled about getting the exact photograph he was looking for. (Some time later, when Taylor first saw the famous Ponting ice cave photo, he was disappointed by how small he and Silas appeared in the photograph.)

The exterior of Ponting's ice cave. Silas Wright (left), Griffith Taylor (right).

Up to now, Scott had made no mention of his intentions for the Pole trip, which only fuelled the rumour mill in the close confines of the hut. Everyone was hoping to be on the Southern Journey and, more importantly, to be picked to actually go to the South Pole.

On May 8, 1911, Scott finally revealed his plans. The expedition would rely entirely on ponies and man-hauling sledges, with the motor sledges and dog teams relegated to a support role on the Barrier. Scott was still going by Shackleton's bad experience with dogs—even though he had been impressed with their excellent performance on the autumn depot-laying trip.

As on previous Barrier trips, Scott ignored the possibility of delays and timed the journey down to the day: the entire journey to the South Pole and back would take 137 days.

In the unlikely event the Polar Party did not return to Hut Point in time to rendezvous with *Terra Nova*—which could only stay in McMurdo Sound until March 10, 1912, or risk being frozen in for the winter—a group would have to remain behind for a second winter, without salaries.

The Southern Party would consist of five teams: one dog team, one motor team and three pony teams. Once they crossed the Barrier, those of the ponies who had survived (hadn't been shot) would be executed at the foot of the Beardmore Glacier, and the dogs would be turned back, leaving three teams of four to manhaul sledges to the top of the Beardmore, which Scott calculated would take two weeks. At the top of the glacier, at an elevation of 9,500 feet, one four-man team would turn back, while the remaining two four-man teams would travel south on the Polar Plateau for another two weeks until approximately 150 miles from the South Pole, when another team would turn back, leaving Scott and three men to carry on to the Pole. Typical of Scott's secretive nature, he wouldn't announce who those three would be until that point in the journey, although everyone expected Scott's close friend Wilson would be one of the party, leaving two positions still to be filled.

Scott calculated that they would need a total of 3,255 pounds of provisions for the four-man units and that the ponies would need 3,741 pounds for their contribution to the journey. Silas spotted a fatal flaw in Scott's plan. The eight-day fall depot-laying trip, where they had been delayed by bad weather and almost ran out of food and fuel, had given him healthy respect for the Barrier. He felt that Scott had not taken into account the days, or possibly weeks, they might be delayed due to blizzards and he wasn't making maximum use of the meat from the ponies. Rather than feed all the pony meat to the dogs, it would be more sensible to cache some of it for human consumption later, because the amount of provisions the returning Polar Party could carry on one sledge on the unsupported return from the Pole would be inadequate. It made more sense to increase the amount of fuel carried on the sledges—perhaps sacrificing other items— so they would have extra fuel to cook the frozen pony meat.

Reluctant to approach Scott directly, and perhaps incur his wrath, Silas expressed his concerns to Wilson and asked that he relay them to Scott:

I had felt that Scott's plans as outlined by him in the winter seemed to me to give little thought to this source of extra food and that I had asked Dr. Bill to raise this matter with Captain Scott. I do not know if he did, but I heard no more and feel bound to say that I was in no position to suggest what items might be dropped to make up for the extra oil required for cooking.

—Wright memoirs

Even if Wilson did relay Silas's concerns to Scott, it's doubtful that Scott would have paid any attention to a twenty-four-year-old physicist when it came to matters of logistics.

Wright has all the training in physics to cope with these ice problems but as yet [they remain] new to him and he has no grip of the larger issues. I feel particularly interested in making a success of this business because it was my own idea to secure a specialist for the work and because it seems to me of the greatest scientific importance.

—Robert Scott, May 19, 1911

By now it was dark even at noon and the stars were visible for twenty-two hours a day. In fact it was lighter at night than during the daytime as at least there was a moon at night, which led to some splendid displays of "mock moons" or paraselenae, which Wilson recorded so beautifully in his watercolours.

Preparing rations for the Southern Journey: Birdie Bowers, Dr. Atkinson and Cherry-Garrard cutting up pemmican.

With temperatures normally below freezing, Wilson was not able to use his watercolors outside. Instead, he would make pencil sketches and write codes for which colour went where, and then complete the painting back in the hut.

May 24, 1911: Scott told Griffith Taylor he wouldn't be going on the Polar Party because there was no time for doing any science on the Southern Journey. "You would only be able to go up the Beardmore and down again, so your time would practically be wasted."[1] More likely, Scott was annoyed with Taylor for his habit of speaking his mind in front of him. Instead, Taylor would lead an expedition to Granite Harbour to the west, much to Debenham's chagrin, as he had assumed he was going to be heading that party. Scott, though, obviously didn't think a second Western Party would accomplish much, as he wrote on October 28, 1911: "It is trying they should be wasting the season in this way."[2]

June 1911: Routine had set in. Debenham worked on cutting up geological specimens on his makeshift cutting table. Simpson and Silas were busy with

Scott in his cubicle. His writing table also doubled as the chart table.

meteorological duties and equipment—most of which was in a constant state of repair, or disrepair. Atkinson was busy with his parasites, Cherry-Garrard worked on putting together the *South Polar Times*, Wilson painted, Lt. Teddy Evans made charts, Ponting made prints, Birdie Bowers took temperature readings and Scott was preoccupied with reading and writing or, as Debenham described it, "inspecting."

Silas was keeping busy on the scientific side and had rigged up the instruments required for measuring air conductivity and penetrating radiation. The gear seemed to work well but required that he sit outside in the frigid temperatures for forty minutes at a time.

> His station is near the rubbish-heap, and is connected by telephone
> to the hut. It is a cold game, as may be imagined, and to man-
> oeuvre in light gloves with delicate screws would try the patience
> of a saint. I never heard of a Saint Silas, and when Wright's light
> blows out, the gentleman inside the hut (with the chronometers)
> blushes at the language carried by the telephone wire. There was
> a yarn (which is not necessary to believe) that the said wire had to
> be drenched with water at regular intervals to prevent the heated
> remarks from fusing it!
>
> —Griffith Taylor[3]

Silas posing by the transit in midwinter. The curses from Silas, who was freezing to death, became more vociferous the longer Ponting took to get this shot.

The Sunday service on July 2 competed with the sound of George Simpson counting out the seconds over the phone as Silas, who was outside, took star shots. Both Simpson's counting and the hymns were drowned out by Silas's curses when the stars failed to co-operate.

Wright was a professor of a vocabulary of Canadian expressions that was the envy of all his comrades. If by chance he should breathe upon the eye-piece of his telescope at a critical moment, thereby causing it to fog—or anything else went wrong—the remarks that our "Silas" addressed to the particular heavenly body under observation were of such a wrathful nature it was reported a star was seen positively to wobble ... but Silas was no wobbler. Never did mortal man persevere at so frigid a task with more consistent resolution. Zero or "fifty below," it was all the same to him.

—Herbert Ponting[4]

On June 1, exactly one year after they set sail from Cardiff, Scott took Silas aside and—to Silas's delight—informed him that he would be part of the supporting party heading south the next summer and would be staying down the second winter. Assured of a place on the Southern Party, Silas set to work preparing instruments for the trip—specifically, the level on the theodolites, because plugs at both ends had broken and been replaced with rubber corks, which he figured would probably contract and harden once exposed to the frigid

A Cooke transit from the expedition. Of the six originally manufactured, only three are known to still exist.

temperatures on the Barrier. The theodolites they had with them were made of a lighter alloy with leather covers on the knobs to prevent flesh from freezing to the metal. In the supply depots out on the Barrier, the leather seals for the fuel oil containers were also hardening and shrinking, resulting in their precious contents slowly leaking out.

Silas was also occupied with keeping the temperamental generator running, which, despite being subjected to numerous curses, refused to co-operate:

The beastly petrol motor is getting in a bad way it now takes a person's undivided attention while the thing is running. It is positively the craziest thing that was ever designed, weighs a good 300 lbs, gives 1/10 HP. The dynamo is also a curious piece of apparatus it weighs about 20 lbs & charges at 5 amps@24 volts. Sunny Jim must have been drunk when he got it.

—Wright, June 13, 1912

June 14, 1911: Debenham and Gran went over to check whether the Hut Point hut was still standing and found Mukaka, the sledge dog who'd gone missing a month earlier. After a few days's feeding, Mukaka helped them on their return to Cape Evans in a blizzard by obligingly pulling

Edward "Marie" Nelson digging out the hut after a blizzard.

the sledge for them. Scott was furious that they arrived back late and in such terrible condition. Even more so with Gran, who had been on the receiving end of Scott's wrath ever since his countrymen had turned up in the Bay of Whales. Fortunately, the return of the missing dog helped to mollify Scott.

With the hut at Cape Evans almost completely snowed under, it didn't shake the way it had in previous blizzards. Although there were many hours of back-breaking work when they had to dig themselves out of the hut after a blizzard, and the extreme cold made trips to the latrines rather trying. Wrote Silas:

It was quite cold and when I went out in my pyjamas [to relieve himself] as usual and came back in less than two minutes I found my nose was slightly frozen. Wind is the factor of chief importance, rather than the temperature.

Boredom was setting in. Everyone's books had been read, reread and swapped among them. Debenham's collection of "six-penny-dreadfuls" were the most popular, with even the erudite Scott scrounging a book or two from Deb. Diaries were largely forgotten, as there wasn't much to record during this period. (Silas's diary for the period mainly mentions wind speeds, temperatures—and not much else.) The exceptions were Scott, Gran and Taylor, with the latter being called upon to provide dates and details when a diary laggard wanted to catch up after a fortnight of idleness.

The monotonous routine at Cape Evans was briefly interrupted by Midwinter Day celebrations. Due to confusion over the international dateline, there was much argument as to whether this day fell on June 21 or 22. The 22nd won out, and sledging flags were hung and liquor and treats were broken out on June 22, 1911.

Crean, Forde and Taff Evans making a sledge.

Everyone had their own sledging flags. Silas had two silk flags bearing a maple leaf and beaver with the motto *LABOR IPSE VOLUPTAS* (labour, self, satisfaction). They eventually ended up in Canada, where mice chewed them up and made them into a bed.

Sledging flags are depicted in films and on TV as being flown on the sledges, but that's something Hollywood directors have dreamed up to add "colour" to a production. In actual fact they were only brought out and hung in the hut on special occasions, such as Midwinter Day or Christmas Day.

Shortly after the midwinter celebration, Wilson announced what was probably the most insane journey of all—the Cape Crozier penguin egg-gathering expedition. Wilson had been obsessed with emperor penguins since the 1901 Discovery Expedition, and was convinced that in embryonic stage emperor penguins were actually reptiles. By studying the embryos under a microscope, he might find evidence of scales, which would prove his theory. This would be difficult to prove, however, as emperor penguins only laid their eggs in the middle of winter. Wilson, accompanied by Cherry-Garrard and Birdie Bowers, would visit an emperor penguin colony to pilfer eggs, then take them back to Cape Evans for dissection.

The nearest emperor colony was at Cape Crozier, 40 miles from Cape Evans, where temperatures in July would be consistently south of minus 40° F. To be out on the ice under those conditions for one month, dragging two sledges in twenty-four hours of darkness, was utterly insane. Silas was dubious as to the wisdom of the trip. He considered it would be "devilishly cold" where they were going, and they would be exposed to far worse winds than at the more sheltered Cape Evans. Even Scott, no stranger to insane expeditions, had reservations—he was concerned that he could lose three men to the elements—but Wilson was insistent, so, reluctantly, Scott let them go.

Midwinter festivities. Silas (left) standing. Griffith Taylor sitting (right).

Bowers, Wilson and Cherry about to depart for Cape Crozier.

The Cape Crozier party left on June 27, pulling 250 pounds per man on two sledges. The temperatures were benign for that time of year, minus 14° F in the daytime to minus 26° F at night—nothing they hadn't seen before on the Barrier, except they were still on the sea ice.

Three days later, they were on the Barrier, where the temperatures had dipped to minus 66° F. Cherry's toes and fingers were already getting frostbitten, as well as Wilson's heel and the sole of one of his feet. Three men couldn't drag two loaded sledges, so they moved them in a relay, doubling the distance they had to travel and compounding the misery.

It was so cold at night, they had to completely button themselves up in their sleeping bags, as any exposed skin would get frostbitten as they slept. In that cocoon, their breath would turn the inside of the bags into a soggy swamp, along with the clothes they slept in, all of which would freeze solid as soon as they broke camp. The frozen sleeping bags were becoming brittle, with Wilson's sleeping bag cracking at both ends, eventually breaking in the middle and becoming useless.

By July 6, the temperature had dropped to minus 77° F, with the snow having the consistency of a gravel driveway, slowing their progress. The thick frozen fog that now enveloped them didn't help, and accurate navigation was all but impossible. On July 10, another blizzard rolled through, elevating the temperature to 6° F. They waited three days for the blizzard to pass, dug themselves out and continued on their way, this time up to their armpits in deep, wet snow.

On July 15, they reached Cape Crozier. Although the entire area was a barren, windswept hellhole, they found a spot on a moraine, overlooking the emperor penguin breeding grounds and sheltered from the wind off the ocean, that they named Oriana Hill, after Wilson's wife. There they built an 8-by-12-foot hut out of rocks, using a sledge as a roof beam and canvas for a roof.

> Cherry had practised building a rock hut at Cape Evans—the remains of which are still evident today.

It was urgent that they immediately locate a few penguins to slaughter for their blubber because, as was typical of previous Barrier expeditions, they had only the bare minimum of supplies and what little oil they had they needed to save for their return journey. Without penguin blubber to fuel their stove, they would have no way of cooking or heating their hut.

Their first attempt to descend the ice foot to the penguin colony was blocked by giant pressure ridges and crevasses, forcing them back to their camp. The next morning they tried again, this time taking a different route down the ice foot by cutting steps into the ice. On the beach, they snuck up to where the emperor penguins were huddled in a large group and pounced on them, collecting five eggs and killing three penguins, which they immediately skinned for their blubber. While shooing the penguins off their eggs, they were occasionally fooled by pieces of ice that were roughly the same shape as a penguin egg. The penguins, in turn, would sometimes mistake a lump of ice as an egg and try to incubate it.

> Of the five eggs they had collected, only three made it back to their camp intact—and all three froze and split on the return to Cape Evans. Wilson never found evidence of reptile scales in the embryos.

Back in the shelter, the penguin blubber was rendered down to oil and burned splendidly, but a piece of hot oil sparked into Wilson's eye, causing him intense pain and temporarily blinding him. Being Wilson, he said nothing to the others and no one knew of his injury until weeks later.

July 22, 1911: The wind was blowing at force 11. Snow was pouring into their hut through the cracks in the rocks, and despite socks and mitts being stuffed into the holes, their shelter continued to fill with snow. They realised the canvas roof was acting as a giant bellows in the wind—every time the canvas blew up, it sucked snow into the hut. Worse, their blubber stove broke, leaving them with no way to cook or melt snow for water, unless they used their Primus cooker and broached the last can of oil, leaving them short on the return journey. Their tent, which was still pitched outside and which housed their equipment, blew away. The next day the canvas roof over their rock hut was shredded by the wind, and what was left of it disappeared. The only bright spot came while they were searching for the remains of the canvas roof: they found their tent.

July 25, 1911: Caching one sledge and some surplus equipment, they abandoned Cape Crozier and headed back to Cape Evans, but made only a mile on their return journey before the wind blew so hard, they had to camp again. It was now so cold that they took more than four hours every morning to dress, make breakfast and load the sledge. They were now walking, frozen zombies, and on some days they slept as they marched.

August 1, 1911: They arrived at the *Discovery* hut at Hut Point. Since the hut had no insulation, and its interior was frozen, they pitched their tent inside. After a few hours's sleep they made it the last few miles over the sea ice to Cape Evans. They had been out thirty-six days. Silas said it took them a quarter of an hour to get the frozen clothes off the Cape Crozier party: "All had been having a gruelling time and seemed to have been marching in their sleep."

Cherry never fully recovered from the Cape Crozier trip, which caused health problems, specifically to his heart. He also suffered from clinical depression attributed to his time at One Ton Depot, waiting for Scott's returning party.

Wilson, Bowers and Cherry-Garrard on their return from Cape Crozier.

The same cold they had experienced at Cape Crozier now gripped Cape Evans, and answering the call of nature was becoming hazardous. Even touching metal was becoming a chore. When it was too cold outside, the men would pee in a bucket in a corner of the hut. Although when Scott was present in the room, they were required to make the trip outside. *Fingertips have now lost all feeling from freezing while handling any metal in the cave and outside when taking the time observations each day.... We touched our record low temperature of −49° F on or about the 5th of July. I got my nose mildly frozen while going to and coming from the pendulum cave 10 yards from the hut.*

—Wright memoirs

July 4, 1911: During a blizzard and minus 20° F temperatures, Atkinson wandered off on his own to read the thermometer installed on the sea ice. He got only 400 paces from the hut before visibility was reduced to zero. He tried to return to the hut but missed Cape Evans completely. It wasn't until 7 PM that he was noticed to be missing. Flares were let off and guns fired, but Atkinson failed to show up. With the temperature rapidly dropping, three search parties were hastily assembled—one sent up the

coast to Cape Barne, the other to Glacier Point and Silas, Thomas Crean
and William Lashly were sent out to Inaccessible Island to look among
the stranded icebergs.

By 1 AM the blizzard had passed, and the moon came out just as
Atkinson staggered back to the hut, badly frostbitten but alive. Pausing only
long enough to get the requisite tongue-lashing from Scott, he collapsed
onto his bunk. It turned out that after missing Cape Evans, he crossed
the sea ice and ran into Inaccessible Island. He followed the coastline of
the island, eventually losing it in the blizzard and arriving at Tent Island,
where he dug a hole in a snowdrift to wait out the blizzard.

> He ought to have been blown into hundreds of little pieces, but
> always like some hardy India rubber ball he turns up again, a little
> dented, with the same tough elasticity which refuses to be hurt.
> And then in the same quiet voice he volunteers for the next, and
> tells you how splendid everyone was except himself.
> —Cherry-Garrard on Atkinson[5]

Not long after Atkinson arrived back at the hut, the blizzard started
again. If he had not been found he would surely have died of exposure
that night.

July 9 to July 17 was just one long, unbroken blizzard. Bones the pony
came down with a form of colic and was a few hours away from getting
a bullet in the head when he got up and started eating again. Oates and
Meares, who would while away the dark hours chatting in front of the
blubber stove, discussed returning to Antarctica and introducing foxes to
the continent for the sport of hunting and their fur, which, they reasoned,
through evolution would eventually turn to a more valuable white coat.

Even though it was dark for most of the day, with daylight being
just a dim twilight for a few hours, Silas kept busy. Later he commented:
"The intelligent man will find lots to do and the unintelligent man (if
unprejudiced) doesn't think about it. There is a class in between which
may find darkness trying." Everyone was keeping an eye on Mount Erebus, as the first hint of the sun returning would show up as a reflection
on her peak.

Oates and Meares at the blubber stove.

The smoke and steam from Erebus would rise up to a height of 4,000 feet before drifting southeast. At that time of year the sun, although below the horizon, would light up the smoke with, as Wilson said, "a mixture of vermillion and yellow ochre."

Although everyone pretty much got along with one another during the long winter, tensions did develop in the hut. Debenham felt that the others were "down" on all things Australian and did his best to dissuade the image of the rough-around-the-edges Aussie, undercut by Griffith Taylor, who delighted in ruffling more than a few feathers. After doing a plane table survey of the Cape Evans area, he claimed the original maps were inaccurate—specifically, the location of Mount Erebus was out of whack. This was an unfortunate statement, because it was Scott himself who had been involved in the original survey in 1902 and he didn't take kindly to Taylor "rubbishing" his maps.

Shrugging off Scott's wrath, Taylor carried on with his survey work. Silas, another colonial, seemed to fit in well. Probably because he knew when to keep his mouth shut, and didn't want to be sent home before he'd finished his magnetic experiments. However, he was wary of Scott's moods, confiding years later: "Scott was very inclined to act depressed over small things. He was up here, or down there and used to get down there with quite small things."

As spring approached and temperatures slowly rose, they were able to get out on the ice to stretch their legs and do more field work. Judging heights and distances was difficult in the Antarctic. With no landmarks or anything familiar to use for scale—with the exception of penguin shit— what they would assume was a 100-foot-high berg could end up being half that. A berg that was thought to be a mile off could end up being 4 miles away. This was an anomaly that would cause problems when they needed to find supply depots while sledging in flat light on the Barrier the following summer.

Size and distance can easily prove fatal in the Antarctic. Once, when Silas, Debenham and Gran were out for a walk around Inaccessible Island, Gran pointed out an emperor penguin on the ice ahead of them. Silas pulled out his Mauser, took aim and was about to squeeze the trigger when Debenham shouted that the "penguin" was actually Lt. Teddy Evans, who was also out for a walk. Later, on the Beardmore Glacier, Silas may have regretted not pulling the trigger when he'd had a legitimate excuse.

August 22, 1911: This was the day the sun was expected to return, but due to a blizzard, the event everyone had been waiting for was a bust. However, they did celebrate with a fine dinner, "with liquids." The Southern Journey was now only months away and everyone was busy with preparations for the trip including Silas:

Day is making small sun dials in place of a magnetic compass for use on the Barrier, when the sun is shining, of course. They work all right by rotating the dial until the shadow of the vertical pin lies on the dial marked in hours and minutes. But the pin must be vertical and the dial horizontal, that is, level with the horizon. In these circumstances, a very accurate bearing is possible valid for November until February and for latitudes from 78° south to the Pole.
But it seldom happens when the sun is shining as well as the horizon [is visible] that there is no other means of maintaining a bearing by scraps of cloud in the sky, feel of sastrugi [ridges in the snow, caused by wind] underfoot of angle of drift snow across the ski. Indeed, to help my navigation I might

Bernard Day's sundial compass.

have to do, I hammered a few copper nails into my ski near to the bow turn up to
mark 15°, 30°, 45° and so on. These proved useful for maintaining a direction but
not for setting a course for which one had to use a magnetic compass.

> The variation caused by magnetism at Cape Evans was about 150° south,
> which means that the north-seeking needle pointed southeast because
> they were south of the Magnetic South Pole.

The sun finally made its appearance on August 24, 1911—125 days
after it had set on March 21. The event was marked by Wilson's discovery of what he thought was a new mineral, but his hope of fame for discovering "Wilsonite" was dashed when, on closer examination by Griff
and Debenham, it turned out to be a pile of frozen bloody seal blubber
regurgitated by a skua with indigestion. (Pukite?)

By the end of August, preparations were well under way for spring
depot-laying parties, with Oates busy exercising ponies on the beach.
There were now only ten ponies left and of them only eight were pass-
ably fit for the journey across the Barrier to the Beardmore Glacier. As

Debenham and Griffith Taylor in their cubicle.

Silas with Chinaman, the pony he was charged with on the Southern Journey.

so much of the success of the mission depended on the ponies, Oates was under tremendous pressure to ensure they would perform. To that end, Silas was dragged out of his magnetic cave and given the task of exercising Chinaman, a pony who already had a reputation as a bastard. Silas noted:

When he is good, he is very good, but he is usually just the opposite thing and he knows how to do that too. He is supposed to be mad and apparently gets the delusion that he is a cross between a rocking horse and a jack-in-the-box. He is moreover a three-geared rocking horse—the slow speed when I'm taking him out, the middle when I am taking him in, the high speed when he takes me in at which time his motion is somewhat eccentric. He has bolted with me several times but to date has not yet bolted from me.

As the scientific staff didn't have time (read: couldn't be bothered) to exercise ponies during the winter, they were assigned the worst of the ponies on the Pole trip. Those who bothered to exercise their ponies got the best ones.

August 27, 1911: Julik, a sledge dog who had been missing for a month, turned up back at the hut, smelling strongly of seal and covered with blood but healthy and happy to join his hairy companions.

September 8, 1911: Despite the fact that it was early spring, when they could experience some of the worst conditions, Scott sent a depot-laying party, with Lt. Evans, Gran and Forde, to locate and dig out Safety Camp and Corner Camp. They returned, reporting temperatures of minus 72° F on the Barrier. The start of the Southern Journey would have to be delayed because there was no way the ponies (or men) could survive such bitter cold.

Coincidentally, Roald Amundsen had set out for the Pole on the same day, running into the same wall of cold, with temperatures down to minus 56° F, forcing him and his party back to Framheim base, at the Bay of Whales five days later, barely alive and in disarray. The Barrier had humbled even the invincible Amundsen.

In spring sledging and in winter, beards were kept as short as possible. The moisture from breath froze the hair to the inside of their helmets. Those with beards would have to hold their head over the stove to melt the ice around their face in order to thaw the flannel helmet before removing it; if this wasn't done, it literally tore the hair from the face.

Silas took over Simpson's duties in the meteorological hut because Simpson was finally being allowed to leave Cape Evans and, along with Scott, Bowers and PO Evans, would go to the Ferrar Glacier to check the stakes put in by Silas in the fall to see whether there had been any movement on the glacier during the winter. (Silas expected there would be none, but to his surprise they discovered the glacier had moved between 24 and 30 feet over the winter.)

During Scott and his party's absence, Bernard Day took over most of the room in the hut to replace the wooden rollers for the motorised sledge. Using the crankshaft at the front of one tractor as a power take-off to operate a makeshift lathe, he was able to turn new rollers, with a stool acting as the rest for his chisel. Sadly, all his hard work would be for

Bernard Day working on a motor sledge.

naught, because on the Southern Journey, the motorised sledges would travel only a few miles on the Barrier before expiring.

Ponting went missing from Cape Evans on September 24. It wasn't unusual for him to wander off and it also wasn't unusual for him to get lost because, as Silas said, he had a poor sense of direction but never would admit it. However, before they sent out search parties, he arrived back at the camp none the worse for wear.

Herbert Ponting returned on *Terra Nova* in 1912. He planned to mount exhibitions of his photos in London and had been discussing with Wilson the idea of exhibiting and selling his photos, along with Wilson's watercolours at the same time. Wilson was reluctant to have his watercolours sold off and scattered to the four winds before he himself got home—preferring instead to wait until he returned, in 1913, to mount his own exhibition, hoping that the market hadn't already been saturated with Ponting prints by then.

Ponting with the dog cart he used for transporting his camera gear.

As the sun rose higher in the horizon, spirits rose. Everyone had survived the winter of 1911 in good health and no one had even caught a cold—probably because even the most virulent virus would have had a hard time penetrating the layer of grime that had built up on their bodies and clothing over the winter. Oates, who was not terribly concerned about his sartorial style at the best of times, had been wearing the same breeches throughout the winter, and by spring, his pants were so stiff with the buildup of seal grease and blubber that he was no longer able to bend while wearing them. Thomas Clissold, the cook, kindly boiled Oates's pants for a few hours, returning them more or less to their softer state.

Pants were a precious commodity, with everyone carefully darning and mending theirs during the winter. The men also kept a close eye on their pants, because an unattended pair of pants could sometimes mysteriously vanish.

Oates's observation back in New Zealand that the ponies were "a bunch of old crocks" proved to be correct. Atkinson's pony, Jehu, was deemed unfit for travel after pulling (or attempting to pull) a sledge for half a mile, and Silas suspected Chinaman might not be up to the task ahead of him either. Jehu ended up getting his second wind, which meant he was fit to go south, which was an act of pony suicide.

After an incident-free winter, they were suddenly plagued with accidents leading up to their departure on the Southern Journey. Clissold was

The "tenements:" Clockwise from bottom left: Cherry-Garrard, Bowers, Oates, Meares, Atkinson.

posing on an iceberg for Ponting when he slipped and fell over 20 feet, injuring his back. (Clissold was eventually invalided out on *Terra Nova* after severely cutting his hand.) Griffith Taylor went out to the Glacier Tongue on a bicycle and ended up "playing himself out," but he couldn't just sit down to rest or he would have got frostbite of the ass. Silas, despite the fact that he was over on Turk's Head Glacier and without his spectacles, spotted that Taylor was in trouble, hurried over to him and was able to assist him as far as Land's End, where he left him in order to get some restorative brandy—preferably without Scott noticing. Scott got wind that something was up, however, and sent a sledge party out to retrieve the embarrassed Taylor, who received a dressing-down from Scott and glares from Wilson.

> He is a person that goes full bore at everything that interests him without a thought as to what has to be done after, or how he is going to get back; a trait which is good enough except for the half dozen people who have to go and nurse him home again.
> —Edward Wilson October 9, 1911

The Southern Journey was about to start and everyone was writing letters home, just in case something unpleasant should happen. Oates had his hands full getting the ponies ready but found time to write one last letter to his mother on October 22, 1911, in which he said:

> Meares upset that they lost Punch, one of the ponies who floated out to sea. He could have been saved if Scott had not been fussing to the extent he was.
>
> Scott has put two or three people's backs up lately and Meares, who looks after the dogs and is a pal of mine, had a regular row with him. Myself, I dislike Scott intensely and would chuck the whole thing if it was not that it was a British expedition and must beat those Norwegians. Scott has always been civil to me and I have the reputation of getting on with him. ·
>
> We hope to start up the Beardmore Glacier three tents of four men each and I am in Scott's tent. Whether this means I am going on the final party or not I don't know, but I think I have a fairish chance that is if Scott and I don't fall out it will be pretty tough having four months of him. He fusses dreadfully. I wonder how the Norwegians have got on this winter? I expect they have had a pretty rough time if they are not all drowned. I expect they have started for the Pole by this [time] and have a jolly good chance of getting their [sic] if their dogs are good and they use them properly. From what I see I think it would not be difficult to get to the Pole provided you have proper transport but with the rubbish we have it will be jolly difficult and means a lot of hard work. The fellows in this expedition are a first rate lot of chaps and I have got on splendidly with them. Anton Melchenko [Omelchenko] the Russian boy who has helped me with the ponies has been excellent he goes back in the ship this time I don't know what they will do without him if those mules come down. Scott wanted me to stay down here another year but I shall clear out if I get back in time for the ship which I hope to goodness will be the case. It will be only a small party to remain next year. Scott pretends at present he is going to stay but I have bet myself a fiver he clears out. That is if he gets to the Pole, if he does not and some decent transport animals come down on the ship I have promised him I will stay to help him have another try but between you and me I think if he fails this time he will have had a pretty good stomach full.

Oates in the Cape Evans stable.

Meares goes home in the ship he is a very good chap although he did buy all those rotten ponies, he told Scott he was going to clear out, whatever happened. I don't think there is any love lost between them.

I am going to try to keep a diary on this journey [Southern Party] I am taking a book and a pencil but don't know if I shall be able to keep it up. If you get this without hearing of the return of the polar party and I happen to be in the party, there is no cause for anxiety as the only dangerous part of the journey is the ascent of the glacier and you will have heard if we get up that safely. The coming back is not nearly so bad.

A final football match on the ice was arranged so that Ponting could take cine film of the action. Debenham twisted his knee in the melee and was confined to bed for a fortnight. Scott, whose nerves were on edge on the eve of their departure, tore strips off Wilson for letting Debenham play.

They were now days from the start of the Southern Journey, and Oates had taken on the irascible Christopher, who flat-out refused to be harnessed to a sledge and made good use of both his hooves and teeth.

Perhaps he had some horsey premonition of what lay before him on the Great Ice Barrier.

VAIDA (Vida or Oldham). Vaida had the dubious reputation of having bitten everyone in the party. However, he took a liking to Scott, who wrote: Vaida was especially distinguished for his savage temper and generally uncouth manners... He became a bad wreck with his poor coat at Hut Point, and in this condition I used to massage him; at first the operation was mistrusted and only continued to the accompaniment of much growling, but later he evidently grew to like the effect and sidled up to me whenever I came out of the hut, though still with some suspicion. On returning here (Hut Point) he seemed to know me at once, and now comes and buries his head in my legs whenever I go out of doors; he allows me to rub him and push him about without the slightest protest and scampers about me as I walk abroad. He is a strange beast—I imagine so unused to kindness that it took him time to appreciate it."

II. THE SOUTHERN JOURNEY 1911

Adventure is just bad planning.

—Roald Amundsen

On October 24, 1911, Bernard Day coaxed the tractor engines to life and the Motor Party slowly lumbered out of Cape Evans, dragging five sledges loaded with three tons of provisions. The bulk of these provisions would be left at Corner Camp to be picked up by the inbound* Pony Party when it eventually passed by.

The Motor Party consisted of Lt. Teddy Evans and Bernard Day on motor no. 1 and Frederick Hooper and William Lashly on motor no. 2.

> **William Lashly**
> Born in 1887, in Hambledon, Hampshire, William Lashly came from a farming family, and after joining the Royal Navy was seconded to Scott's 1901 Discovery Expedition and was subsequently assigned to the 1910 Scott Expedition.

Those who would be in the following pony parties were scornful of the primitive motors and sent them off with much good-natured jeering and catcalls. Almost immediately, the motors fell short of expectations.

---

* For the purposes of clarity, the word *inbound* will indicate the Southern Party's journey towards the South Pole. *Outbound* will indicate the return journey back to the coast.

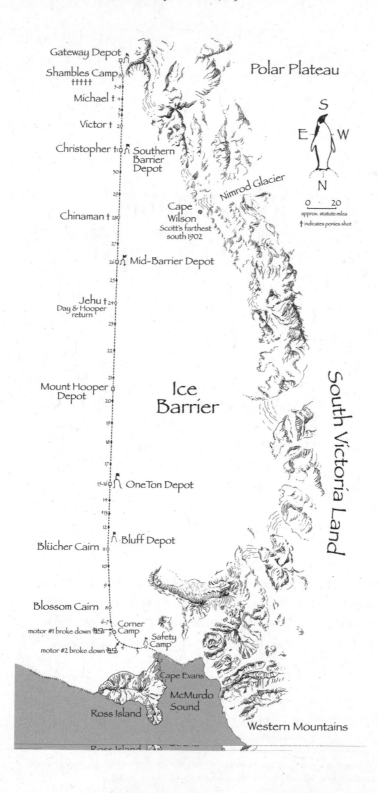

Gateway Depot

Shambles Camp
†††††

Michael †

Victor †

Christopher † Southern
Barrier
Depot

Chinaman †

Polar Plateau

Nimrod Glacier

Cape
Wilson
Scott's farthest
south 1902

Mid-Barrier Depot

Jehu †
Day & Hooper
return

Mount Hooper
Depot

Ice
Barrier

One Ton Depot

Blücher Cairn

Bluff Depot

Blossom Cairn

Corner
Camp
motor #1 broke down
Safety
Camp
motor #2 broke down

Cape Evans
McMurdo
Sound

Ross Island

Western Mountains

South Victoria Land

approx. statute miles
† indicates ponies shot

0   20

Motor sledge on the sea ice. Ironically, even before they left Cape Evans, Scott had washed his hands of the motors, writing: "The motor programme is not of vital importance to our plan and it is possible the machines will do little to help us, but already they have vindicated themselves."[1]

The front cylinders of their air-cooled engines would get too cold, while the rear cylinders would overheat, forcing them to make regular stops to cool the engines. Just starting them again was a delicate business, involving heating the carburetor with a blowtorch. They didn't blow themselves up, but the tracks were giving them grief: the sea ice between Cape Evans and Hut Point was so smooth, the motor sledges had a tough time getting traction, which chewed up the wooden rollers that Day had spent so much time constructing. They eventually gave up and camped for the night a mile from Razorback Island. The next day they barely made 3 miles and that was only because they physically pulled the tractors themselves.

On October 26, Scott and a party of seven others took pity on the Motor Party and turned out on the ice to help them with their loads, but in fact the men of the Motor Party were able to coax the tractors to Hut Point without assistance.

On October 27, both tractors left Hut Point and made it onto the Barrier, where the big end brass of one of the cylinder connecting rods broke on motor no. 2. Day and Lashly worked for eight hours trying to fix it, all the while cursing the person who had dreamed up motor sledges for the Antarctic (Scott). They were able to repair the engine, but temperatures had plunged, so they camped for the night on the Barrier. The next day they only made it a few miles before a connecting rod bust through a piston on motor no. 2. It was decided the tractor was not repairable and abandoned. As they were still short of Corner Camp, a makeshift depot was built, where they left as much of the supplies from motor no. 2 as they could, including Silas's skis. The party remained at the depot throughout the next day, trapped by a blizzard. On October 31, they dug themselves out and crawled south with motor no. 1. On November 1, 1½ miles from Corner Camp, the engine on motor no. 1 seized. After a few hours of tinkering they coaxed it back into life and crawled into Corner Camp the next day, where they deposited dog food and sacks of oats. Just 1½ miles farther south of Corner Camp, the big end brass on the sledge's engine went, and it was abandoned. The motor sledges had lasted all of ten days. The Motor Party continued on foot, pulling 740 pounds on a 10-foot sledge, with hundreds of miles of flat, featureless Barrier ice ahead of them. At one point on the march, Hooper wrote to his fianceé back in England:

> By this time things were getting a bit uncomfortable, our sleeping bags were frozen hard & we were getting very weak, craving for food. It's all one's got to think of, on the d—rotten Barrier, nothing to see but yourself, the sun and the snow. You may laugh when I tell you that many a night after we camped I felt as though I could cry my eyes out, absolutely worn out. We are all the same. Many a time I wished I had never left England."[2]

Back at Cape Evans, the members of the main Southern Party—consisting of Scott, Dr. Wilson, Dr. Atkinson, Lawrence Oates, Birdie Bowers, Silas, Cherry-Garrard, Patrick Keohane, Thomas Crean and PO Evans, along with ten ponies—were assembled and ready to follow in the motor sledges's wake. At 11AM, on November 1, 1911, Oates assembled the ponies in their harnesses and the Southern Party shambled out of Cape Evans.

Cherry's pony Michael being harnessed to a sledge.

The party spent the first night of the Southern Journey at Hut Point, although Silas didn't get much sleep. His sleeping bag was next to Chinaman, who snored loudly. Silas wrote: "The three ponies in the hut made such a devil of a noise all night and I was kept busy swearing at them."

They set off the next day for the slow march across the Barrier. The three weakest ponies—Jehu, Chinaman and Jimmy Pig—were with Silas's party, which included Atkinson, Cherry and Keohane. Their leisurely pace earned them the nickname "the Baltic Fleet." There was much speculation on who was older—Silas or Chinaman—with no one willing to place money on the answer.

The Baltic Fleet, under Admiral Rozhestvensky, was sent by the tsar to reinforce the Russian fleet in the 1904–05 Russo-Japanese War. Sailing from the Baltic Sea, they took so long to reach the Far East, they arrived too late to prevent a Japanese victory. While making a run for the safety of the Russian port of Vladivostok (home port of *Khlebnikov*), they were engaged by the Japanese fleet and decimated.

The Southern Party on the Great Ice Barrier.

Due to their sluggish pace, the polar Baltic Fleet would leave camp first thing in the morning before the others, followed by Oates, PO Evans and Crean, with their ponies Christopher, Snatcher and Bones. They were followed by Scott, Bowers and Wilson, with their ponies. If all went according to plan, every team would eventually arrive at the final camp of the day at the same time.

Early in the journey, night marching was favoured so the ponies could rest up in the daytime, when temperatures were warmer and the snow was softer—which tended to slow their progress. Unfortunately, the lower temperatures at night made hauling sledges more difficult, as the granular snow put more drag on the sledge runners.

Silas did an intensive study of the effect of ice crystals on sledge runners, specifically on friction, which occurred at different temperatures. He discovered that sledge runners melted to a small degree the millions of ice crystals they slid over. He experimented on what would be the optimum temperature for sledging to have the least friction. During the summer on the Barrier, the best temperature was minus 17° F to plus 5° F, next best between 5° F and 15° F and less so as temperatures approached the freezing mark (32° F). The higher the temperature, the more snow melted due to heat generated from friction between the ice crystals and the runners— snow that would turn into ice buildup on the sledge runners, with even a tiny amount causing undue drag on the sledge. Silas theorised that this ice was formed when dark wooden runners warmed by friction and radiation from the sun sank into deeper, colder snow. This condition was most noticeable on the Beardmore Glacier, where they would be constantly stopping to scrape ice buildup off the sledge runners.

The daily per man as measured for the Summit Party:16 oz. biscuits, 12 oz. pemmican, 2 oz. butter 0.57 oz. cocoa, 3 oz. sugar cubes, 0.86 oz. tea; Total: 4,889 calories. (The United States Forest Service recommends that the daily intake for firefighters working on a forest fire be at least 7,000 calories.)

On November 4, they came across the first of the abandoned motorised sledges. As they crossed the Barrier, they built snow cairns with flags between food caches to assist them and the Polar Party on their return. Amundsen put his depots exactly 1° (60 miles) of latitude apart. With an accurate sledgemeter, finding his depots in a blizzard would be relatively easy. Scott's depots were laid in a more haphazard fashion, at seemingly random intervals—ranging from 8 to 102 miles apart.

Dogs relaxing at a camp on the Barrier.

Silas's sledge, pulled by Chinaman, contained all the summit rations needed for the four men who were to go on to the Pole. The rations that were to be left at the supply depots were strictly apportioned according to Scott's calculations as to where they would be on which day during both the inbound and outbound journey, leaving no margin for error in case they were delayed due to accident or bad weather.

November 7, 1911: When they got 1½ miles south of Corner Camp, the Southern Party came across the last of the abandoned motor sledges. Scott wasn't concerned. He'd fallen out of love with his secret weapon and never considered Day and his Motor Party to be part of the race to the Pole (even though the Motor Party manhauled a sledge farther than anyone else on the Barrier).

By November 8, 1911, at 78°23' S, Cecil Meares and Demetri Gerof, with the dog team, had caught up with the main Southern Party. But instead of receiving a hearty welcome, Scott was furious with them. The dogs were supposed to rendezvous with the Southern Party farther south, at 80.30°—Mount Hooper Camp. Scott had wanted the dogs to remain back at Hut Point longer, putting less pressure on critical food supplies. Now the dog team was with the slower, main Southern Party, and would be burning both their own and the Barrier rations unnecessarily.

That the dog teams were performing so well and proving their superiority over pony transport was now the 800-pound elephant seal in Scott's tent—a reminder that Amundsen was using only dogs and was most likely ahead of them on the Barrier.

In fact, Amundsen was 100 miles farther ahead of them at 83° south. Amundsen wrote that day in his diary: "We are going like greyhounds over the endless flat, snow plain." The dogs didn't really have much choice—Amundsen was a relentless driver of dogs. If a female dog went into heat during the trip, she was shot. A dog that was pregnant and unable to pull her weight was removed from the team and shot. Amundsen will never be a poster boy for PETA.

Meares, Demetri and the dogs couldn't have travelled any slower. Doing the math: Scott & ponies—10 to 13 miles per day. Dog teams—17 to 20 miles per day, and that's without pushing the dogs. The only way Meares could have met Scott's original rendezvous without having the dogs kill one another with boredom would have been to let them stop to sniff every pony turd. Even Silas was impressed with the ease the dogs were able to pull a sledge, compared with the glacial pace of his antique pony, Chinaman. Writing: "In these conditions, dogs are better than ponies and better even than men since they carry their own rations in the form of the weaker members of the teams and ready to be sacrificed at appropriate intervals."

Now accompanied by the dog teams, they all pressed on, with the weather in their favour, but the good weather brought a new set of problems. The sun was shining for twenty-four hours a day and snow blindness was a real threat on the dazzling white and featureless Barrier. Even though they were marching at night, the sun was still high in the sky, as it was close to the Austral midsummer. Silas's most vivid memory of that period was the complete silence of the Barrier. Unlike the coast, which was alive with the sounds from the gulls and other wildlife, here there was nothing except the creaking of the ponies's leather harnesses and the occasional "Barrier hush."

"Subsiding crush" or **"Barrier hush"**: A phenomenon where the weight of a loaded sledge will break through the crust of compacted snow lying over the softer snow beneath, with the air beneath expelled in a long "husshh." Debenham described the noise as one that begins and dies away in the distance in a most eerie fashion.

Custom-made pony snowshoes proved sketchy because they were hard to keep attached to an animals's hooves.

Chinaman briefly bolted from Silas on November 9, perhaps having seen Meares cleaning his rifle and eyeing him up. Meares was of the opinion that more ponies should be shot to provide food for his dogs. Silas had become suspicious that his pony might meet with a "hunting accident" when his back was turned, and he'd been keeping a close eye on Meares. Silas wrote in his diary: "Meares was not regarded kindly by the Baltic Fleet as we thought we could see his eyes fixed gloatingly on our decrepit ponies as food for his dogs." If a bullet from Meares's rifle didn't kill Chinaman, the Barrier would. He was pulling a sledge loaded with more than 400 pounds of supplies over rough terrain and loose snow. Some days he'd sink into the snow up to a foot or more. Silas felt sorry for his pony, and did what he could to make his life more bearable: "Had to camp as Chinaman all in. Tired out poor devil! Now munching happily."

It wasn't just bad snow conditions that made the going tough for the ponies—the glare off the snow was making them, as well as the men leading them, go snowblind. The ponies did have makeshift "snow goggles," which were just rope curtains draped over their heads; these helped after a fashion, but proved too tempting a snack for the hungry beasts—Christopher's goggles ended up being eaten by Bones. As for the men, Silas, fortunately, had his own custom-made pair of snow goggles, but even those eventually proved ineffective, especially on his return across the Barrier.

November 12, 1911: They reached Blücher cairn, where Forde's pony, Blücher, had been killed on the autumn depot-laying party. (By coincidence, it would be exactly one year later to the day that Silas would discover the tent containing the Polar Party's frozen remains.)

On November 17, 1911, at a point 11 miles south of One Ton Depot, they passed the exact spot where Scott, Wilson and Bowers would meet their end 133 days later. Silas made an inadvertent prophetic entry in his diary that day: "New routine started. We (the funeral cortege) off at 8 PM,

others at 10 PM. All stop for lunch.
Trying to make thirteen miles per
day."

On November 21, 1911, the
Southern Party caught up with the
Motor Party (minus their motors),
who had been waiting for a week
at Cairn Depot. The fact that Scott
and everyone else looked fit, well
fed and rested didn't sit well with
Frederick Hooper:

Pony snow goggles.

> The pony party up to this time has not done any work, only walking
> along side of the ponies' heads, & we poor Manhauling Party have
> been pulling 1000 lbs on a sledge over a very bad snow surface,
> sinking in about 8 in. over our boots every time we moved.[3]

Amundsen, meanwhile, was 360 miles farther south and more than
9,000 feet higher, having already reached the Polar Plateau by way of the
Axel Heiberg Glacier. It was on this day that he shot twenty-four of his
sledge dogs, leaving eighteen dogs to take him to the Pole and back.

Scott's dogs were also performing splendidly, considering they were
on short and, in many cases, inadequate rations, which forced the dogs
to lower their culinary standards.

Silas made reference in his November 19, 1911, diary entry to "dumping
together," which meant the party would empty their bowels in the same
spot, for the benefit of the dogs.

On November 25, at 82°80' S, Scott ordered Hooper and Day, along
with two played-out sledge dogs, Stareek and Tsigane, to turn back to
Cape Evans. Hooper and Day had walked 200 miles farther south than
was originally planned and were by now heartily sick of the Barrier and
more than happy to see the last of it.

Scott gave Hooper and Day strict instructions that if Meares's faster dog team was not back at Cape Evans by the time they returned, they should make up a party of four and go to One Ton Depot with more food for the returning Polar Party. Hooper and Day certainly hoped the dog teams got back, as neither of them relished the thought of dragging another sledge back out on the Barrier.

Conditions on their march south had been unpleasant for the Motor Party, but that was nothing compared to their return trip north, with Hooper suffering from severe snow blindness, and both he and Day coming down with acute rheumatic pains when temperatures went up and their clothing and sleeping bags became soaked.

Tsigane trotted alongside their sledge, but Stareek was restless and spent the whole of the first day on the homeward journey pulling to the south. On November 25, 1911, he chewed through his trace and ran south—looking for his friend, Bill Wilson. Hooper and Day assumed he wouldn't last two days out on his own and kept going. Incredibly, Stareek returned to them on December 12—nineteen days later and 200 miles from where he had left them. This was an incredible feat for a dog of his age, considering there was nothing for him to eat during his time wandering the Barrier. On his return, he reasserted his position on the team by kicking Tsigane out of his bed on the sledge. Unfortunately for Stareek, in his absence his biscuit ration had been given to Tsigane. Eventually, when the last of the dog biscuits were gone, the dogs had to exist on Day and Hooper's excrement.

Stareek was one of the older dogs and used to belong to a trapper on the Amur River in Russia. Wilson described him as "quite a ridiculous 'old man' and quite the nicest, quietest, cleverest old dog gentleman I have ever come across: He looks in face as though he knew all the wickedness of all the world and all its cares and as though he was bored to death by both of them—he's a dear old thing."[4]

The Southern Journey continued. It was now a slow plod south, with Scott anxiously recording their progress in his diary and comparing it to that of Shackleton a few years earlier. He also recorded the condition of their ponies, confident they'd all make it past the spot where Shackleton "killed his first animal."[5] Unfortunately, Atkinson's Jehu didn't make it. On November 24, at the end of the day's march, Jehu was led away and shot.

Four days later, on November 28, 1911, Silas marked the untimely passing of his pony:

Chinaman died tonight of senile decay complicated by the presence of a bullet in the brain. Poor old devil, he never shirked and was capable of reaching the Beardmore. Dogs had to be fed was the trouble. He was the smallest and the oldest of the lot and the first to cross every degree of latitude. Would eat some of him only if Atch refuses.

He ended up eating him.

The next day they moved on, leaving a few pounds of Chinaman for the dogs, and a sledge at a food depot. Silas was now manhauling a sledge along with Lt. Evans, Lashly, and Atkinson. They were now leading (breaking trail) for the dog team with Scott, Bowers and PO Evans following behind with their ponies. Silas had been hungry when walking beside Chinaman, but now that he was pulling a sledge, he became ravenous.

Sledging rations, which were based on Shackleton's 1907 rations, were proving inadequate to sustain them under such strenuous conditions.

"Spell-ho" on the Depot-Laying Party. According to Bowers: "Lunch time is the worst in the day for us if the weather is at all cold as it is necessary to wait for the beasts to finish their feeds and eat some snow. After a march and camping, one's body is generally pretty warm all over, as soon as exercise ceases.... After lunch however I found my feet often got stone cold with sitting in the tent waiting for the beasts to finish...."

Shackleton's sledging ration was 34 oz. a day, which even Shackleton admitted was far from enough. On the Beardmore in December 1908, Shackleton's Polar Party—consisting of himself, Frank Wild, Eric Marshall and Jameson Adams—was reduced to supplementing their meagre rations with pony fodder.[6]

Scott, meanwhile, was congratulating himself on his portioning of the rations: "We have all taken to horse meat and are so well fed that hunger isn't thought of."[8]

He obviously didn't hear Silas's tummy rumbling.

But it wasn't rations that was uppermost on Scott's mind. It was Shackleton, and Scott was marching as if a man possessed, determined to beat Shackleton's southernmost record, which should have been a piece of cake—Scott's party had four times the pulling power of Shackleton's. At every stop Scott would pull out his copy of Shackleton's sledging diary and compare their time and distance with Shackleton's in 1908.

The sun got stronger the farther south they went, with Silas now snow blind in one eye, which made steering a sledge a little difficult:

December 1, 1911: Christopher joined Chinaman in pony heaven. Silas felt they should have shot Christopher first and kept Chinaman longer, as Chinaman was still going strong when they shot him. However he wasn't terribly upset to see Christopher meet his end, writing: "The manhauling party were feeling very hungry themselves and appreciated the scraps of pony meat that escaped the jaws of the dogs."

Snow blindness is sunburn to the cornea and may not be noticed until hours after overexposure to the sun. Symptoms range from bloodshot eyes to outright pain; eyes feeling like someone threw sand in them; and eyes swelling shut. In very severe cases, snow blindness can result in permanent blindness.

Silas's previous concern over the ponies' welfare was now a distant memory, writing on December 2, 1911: "Had pony meat for breakfast and dinner—damn good stuff—feel almost full tonight. Hope I don't have to stay in Teddy's tent, am sure to have a row sooner or later."

Silas had come to dislike Lt. Teddy Evans. He felt he was a slacker and a drag on the party, especially when it came to pulling a sledge. Unlike the other Evans—PO Taff Evans, a large, cheerful man who seemed capable of doing anything required—Teddy had a reputation as a shirker. Even Debenham, who was not in the Polar Party, was uneasy around Evans, writing in his diary on November 14, 1911: "He [Teddy Evans] is great fun in company but I don't like being alone with him—his confidences are too overwhelming and ill-advised."[7]

December 3, 1911: The weather had deteriorated to the point that Silas's party decided to camp and wait out the blizzard. He was surprised when Scott turned up with his ponies and was "sick about our stopping." In a snit, Scott and Bowers continued on, leaving Silas and his companions scrambling to break camp and follow them. Silas felt this was completely unfair because it was almost impossible to keep one's direction in a blizzard—especially while manhauling a heavy sledge. Silas also wondered why there was no assistance from those of the party whose ponies had not been shot—which freed them up to lead the way, relieving those who

Sastrugi provided one way of navigating in flat light conditions. They're small snow ridges formed by wind, sometimes looking like frozen ocean waves. As they are formed by the prevailing wind, they are handy for ensuring you're travelling in a straight line.

were still manhauling from the added burden of navigating while pulling an 800-pound sledge. He wrote:

Light after cairn too utterly awful for words. I was steering by sastrugi alone. It is impossible to steer well and pull well at the same time and don't see why Scott could not have steered for us on ski.

December 4, 1911: The carnage continued, with Cherry's pony, Michael, shot, which upset him greatly, as he had become very fond of Michael. Silas sympathised: Michael was a neat, attractive pony with few if any vices and was considered the most pleasant of the herd, but that didn't prevent Silas from popping bits of Michael into his hoosh that night.

Despite their inadequate rations, Bowers always kept a biscuit from his ration to share with his pony, Victor. Even on the evening his pony was to be shot, he gave Victor his last biscuit as he was led away to be executed.

December 5, 1911: The Southern Party was camped within a day's march of the base of the Beardmore Glacier, waiting out what they assumed would be a short blizzard. With the snow came high temperatures and the resulting pools of water that formed on the floor of their tents, soaking sleeping bags and clothes. They lay shivering for hours in puddles of cold water while the wind whipped around the tents. The blizzard lasted three days, with the temperature outside climbing to 2° F, making conditions inside the tent even soggier. While waiting out the blizzard, Silas took the opportunity to write a letter home:

Dec. 7, 1911 Lat 83° 20' abt. 12 miles from Beardmore Glacier

Dear Dad,
All went well up to a few days ago or Dec. 3rd. Since then almost constant blizzards. Have had 72 hours blizz. here already & still going on. Snow mixed with rain, so everything soaked & now lying in pools of water. Don't expect the ponies will do much in this snow & will probably sink in right up to their bellies. Chinaman shot in 82° 10' & since then we have been manhauling. Get horribly empty about 1½ hrs. after lunch or breakfast. Day we came in had 11hrs. between lunch and dinner & was

Camp on the Barrier with pony walls.

famished. Lunch consists of 3 biscuits, 1 oz. of butter & 1 oz. Chocolate. The old craving for apples has returned & I'm going to ask you if they can be got to Lyttelton by Dec 10 to have two or three boxes of Northern Spies sent down per Terra Nova. The motors were of little use going only 35 & 45 miles respectively from Cape Evans. Chinaman was the second pony to be shot though he was perfectly capable of getting along this far & we have now 5 left with about half a day's food for them. Dogs will still be with us for a couple of days & will take this letter back. The surfaces have been much worse than we had any reason to expect, but if it were not for the last 3 days blizz. We should have been to Shackleton's time though later starters. At first our time on the march hovered around −20 but now can hardly be below zero. Am writing this in a recumbent position with the tent space so contracted by drifted snow that it is now only ⅔rds. size. We clear the snow away three times a day, too. Started on the S. ration today. We all miss the stick of chocolate & think the ration should be twice as big. Am now cook to the man-hauler's tent and have to go very easy with the oil on account of the wasteful habits of my predecessor [Teddy Evans]. Our marches since "One Ton" depot have been 15m. a day, except when held up by blizz's, so that the ponies have done well—also dogs.

8 p.m., Dec. 8

Still here—practically raining now, surface awful. One sinks in never less than 18 ins and usually 30 ins. Tried pulling sledge on ski. Can just manage 175lbs. per man. But it will be awfully hard work & slow work unless something happens shortly. Ponies go up in to their bellies every step. This letter will go back about tomorrow per Mr. Meares & dogs. Wind ceased now but snowing & raining just as hard as ever. Wish I had moccasins & snow shoes down here as I would like to convince Capt. Scott of their superiority over ski. They could have been used with advantage for ⅔rds. of the distance. Please ask Brown [brother Brownie] to send me a pair of long, narrow snow shoes for next year that I may try to convert him.

Far to the north of the Southern Party, Hooper and Day were also having a rough time with the weather but had finally reached One Ton Depot, exhausted and starving. That depot was meant for the other returning parties, so they continued on with nothing but three biscuits a day to keep themselves and two dogs alive for the 33-mile march to Bluff Depot.

For the Polar Party, it wasn't until December 8 that the wind dropped enough for them to dig themselves out of their tents and locate their sledges, which were under four feet of wet snow. Not good news for the party, but worse news for the remaining ponies, who sank in wet snow up to their bellies with every step, alternately dragged and flogged as they struggled to pull the overloaded sledges through the muck. They made just 5 miles in eleven hours. For the ponies, their misery was to end in a matter of hours. For the men, it was just beginning.

12. THE BEARDMORE GLACIER

You get a darn sight more from people when you are reasonably human with them than when you are sitting on a pinnacle and are remote from the remainder.

—Silas Wright

The Beardmore Glacier is 120 miles long, 40 miles wide in places and rises to an elevation of 9,000 feet. In the early twentieth century it was the only known route to get from the Great Ice Barrier to the Polar Plateau. On December 9, 1911, Scott's Southern Party reached the foot of the Beardmore and made camp at a spot they named Shambles Camp, where the 5 remaining ponies were led away and shot. After the last pony dropped to the snow, Edward Wilson turned to Lawrence Oates: "I congratulate you, Titus." Scott added: "And I thank you, Titus."

No one said anything to the ponies lying on the snow with holes in their heads.

A dreadful day and worse for the main party and for the ponies who were all shot at the end of this march. Our camp was at the top of the "divide" with Mount Hope to the east and preparations were made for the start of manhauling from December 10th, except for the dog teams, which the Owner has decided to bring farther than he had originally planned.

—Wright memoirs

In addition to the dog team, there were now three manhauling parties:

1. Scott, Wilson, PO Taff Evans and Oates
2. Lt. Teddy Evans, Atkinson, William Lashly and Silas
3. Birdie Bowers, Cherry-Garrard, Thomas Crean and Patrick Keohane

Night camp on December 10 located north of Granite Pillars. Sixty-nine days later Taff Evans was to collapse and die just south of this camp during the Polar Party's return from the Pole.

Each four-man sledge was loaded with 800 pounds of supplies and equipment, which meant each person was pulling 200 pounds. Scott's team was the fastest, followed by Bowers' team. Silas considered his to be the weakest sledge team, as Evans and Lashly had manhauled 400 miles since their motor sledge broke down and Atkinson and Silas had dragged a sledge since their ponies had been shot twelve days earlier. All were pretty much exhausted. No one wanted to show it, though, because they were well aware that Scott was still making up his mind about who would be accompanying him on the final dash to the Pole.

It was on the Beardmore that the first signs of scurvy appeared. The men had been existing on a poor diet for the past month and were sweating profusely as they dragged fully loaded sledges through wet snow—possibly losing what little ascorbic acid they had in their system in their sweat. (South African miners were known to get scurvy through excess sweating—a process known as "exuding.") The snow on the lower Beardmore was so soft that sledge runners couldn't carry the load and sledges sank to their uprights, with much of their load submerged in wet, clinging snow. Men sank up to their knees and had to lift the sledges over the soft patches. It was here that Scott crossed Silas and William Lashly off his list of those who would be accompanying him to the South Pole, writing in his diary on December 10, 1911: "Atkinson says Wright getting played out and Lashly not so fit as he was owing to the heavy pulling since the blizzard. I have not felt satisfied about this party."[1]

Regarding Atkinson's comment that Silas was "getting played out," Silas reflected years later that it was possible he was suffering from the increasing altitude on the ascent of the Beardmore. Or he may have been suffering from malnutrition. He had written in his diary two weeks before: "The man-hauling party was very, very, hungry after a little over a month on our way."

December 11, 1911: At Lower Glacier Depot, Cecil Meares and Demetri, with their dog team, were turned back; they deposited part of their load of supplies on the three other manhauled sledges, much to the chagrin of Silas's team. In the current snow conditions, the extra weight made dragging the load even more difficult for them. Scott predicted that Meares and his dogs would be back at Hut Point by December 19, although in actual fact they didn't arrive until January 4, 1912.

Back on the Barrier, they had already been burning more calories than they were taking in, but here on the Beardmore they were burning up far more. (Much later, Silas thought that he and his party didn't recover from their time ascending the Beardmore until weeks after they returned to Cape Evans.)

Conditions on the Beardmore worsened and tempers were getting frayed, with Silas feeling that Teddy Evans wasn't pulling his fair share of the loaded sledge. On December 12, Silas wrote in his diary:

Same surface and trouble. Made about S 20° W four and a half miles on ski. Have only seen a half dozen crevasses so far on account of deep snow. Lost one hour on owner's sledge today. Looks bad but Teddy and Lashly had pulled all the way from Corner Camp. Teddy a quitter.

At this point on the Beardmore, Meares, Demetri and their dogs were sent back.

Coincidentally, in 1908, at roughly the same spot on the Beardmore Glacier, Frank Wild was feeling aggrieved at what he felt was Eric Marshall and Jameson Adams' lack of effort in pulling the sledge, and he wrote:

> Neither A. nor M. have been pulling worth a d--, & consequently S [Ernest Shackleton] & I have to suffer. I am now quite certain we are pulling two thirds or more of our load. If we had [Ernest] Joyce and [George] Marston here instead of these two grub scoffing use-less beggars we would have done it [reach the Pole] easily.[2]

Scott's party continued their own struggle on the Beardmore. Wilson came down with an acute case of snow blindness, due to his constant sketching of the landscape every time they stopped for a rest. Even though he could only barely see out of one eye, he still kept on sketching.

A crude cure for snow blindness was to soak a rag in tea and bandage the eyes as a blindfold.

December 13, 1911: That morning, Silas's team covered barely half a mile. The snow was so soft and deep that they were sinking up to 4 feet in the mush and reduced to relaying half-loads and then returning for the remainder. Scott didn't help, returning to Silas's team and demanding to know what the delay was. He had been keeping a relentless pace to make up for time they'd lost during the blizzard at the base of the Beardmore and was upset that the slow pace of Silas's team could prevent him from beating Shackleton's farthest south.

Silas discovered he could do better by pulling at an angle of about 15 degrees to the side, getting a grip on the surface without his ski sliding back. As Silas noted in his memoirs, Scott said to Bowers: "See, that's the way to do it." Bowers replied that he thought there was a loss of pull due to the angle. Silas was about to protest but wisely decided to keep his mouth shut. Tempers were now at their most strained and they still had most of the length of the Beardmore Glacier to climb.

Mount Cloudmaker was named by Shackleton. It was unique due to its bare rock face, which absorbed the sun's rays, heating the surrounding air, causing it to rise and condense into a cloud that always seemed to hover over the peak.

The frozen surface of the upper Beardmore Glacier.

On December 14, 1911, un-beknown to them as they continued their slow progress up the glacier, Amundsen had reached the South Pole.

The next day, they were at Mid-Glacier Depot, near Mount Cloud-maker, when the deep snow finally gave way to hard ice. Silas recalled, "Scott looked up at the glacier, say-ing: 'Well, there are the crevasses, someone has to fall into one first.' By co-incidence, he was the first to do so."

84° 34' S. Went all day helter-skelter over, under, in and through crevasses. Scott set a hot pace. May I never again be the only long-legged one in such a team. All did their best but I am damn sure I had to provide the extra speed. Slipping all over on the thumbprint ice even with crampons. Nobody ever down [a crevasse] the full length of a harness, but legs, etc. in every few yards.

—Wright, December 19, 1911

Amazingly, no one broke a leg in a crevasse. The surface was improv-ing, though, with only light snow covering the ice, which made it easier to spot the crevasses, and they were making good time. Silas, the ice ex-pert, was expected to know about crevasses, but to date his knowledge of crevasses was mostly from seeing the inside of them, writing: "Crevasses are not regular at all and you can have two members of the same party down two different crevasses at the same time, and the sledge down a third, if you're not careful, too." Sometimes they inadvertently camped on a crevasse, which would then reveal itself in the middle of the night, as they melted the snow beneath them.

Atch nearly all in at finish though a very short day—less than eight and a half hours march. Our sledge is slow and can't keep up with the owner's. Teddy, that damn hypocrite, as soon as he sees the owner's sledge stopped and they are watching us come up, puts his head down and digs in for all he's worth.

—Wright, December 19, 1911

Even Cherry-Garrard was losing patience with Teddy Evans, writing in his diary on December 14: "Wright wanted to push Teddy Evans down a crevasse... It is a pity he didn't." That same day, Frederick Hooper and Bernard Day finally reached Hut Point and were dismayed to find the dog teams weren't there. It meant they would have to return to the Barrier to provision One Ton Depot.

Back on the Beardmore, excitement among the group was mounting because the next day they would be approaching the top of the glacier—where they would find out which of the remaining two support parties would be sent back. It was typical of Scott that no one had been let in on his plans, and if Wilson, his only confidant, knew, he never let on. Silas thought he had a pretty good shot at being included because he had the best skills when it came to navigating without a compass in whiteout conditions—handy at 90° south and even handier on the solitary, unsupported long march back across the Barrier to Cape Evans. Lt. Evans had experience in navigating, as did Oates, so technically, Silas had a one-in-three chance of being included in the final Polar Party. Spirits were high. As they hadn't seen any sign of Amundsen on the Beardmore, everyone was pretty sure that either some disaster had befallen Amundsen's party or they had fallen behind.

Scott himself was full of hope all would be well and that the Pole would be reached first, especially as we had always thought that Amundsen would travel by the Beardmore Glacier and we had seen no signs of him on the glacier. In fact, we were cock-a-whoop with no real misgivings even about the bug-bear of scurvy.

—Wright memoirs

On Wednesday, December 20, 1911, 283 miles from the South Pole, Scott revealed his choice. Silas was devastated writing in his diary that night: "Atch, Cherry, Keohane and I turn back tomorrow night. Scott a fool. Teddy goes on. I have to make course back. Too wild to write more tonight. Teddy slack trace ⅞th of today."

It wasn't being cut from the Polar Party that most upset Silas; it was that Teddy Evans, whom he considered wasn't pulling his weight, was to carry on and quite possibly be on the final Polar Party. Silas was later to comment:

I was quite, quite certain that there were at least two people, maybe three who were going on, and were not in as good condition as I was … I'd say I thought more highly of myself and my condition than maybe Captain Scott did.

In his memoirs, Silas reflected further on that day:

And here it was that the Owner told us that Atch (in charge) Cherry, Keohane and I were to return. Cherry was, I know, very disappointed and so was I. The reason for my disappointment was that I was quite certain that both Cherry and I were in better shape than at least one who was chosen to go on. I must have shown my disappointment since the owner, most kindly, softened the blow by pointing out that I would have the responsibility as navigator of the party, of seeing that we did not get lost on the way back. It did soften the blow to a great extent. I was not entirely happy but soon recovered and indeed, probably took this responsibility too seriously.

On December 21, 1911, at Upper Glacier Depot, Silas's party bade farewell to the others and prepared to turn back. Scott wrote: "We made our depot this morning then said an affecting farewell to the returning party, who have taken things very well, dear good fellows as they are."[3]

The two parties who remained would be pulling 190 pounds per man:

1. Scott, with Wilson, PO Evans and Oates
2. Lt. Teddy Evans, with Bowers, Lashly and Crean

Wilson handed over a few items for the others to take back, writing in his diary: "It was wretched parting from the others. Atch took my watch back, as they were short and only had one. Silas took my sundial." Cherry gave his pyjama trousers to Wilson and a pouch of tobacco to Oates, along with a spare pair of finnesko to Bowers. They said their final farewells, and Silas and his party turned north.

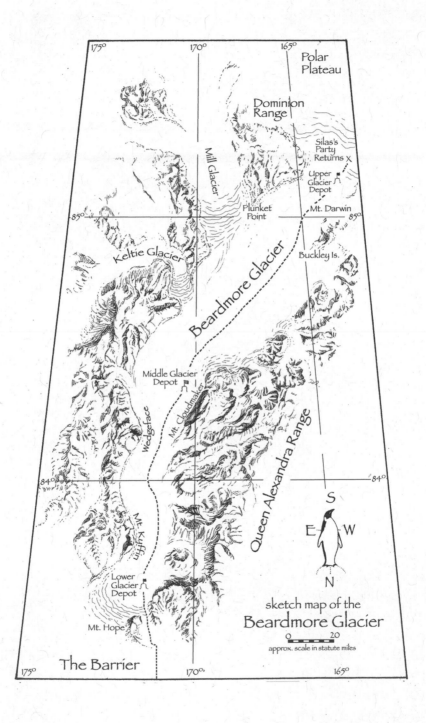

sketch map of the
Beardmore Glacier

approx. scale in statute miles

13. SILAS'S RETURN FROM THE BEARDMORE

Last time I take on a job like this.

—Silas Wright

Silas now had to navigate for his party back down the Beardmore Glacier and across the Great Ice Barrier to Cape Evans. They made good time descending the glacier until December 23, 1911, when the tracks made on their ascent were obliterated by blowing snow and Silas had to navigate blind through a mass of hidden crevasses. Silas wrote in his diary: "So much for my navigation—and all Atch said was, 'Which direction do we go now?' My reply was: 'Oh, straight ahead.'"

Patrick Keohane set the record for falling into crevasses—disappearing down eight in fifteen minutes. Atkinson fell head-first into a crevasse and as he was being hauled out by his sledge harness, the attached sledge dropped into another crevasse. They decided to call a halt and assess the situation.

Needless to say, I was feeling very badly about having led our party astray amongst the seracs* north of the Cloudmaker. There was little excuse for this except the fact that we had taken no bearings at the depot which would have helped us and the undoubted fact that it is much easier to see and avoid trouble going up than going down a glacier like the Beardmore. And it has been little satisfaction that Teddy Evans's party as well as Scott's own party were not free from similar troubles in about this area.

—Wright memoirs

---

* Seracs are the ridges on a glacier formed by the resulting pressure where two glaciers meet.

Silas gingerly led the party out towards the centre of the glacier, where they found better ice conditions and fewer crevasses. They made the Mid-Glacier Depot opposite Mount Cloudmaker on Christmas Eve, with half a day's rations to spare and everyone's limbs intact. Unfortunately the hard glacial ice was tearing their sledge runners to pieces, slowing their pace and meaning they'd have to stretch out their already pitiful rations.

December 25, 1911: Silas's group celebrated Christmas by breaking out the special Christmas rations that Birdie Bowers had given them, which thoughtfully included such delicacies as chocolate, raisins and even four small cubes of Christmas cake.

A few miles south, in Scott's party, William Lashly celebrated Christmas by falling into a crevasse, almost dragging Bowers and Crean in with him. That night, Bowers broke out their own Christmas rations, and they feasted on plum pudding, raisins, caramels and ginger.

December 28, 1911: Silas and his party made Lower Glacier Depot, where they swapped their battered 12-foot sledge for a cached 10-foot sledge with runners that hadn't been scored by glacial ice and pulled more easily. The next day they were finally off the Beardmore and onto the Barrier but only had seven days's rations to carry them the 43 miles to South Barrier Depot. With supplies so short and depots spread so far apart, it was essential that Silas get them across the Barrier as quickly as possible, in case they were hit by a multi-day blizzard. Keohane had been complaining of an upset stomach—probably due, Atkinson assumed, to eating too much Christmas dinner and it would soon pass, but it persisted. A day later, Keohone was suffering from full-blown dysentery and unable to pull the sledge. To make matters worse, the snow was back to being soft and deep, which slowed them down considerably. They eventually stopped for the day and gave Keohane a liberal dose of brandy. From notes

On the return from the top of the Beardmore: from left, Keohane, Atkinson and Cherry-Garrard.

Camp on the Beardmore. Silas calculated that if their sledge runners had been in better condition, they could have made an extra 5 miles a day.

left by Cecil Meares at the depots and picked up by Silas's party, it appeared that Meares and Demetri's dog team wasn't having a much better time of it. Bad weather, lousy snow surfaces, food shortages and exhausted dogs. But so far, no dysentery…

It was vital to Scott's plans that the dogs got back safely, as he needed them to take him the last few miles from One Ton Depot to Hut Point on his return. He had given Meares instructions to bring a dog team back from Hut Point to One Ton Depot on March 3, 1912, and wait at One Ton to meet his returning Polar Party. But the dogs had travelled farther south than originally planned and now, on their return, were worn out from their arduous journey, with no guarantee they'd have enough food even to last them to Hut Point.

On January 1, 1912, Silas's party celebrated New Year's Day with one extra sledging biscuit each. Temperatures were varying from between minus 17° F at night to plus 20° F in the daytime, which softened the snow, making pulling the sledges difficult, with sweat from the day's labour quickly freezing at night.

Would give anything for a full tummy. If we can keep our present average will be in One Ton Depot in about two weeks. Hope to heaven it is laid out by that time or we

may have to make Hut Point on half rations or less. Full ration God knows leaves one
empty enough. I get hungry again one hour after lunch. Am certain could do more and
better work on a bigger ration.

—Wright, January 1, 1912

But Silas kept up a relentless pace, worried the weather would turn on them. As a precaution, they were putting aside a few extra rations every day in case they became trapped on the Barrier by a blizzard.

Silas's ski boots were disintegrating, and he was worried they wouldn't last until Hut Point. The weather, which remained clear and sunny, was making it difficult for Silas to navigate in the relentless glare, and he was feeling the effects of snow blindness. Years later, Silas wrote of the difficulties of navigating on the Barrier:

Judgement of size and distance are interesting. Our classical example was in mistaking
pony droppings for a sledge party miles away. This difficulty of not knowing for what
distance the eye was focused was most disturbing to us in periods when we never saw
the horizon for days on end. In trying to pick up depots, we often found ourselves
looking up into the sky at any angle up to 30 deg. [degrees] In such conditions also,
I personally found my eyes were not focused for infinity; Depots, when they became
visible (by focusing correctly) positively hit the eye. On other occasions, I have taken
the party between two 10 ft. high snow cairns a few feet apart without the remainder
of the party seeing them at all.

Silas and his party slogged on, Silas thinking of nothing more than putting one ski in front of the other and dreaming of food.

…tried a bit of pemm. [pemmican] in tea at lunch. Makes a tremendous difference
& makes the measly 5 lumps of sugar almost tasteable. Wish we had food like cocoa
instead of this beastly rotten tea we have (Coopers) The only taste one gets is of hotness
and wetness.

—Wright, January 3, 1911

The camps they were aiming for were hard to see even in good light, because they had been drifted over by numerous blizzards since they were laid on their outward journey. On the night of January 6, 1912, Silas wrote in his diary:

All day, light too awful for words. Trying to follow dog tracks and eyes now very sore. Short hours, even Atch who had nothing to do but pull felt the strain of a bad light. Last time I take on a job like this.

Occasionally he would get lucky and spot "mundungous" (pony droppings), a sign they were on the track of the outward journey.

January 7, 1912: Disaster. Silas got lost:

I turned a complete circle and came back to meet our own tracks on a dreadful day with no horizon, no wind, no sastrugi or drift to help the navigator. I was terribly ashamed of myself as I had been picking up, quite regularly, all the snow cairns and depots laid on the outward journey. I guess it was time for a jolt to my "ego." This experience shook me to such an extent that I lost all confidence and soon had to suggest to Atch that, until conditions improved, we had better camp.

Fortunately, conditions did improve the next day and Silas was able to get his bearings, but he was much chastened by the experience. It was frightening for him to think of what would have happened had they got lost on the Barrier.

On the Polar Plateau, Scott's party was still going strong and Scott gleefully recorded in his diary that he had passed Shackleton's farthest point south. As far as he was concerned, they were the first humans to get this far south.

On January 10, 1912, Silas's party arrived at Mount Hooper, to find the food cached there somewhat more depleted than it should have been. This was most serious and could mean the difference between life or death on the Barrier. The speculation was that it had to be Meares who had taken more than he was entitled to. After all, he'd been reckless with feeding more pony meat to his dogs than he had been allocated. Silas was furious:

Sixty miles to next depot, two weeks grub about. Meares only two weeks ahead of us in a great panic. Has taken a lot of our grub, which makes it doubtful if we can afford to go on beyond One Ton if depot is not laid. Damn him! Took fifty biscuits for two men doing no work to go sixty odd miles. A blizz will make it impossible to go straight through as One Ton is one hundred fifty miles from Hut Point.

Years later, Teddy Evans disputed the widely held belief among the other members of the returning parties the Meares and Demetri took more than their allotted share. In a lecture at the Royal Albert Hall in London, he claimed that Meares and Demetri travelled back on short rations, voluntarily omitting one meal per day. Evans, however, was no slouch when it came to taking more than his share of rations.

There may have also been some jealousy in that Meares and Demetri could sit on their sledge, letting the dogs do all the work, while Silas's party had to manhaul their sledge from the top of the Beardmore. Conversation in their tent was dominated by speculation as to how much food, if any, would be left for them at One Ton Depot, and if their rations would indeed last until One Ton, which was now fondly called the "Great Hoosh." One night, Cherry sat bolt upright from a deep sleep, declaring: "Within a yard of the Great Hoosh!"

On January 13, 1912, they were hit by a fierce blizzard, with visibility reduced to near-zero, but Silas kept them moving. To slow down while rations were this short would have been suicide. If One Ton had not been resupplied, the best they could hope for was that Meares had left some dog biscuits behind. Two days later, on January 15, they made One Ton depot, which, to their relief, had been resupplied four days earlier—not by Meares's dog team, but by Bernard Day, Edward Nelson, Frederick Hooper and Thomas Clissold, manhauling a sledge. They gorged themselves, with Silas eating a full day's rations in one sitting. Atkinson and Keohane immediately came down with dysentery.

It was here that Atkinson decided to re-apportion the rations, leaving twice what they were taking for the following second supporting party, which annoyed the ever-hungry Silas, who wrote:

*I'm damned sore at Atch. He insists on leaving for the second party two to three times as much grub as we take. They for instance pick up 3 weeks + biscuit here. If they had half starved like us they would [already] have 2 1/2 times the ordinary ration to go in on."**

---

*Handwritten postscript in memoir: "comment: Jolly good thing they did have the extra grub, wrong again CSW."

Silas's party left on January 16, for Bluff Depot, 33 miles away. That same day, 10 miles from the South Pole, Bowers spotted Amundsen's black flag in the distance.

Even though Atkinson was suffering from a severe case of dysentry, he was determined to do his part and declined Silas's suggestion he stop pulling on the sledge. It was a noble gesture, but it slowed them down even more. Fortunately, they now had plenty of rations, so they could afford to take their time.

Silas blamed the dysentry on the richness of the food they were now eating, and wrote of Atkinson, "Wish he would give the hoosh a steady for a couple of days and fill up on biscuits and cocoa." Silas later speculated that considering that they had all eaten the same kind of rations, perhaps the problem was that Atkinson and Keohone hadn't cleaned out their own meal pans properly. Finally, on January 24, they were within sight of Observation Hill and two days later reached the safety of Hut Point.

We reached Hut Point without any further difficulties on January 26, 1912, chalking up an average for the return of about 16 statute miles a day. How we looked forward to a bath at Cape Evans! But it was not to be until the following day since Ponting made a claim [sustained by Simpson] on our bodies to take part in a cinema record of our arrival up the icefoot at Cape Evans, filthy as we were, unshaven and with our hair uncut and with sledge firmly attached behind us. Art not for art sake, but for publicitys!

—Wright memoirs

Simpson remembered their return:"Getting up to them I could recognize no one and Ponting admits that he took them for strangers and thought at once of the Norwegians."

Despite the conditions they had encountered on the Barrier, Silas and his companions had no doubt in their minds that Scott had made it to the South Pole and that the party was on its way back. Right then, however, their most pressing task was to enjoy the first real cooked meal they had had in three months.

Overate. Unhappy.

—Wright diaries, January 29, 1912

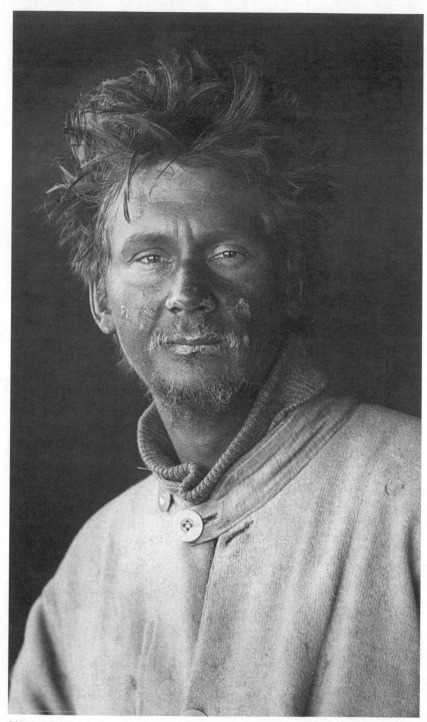

Silas Wright on his return to Cape Evans from the Southern Journey.

14. THE SOUTH POLE AND RETURN JOURNEY

The rapid closing of the season is ominous.

—Robert Scott, February 25, 1912

December 28, 1911: The two remaining sledge parties reached the Polar Plateau. The sun had come out and temperatures were practically tropical at minus 3° F to minus 10° F. Unfortunately the surface was bad for pulling sledges, and Lt. Teddy Evans's team was having a tough time. Scott put that down to their being "stale" and their sledge frame distorted by "bad strapping and bad loading."[1]

By December 30, even though temperatures were falling, they were making good time and were back on Scott's schedule. (The six days they had lost at the bottom of the glacier could no longer be blamed for the delay in their getting back to Cape Evans.) Ironically, on this day and at that latitude, Amundsen was passing them 75 miles to the east on his way *back* from the South Pole.

December 31, 1911: To lighten their loads, they cut the sledges down from 12 feet to 10 feet, and in the process, PO Taff Evans cut his hand. Normally it wouldn't be an issue, but at those temperatures and in their weakened states, it was a serious matter and Evans concealed the injury from the others, as he felt it would surely disqualify him from a position on the final Polar Party.

On January 3, 1912, when they were 146 miles from the South Pole, Scott announced the makeup of the final Polar Party. Edward Wilson, PO Taff Evans, Lawrence Oates and Henry Bowers were going on with him, while William Lashly, Thomas Crean and Lt. Teddy Evans would be turning back. It was a shock for everyone: that Wilson and Taff Evans were selected wasn't a surprise, and even Oates made sense. The inclusion of Bowers did not, for he would be the fifth man. Everyone had assumed Scott would take three men with him. After all, the provisions for the Polar Party had been calculated to sustain four men, not five. That Bowers was chosen to go on to the Pole was puzzling. He would be the only member of the party on foot, as he had abandoned his skis farther back at Three Degree Depot—presumably because he hadn't expected to be on the Polar Party. Birdie Bowers, at twenty-nine years of age, was the youngest of the group. Wilson was thirty, Oates thirty-two, PO Evans thirty-six, and Scott the oldest, at forty-four.

Five in a tent was like being "packed like a bundle of snakes"—Birdie Bowers commenting on what it was like to be five to a tent on a 1911 autumn depot-laying journey. PO Evans's size and weight was such that it must have been impossible for him to stretch out in a tent with four companions, which would lead to cramps and sleeplessness.

January 4, 1912: Teddy Evans, Crean and Lashly watched Scott's party disappear over the horizon and then turned north. There were now only the three of them to drag the sledge, and at every supply depot on the way back they would have to open all the cached rations and extract three-fourths of the rations, instead of the planned for four-fourths—not an easy task in sub-zero temperatures.

For Teddy Evans's party, it was going to be a long, difficult 750-mile slog home.

Scott, on the other hand, was brimming with confidence and calculated that despite deteriorating snow conditions, his team would reach the Pole in ten days, even though logistics had become more complicated. Tasks that were normally routine—such as cooking—became trickier with five in a tent. Scott wrote on January 5, 1911: "Cooking for five takes a seriously longer time than cooking for four; perhaps half an hour on the whole day. It is an item I had not considered when re-organising."

The wound on PO Evans's hand had been revealed on January 7 and was now seriously infected. Evans should probably have rested for a day or two, but they were almost at Shackleton's farthest point south, and Scott was anxious to beat Shackleton's time, or at the very least match it. They finally reached that point, 88°23' S, or 97 geographic miles from the South Pole on January 9, 1912—the exact spot where Shackleton had turned back on January 9, 1909. It was a lopsided victory. Shackleton's party was made up of three men and was unsupported. Scott's party was five and had been supported until the last few miles.

> Scott was always suspicious that Shackleton had faked his farthest south and on January 9, 1912, wrote in his diary, "beyond the record of Shackleton's exaggerated walk." (The manuscript of that diary is in the British Museum. Some two hundred entries were excised from Scott's original diaries prior to the publication of *Scott's Last Expedition*.)

January 15, 1912. Twenty-seven miles from the Pole, they lightened the load on the sledge by dropping off more supplies, to be picked up on their return trip. The next day, Bowers spotted a black flag in the distance. As they got closer they saw it was marking a cairn. When they reached it they saw tracks of men, sledges and dogs. Scott was deflated. Amundsen *had* beaten him to the South Pole. All that was left was to press on and confirm it.

> To ensure they really had reached the South Pole, Amundsen's party set a sledge upright at 89°59' S. From there, one man set out in each of three directions—east, west and south—for 11 miles.

On January 17, 1912, Scott's party found Amundsen's tent, with the Norwegian flag flying from the tent pole. Inside was a note from Amundsen, signed by all his party, as well as a letter to King Haakon,

which Amundsen asked Scott to deliver should something nasty happen
to him before he got home.

> Dear Captain Scott, as you probably are the first to reach this area
> after us, I will kindly ask you to forward this letter to King Haakon
> VII. If you can use any of the articles in the tent, please do not
> hesitate to do so. The sledge left outside may be of some use to you.
> With kind regard, I wish you a safe return.
> Yours, Roald Amundsen

Unfortunately, they didn't find the sledge, and indeed it would have
come in handy on the return journey, as the runners on their sledge were
by now in poor shape.

Scott's party gathered around Amundsen's tent at the South Pole. From left, Scott, Oates, Wilson,
Evans. Photo by Bowers.

They stayed long enough to take sights, plant the Union Jack and take
some photographs. That night, Scott wrote in his diary: "Great God! This
is an awful place."[3] One wonders if Scott would have made the same diary
entry if he had beaten Amundsen to the Pole. Of the group, PO Taff Evans
was the most crushed. He had hoped being first to the Pole would bring
him promotion and the wealth that would surely follow. Oates did it for
the glory of the regiment. Wilson was more pragmatic and wrote: "He
has beaten us in so far as he made a race out of it. We have done what we
came for all the same and as our programme was made out."[4]

They took some sights to confirm they actually were at the geographic South Pole and turned north for the 900-mile journey back to Cape Evans.

When their chronometer watches were retrieved by the search party the following year, they could not be restarted, so it was unknown how accurate they were. This cast some doubt on the exact longitude reached by Scott. Ironically, if the remains of the Polar Party were never found by the search party, Amundsen's claim would certainly have been cast into doubt.

On their inbound journey they had struggled for weeks against the constant winds that swept north off the Polar Plateau. Finally the wind was at their backs, and they could hoist the sail over their sledge. There were days when they virtually flew over the Plateau, but temperatures were dropping, sometimes as low as minus 30° F, and with the exception of Bowers—who seemed immune from the cold—everyone was suffering from some form of frostbite. The intensity of the light was also becoming a problem, going from dazzling to flat, making navigation difficult and causing snow blindness. Scott had expected to follow their inbound tracks on the way back, but in many places, blizzards had obliterated all traces of their journey, although they were still more or less on course and making pretty good time. Bowers finding the precious pipe he'd lost on the way in was taken as a sign that things were looking up.

The good cheer didn't last. Ninety miles north of the Pole, they had to stop to thaw out Evans. Frostbite was tearing him up, and even Oates was starting to flag, with badly frostbitten toes. Food supplies were running low and it was touch and go if they would make it to the next depot. To compound their problems, Wilson had hurt his leg and Scott had fallen, injuring his shoulder—perhaps dislocating it. Bowers, who was in the best shape of all of them, suddenly seemed to lose interest in the whole show and wrote his last diary entry on January 29, 1912.

January 31, 1912: At Three Degree Depot, they stopped to pick up Bowers's skis, which had been left here a month before, on December 31. Bowers, with his short legs, had walked a total of 180 miles on foot, while the other three were on skis. However, of the five men, Bowers was probably in the best physical condition, with Evans the worst. The infection on his hand was spreading, and he had lost two fingernails the previous day.

On February 3, 1912, they reached the edge of the Polar Plateau and were looking down the Beardmore Glacier. It appeared that they'd experienced the worst—it was downhill from here on and there were numerous food caches on the way. But temperatures were already a few degrees colder than on their inbound journey. Winter was coming on fast.

At Wilson's suggestion, they stopped on the glacier to poke about among the rocks, collecting fossil-bearing specimens—adding 30 to 40 pounds of rock to their sledge, which did nothing to speed up their progress.

> I have at home "Glossopteris," a fossil from one of the rocks Wilson collected, found by Silas when they picked through the rocks. It weighs only a few ounces, but still ...

South of Mid-Glacier Depot, they got lost again and spent twelve hours wandering among crevasses and ice pressure ridges. They were down to their last meal and had no idea where they were. It was taking longer for them to go down the glacier with half a sledge that was carrying only some rocks and instruments (certainly no food) than it had for them to go up it with a 12-foot sledge loaded with 800 pounds of supplies. The runners were getting badly scored and torn up from all the wandering on the glacial ice, and the scraping and sandpapering they did to the runners when they camped was making them dangerously thin. Silas had warned of this very thing on the inbound journey—a scored sledge runner drastically reduced the distance they could travel in a day on the Barrier, and a scored sledge runner on cold, gravelly snow was a disaster.

Overall, they were making an erratic course down the glacier, taking twice the time Silas and Teddy Evans's party had taken to descend, despite the fact that Evans's party had three men pulling a sledge and Silas's four. Scott was beginning to show signs of panic, writing in his diary on February 3, 1912: "Have decided it is a waste of time looking for tracks and cairn, and shall push on due north [towards Mount Hooper] as fast as we can."[5]

This proved to be a fatal mistake. The very next day, both Scott and Evans fell down a deep crevasse. They were hauled out, seemingly all right, but the fall appeared to rapidly worsen Evans's already worrying condition. His hands were now so frostbitten that he was unable to help with setting up or breaking camp, and he was now so weak that he could barely pull the sledge. Scott had little sympathy, and wrote on February 16, 1912: "Evans has nearly broken down in brain, we think. He is absolutely changed from his normal self-reliant self. This morning and this afternoon he stopped the march on some trivial excuse."[6] If Evans had been a pony, Scott would surely have shot him by now.

Scott's callous attitude can't have been lost on Evans. On the morning of February 17, 1912, Petty Officer Edgar "Taff" Evans unhitched himself from the sledge for the last time and walked alongside, quickly falling behind while the others plodded resolutely on, making no effort to assist him or even look back. It was only after they'd stopped for lunch that they noticed Evans had failed to show up and went back to look for him. They found him on his knees in the snow, his clothing in disarray and unable to walk. Oates remained with Evans while Scott, Wilson and Bowers returned to get the sledge. It must have been an agonising wait for Oates—to watch his friend live out his last hours in front of him, while his own health was only marginally better. By the time the others returned with the sledge, Evans had slipped into a coma. He never regained consciousness, and died in the tent later that evening. They paused only long enough to bury Evans and moved on. Scott marked Evans's passing in his diary:

> It is a terrible thing to lose a companion in this way, but calm reflection shows that there could not have been a better ending to the terrible anxieties of the past week. Discussion of the situation at lunch yesterday shows what a desperate pass we were in with a sick man on our hands at such a distance from home.[7]

Evans may not have died directly as a result of the fall in the crevasse on the Beardmore Glacier. Later medical studies have supported the theory his disorientation and eventual death were from a brain hemorrhage made worse by his being in a "scorbutic state" (scurvy) .*

*A.F. Rogers. M.D., "The Death of Chief Petty Officer Evans", *The Practitioner*, London, 1974.

Mount Fox and the Granite Pillars serve as Taff Evans's tombstone.

In other words, it was a relief to be shot of Evans.

They arrived at Shambles Camp the next day, where they picked up a supply of frozen horsemeat and had a fine dinner of boiled pony.

The wind was light and they made decent time, but it was cold. Really cold. Minus 30° F and in some cases minus 40° F, meaning the snow had the consistency of gravel, which, combined with scored sledge runners, slowed their progress to a crawl.

Often on the Barrier they would lose their way. Wilson noted in his diary on February 23, 1912: "Bad day off the tracks. We had thick weather and got no cairns. Lost much time in discussing navigation. We were too far out and had to come well in."[8]

The awful realisation they had got themselves into a serious pickle was beginning to sink in for Scott, who wrote on the following day: "I don't know what to think, but the rapid closing of the season is ominous."[9]

They still had a long way to go to the safety of One Ton Depot, where the dog teams would be waiting, but Scott made a curious entry in his diary on March 7, 1912: "We hope against hope that the dogs have been to Mt. Hooper [depot] then we might pull through. If there is a shortage of oil again we can have little hope."[10] This would indicate that Scott had given Teddy Evans instructions to send the dog teams *south* of One Ton.

That same day, Wilson, who up to now had been the most upbeat of the group—sketching and writing in his diary the whole trip back—suddenly stopped keeping a journal.

From here on the only written record of what transpired was in Scott's journals, with his entry for March 10, 1912: "Yesterday we marched up to the depot, Mt. Hooper. Cold comfort. Shortage on our allowance all round. I don't know that anyone is to blame. The dogs which would have been our salvation have evidently failed."[11]

As their spirits lagged, so did their daily mileage. Seven miles a day became six, which then became four. Even in the best of conditions, Scott was subject to depression and mood swings. To lose the Pole to Amundsen must have been devastating, and a depressed man can lose all perspective on reality, his diary beginning to take on a decidedly gloomy tone. Oates, whose legs had been ravaged by frostbite and who was now barely able to walk, received the same sympathy from Scott that Evans had received. On March 10, 1912, Scott wrote: "Titus is the greatest handicap. He keeps us waiting in the morning until we have partly lost the warming effect of our good breakfast, when the only wise policy is to be up and away at once; again at lunch."[12]

Like Silas's party, Scott's party discovered that the food caches were shorter of food and fuel than they should have been. Meares insisted his dog party had gone short, Silas's party took only what it had been allotted, and Evans's party only comprised three men instead of four. Unless Leopard seals were roaming the Barrier, one of the returning parties had taken more than it should have.

By now, Oates's feet were so badly frostbitten that it was obvious that even if the men made it off the Barrier alive, his feet would have to be amputated. He struggled on, never complaining, but had become uncharacteristically quiet.

When it seemed things couldn't get worse, they did. Scott had been relying on the usual southerly winds being at their backs on the return, when suddenly and unexpectedly, the wind shifted to blow from the north—right into their faces. Within hours, they were being battered by a fierce headwind and the temperature fell off the chart. There is an indication that Scott might have considered suicide when it was becoming obvious things had reached rock bottom; he wrote on March 11:

I practically ordered Wilson to hand over the means for ending our troubles to us, so that any one of us may know how to do so. Wilson had no choice between doing so and our ransacking the medicine case. We have 30 opium tabloids apiece and he is left with a tube of morphine.[13]

A blizzard was blowing when they made camp on March 16, 1912, and settled down to sleep. The following morning, the blizzard was still raging. Oates crawled out of his sleeping bag and made for the tent opening, allegedly saying, "I am just going outside. I may be some time." Whether

Oates really did say those words is highly suspect. Scott was the only one still keeping a diary and was carefully putting his own spin on events. Prior to the Southern Journey, Oates had nothing but contempt for Scott and considered him grossly incompetent. In light of what had happened in the past few weeks, it would seem likely that Oates's last words would be a little more forceful. Did Scott make up Oates's last words? Did Oates actually say: "Sod you lot, I'd rather die outside in a snowdrift than in this tent with you." Regardless, no one tried to stop him, even though they knew he wasn't just going out to relieve himself. He limped outside and disappeared into the blizzard. It was Oates's birthday—he was 33 years old. All he left behind was his sleeping bag and his diary, with instructions that in the event his diary was found, it be sent to his mother. (Whether Scott thumbed through it is unknown.)

after Dollman
1913

Oates leaves the tent and walks into the blizzard. Oates's mother was so bitter at what she considered the senseless death of her son that she never revealed the contents of his diary, and as per the instructions in her will, Oates's diary was burned, unopened.

The blizzard passed the next day. The party, now down to three men, limped on, with Scott making only brief diary entries. March 18: "My right foot has gone, nearly all the toes." March 19: "Amputation is the least I can hope for now, but will the trouble spread?"[14]

By March 21, they were within 11 miles of One Ton Depot when another blizzard and frigid temperatures forced them to make camp and wait it out. Temperatures were hovering around minus 40° F, and they had only two days of food and a few drops of fuel left, but if the blizzard passed quickly, they still might make the depot. Scott wrote that Wilson and Bowers would push on to One Ton for fuel. Two days later, the blizzard hadn't let up and it was too late. There was not enough food or fuel to support any of the party to press on or, for that matter, to survive much longer where they were.

They lay quietly in the tent as the blizzard raged outside. Wilson and Scott's legs were dead from frostbite, and everyone's fingers had turned blue and blistered, with cheeks and noses a sickly yellow colour. While Bowers and Wilson stared at the tent canvas flapping in the wind, waiting for death, Scott was busy writing letters—more than a dozen—to wives, mothers, J.M. Barrie, etc. He had unwound the lashings around his finnesko and dipped them like lamp wick in the last of the Primus spirits in order to give him a feeble light by which to write his final words on April 29, 1912:

> We took risks, we knew we took them; things have come out against
> us, and therefore we have no cause for complaint, but bow to the
> will of providence, determined still to do our best to the last. Had
> we lived, I should have had a tale to tell of the hardihood, endurance,
> and courage of my companions which would have stirred the heart
> of every Englishman. These rough notes and our dead bodies must
> tell the tale, but surely, surely, a great rich country like ours will see
> that those who are dependent on us are properly provided for.
>
> —Robert Scott

In 1909, when Scott was in France, he'd held a conversation with French polar explorer Jean-Baptiste Charcot. Scott asked Charcot: "What would be your last wish if you were fated to die in the Antarctic? Would you prefer your body being brought to Europe, or that it should rest beneath the snows?" Charcot replied, "I would prefer to be buried on the field of battle." Scott agreed, "I also would prefer that."[15]

At least one thing went right for Scott.

PART III

1912 - 1914

THE SEARCH FOR SCOTT AND
THE RETURN HOME

15. THE DISASTER

The most God-forsaken country this is. If I ever get
clear of it, I never want to see it again.

—Silas Wright

Cape Evans, January 1912: Silas and his companions congratulated themselves on marching a total of 1,400 miles and making it back more or less
intact. They were convinced that Scott had reached the Pole and was also
on his way back. They gorged on food and drink and revelled in the sounds
of Cape Evans—the raucous skuas and chatty penguins were a welcome
relief from the funereal silence of the Great Ice Barrier.

On reflection, Silas felt he might have been a trial to his returning
party, by urging them to take longer marches to get to One Ton Depot
as quickly as possible in case the weather turned and they were trapped
out on the Barrier. The experiences of Lt. Teddy Evans's party of three,
who were still out on the Barrier, proved that Silas was right to hasten
their return.

Evans's party was experiencing temperatures of minus 73° F, and Evans
himself was desperately weak, turning black and blue along with several
other gruesome colours—classic symptoms of scurvy. Thomas Crean and
William Lashly were reduced to pulling Evans on the sledge and were
getting played out themselves. They got as far as Corner Camp, 35 miles
from Hut Point, and could go no farther. They had a choice: either stay
at Corner Camp and watch Evans die or someone would have to make a
dash to Hut Point to get help. Even though a blizzard was starting, Crean

The second Western Geological Party on their return to Cape Evans. From left: Forde, Debenham, Taylor and Gran.

left Evans in a tent with Lashly and started out walking for Hut Point. Evans later wrote: "Very seriously and sadly, they re-erected our tent and put me once again inside. I thought I was being put into my grave."

Meanwhile, Atkinson and Demetri had already left Cape Evans to meet Lt. Evans's returning party, but only got as far as Hut Point before being stopped by the blizzard. They decided to remain at Hut Point until the blizzard passed and were shocked when Crean burst through the door at 3:30 AM with news of Evans's illness. Crean had walked 34 miles in eighteen hours through a blizzard—a polar record that still stands. The fact that Crean was the biggest and toughest member of the party saved Evans's life. A lesser man probably would not have survived that trek.

They had to wait until 4:30 PM the following day for the worst of the blizzard to subside before they set out for Evans and Lashly. Even then, they were battered by another blizzard and only by luck found the tent, which by then was almost completely buried in snow.

If Teddy Evans had been a few miles farther south, he would surely have died. Shackleton's Ross Sea Party got into the same kind of pickle in 1908. Spencer Smith, who came down with scurvy, was carried 300 miles on a sledge, but died within a mile or two of Hut Point.

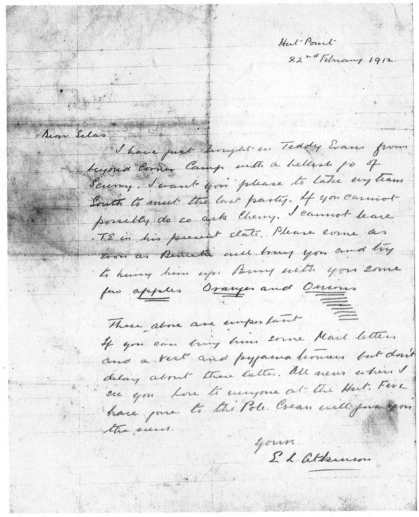

Atkinson's note to Silas.

Once they arrived back at Hut Point, Atkinson sent Demetri, Crean and a dog team to Cape Evans, with a note requesting medical supplies for Evans, along with a request that Simpson (now the ranking officer at Cape Evans) send Silas or Cherry to Hut Point to join Demitri on the dog team being sent south to meet Scott's returning party at One Ton Depot. It was of the utmost importance that they meet Scott's Polar Party and escort them in. *Terra Nova*, which had arrived back from New Zealand on February 4, 1912, would have to leave in a matter of days or risk being frozen in for the winter.

But it was Cherry and Demetri who went on to One Ton Depot, with Silas staying behind, at Hut Point.

On *Terra Nova*, another attempt by Captain Pennell to reach Campbell's party at Evans Coves was thwarted by a gale that lasted two days, coupled with unusually heavy ice that prevented the ship from getting close to the coast. Temperatures were dropping and *Terra Nova* was in real danger of being trapped in the ice, so the ship sailed back to Cape Evans on February 25, 1912. Once there, the ship was turned around and sent to Hut Point to pick up the sick Evans, who was being looked after by Atkinson.

Terra Nova arrived at Hut Point, unloaded supplies in case Scott's Polar Party was stranded there for any length of time, and picked up Evans to transport him home. He was wrapped in a sleeping bag and hauled aboard the ship by rope. Griffith Taylor described him as looking "more like a corpse than a live man."

George Simpson was packing his gear in preparation for leaving on *Terra Nova*. The Indian Met Service had lent him to the expedition for only a year, and he was happy to be leaving.

Herbert Ponting, Cecil Meares, Bernard Day, Robert Forde, Thomas Clissold, Anton Omelchenko and Griffith Taylor were also leaving on the ship. Like Simpson, Taylor was on loan from his (Australian) government only for a year. Taylor was pleased to be going; he had found Scott's style of leadership rather restrictive and was anxious to get back to a less formal atmosphere. Meares was anxious to go as well and claimed the ship brought news that his father had died and he needed to clear up the estate. Forde was still suffering from severe frostbite, and Clissold had cut himself badly. Day's motor tractors were either at the bottom of McMurdo Sound or disabled somewhere on the Barrier, so there was nothing for him to do. Anton's ponies had all been shot, so there was no reason for him to stick around either. Ponting was anxious to get home to make some money on the lecture circuit and exhibit his photographs. Silas was a bit disappointed that Ponting took with him his cine camera, "which, I suppose, belonged to him personally."

Before they could embark everyone, another gale blew up and Captain Pennell ordered the ship out to sea where there was room to ride out the storm. Unfortunately, a broken cog was discovered in the capstan's gears and they couldn't raise the anchor. They tried to engage the capstan with the steam winch, but that just stripped the remaining cogs. By 6 PM, in freezing temperatures and gale conditions, they finally raised the anchor

Terra Nova at Cape Evans prior to her return voyage to New Zealand, where she would spend the winter before returning in the spring of 1913 to pick up those who would be remaining behind at Cape Evans.

with a series of pulleys attached to the steam winch, and *Terra Nova* headed out into the relative safety of the Ross Sea.

On March 1, *Terra Nova* made another attempt to relieve Campbell's Northern Party—and the ship's propeller got jammed in the ice. After much bashing at the ice jam with steel rods, the crew eventually freed the propeller. By now the temperatures were dropping so fast that the open ocean would freeze over in a matter of minutes. They gave up and returned to Cape Evans on March 4, 1912.

Pennell didn't want to risk his ship in these waters any longer, and on March 7, 1912, *Terra Nova* picked up those who were leaving Cape Evans, and headed back to New Zealand.

Cherry and Demetri had arrived at One Ton Depot four days earlier, on March 3. Following Scott's orders, they had set up camp and waited. And waited. But there was no sign of the Polar Party and the weather was deteriorating by the day.

They waited at One Ton for six days as temperatures dropped and winds blew to force 8. Visibility was so bad that Scott could have passed within feet of them and they wouldn't have seen him. Demetri was worried that the dogs were losing their coats and needed more food, so Cherry fed them extra, leaving them barely enough for the return journey. Then Demetri fell ill, complaining of pains in his head and losing the use of his right arm. Cherry himself was suffering from chest pains. In his log he wrote of temperatures of minus 40° F at the end of the day, falling at a rate of 20° F per hour. Which, according to Silas: "Allowing for a bit of exaggeration, this is not good sledging weather."

By March 10 it was clear that staying out there any longer would be pointless. The Barrier was a maelstrom of blowing snow and they were running out of food for both themselves and the dogs. Even though Birdie Bowers and Edward Wilson were two of Cherry's dearest friends, and had been his companions on the insane Cape Crozier emperor penguin egg expedition, he had no choice but to pack up and leave. Down to their last biscuit, they arrived at Hut Point on March 16, 1912, but were prevented from carrying on to Cape Evans due to the blizzard having blown the ice out into Erebus Bay.

Demetri was sick, Cherry had little experience of dog driving and was very short-sighted. In the circumstances he had no alternative but to return and I am sure he did the right thing, especially since this journey was arranged by Scott, in order only to enable him to meet the Terra Nova *before she had to leave for New Zealand.*
                                                                    —Wright memoirs

Cherry's account of the plunging temperatures and winter conditions at One Ton worried Atkinson, but he felt duty bound to attempt one more trip to One Ton to meet the Polar Party, which Cherry agreed to. But before he could get his gear on, he collapsed from a combination of exhaustion and a heart condition.

With both Demetri and Cherry out of the picture, Keohane and Atkinson set out manhauling a sledge to One Ton on March 27. (Gran had pronounced the dogs exhausted, frostbitten and unfit for further travel that season.) The weather on the Barrier was so terrible they made only a few miles before being forced back to Hut Point.

It was not only Cherry who was haunted by thoughts of how things could have been different. In later years, Silas always felt badly about Cherry-Garrard and Demetri's time at One Ton, saying: "It always worries me. I should have had that job."

Despite the disaster that appeared to have befallen the Polar Party, as far as everyone was concerned Amundsen had not reached the Pole. None of the support parties had seen any sign of him on the Beardmore Glacier, so it was assumed he had never made it that far south. It never occurred to anyone that he might have reached the Polar Plateau by using a different glacier.

On April 10, 1912, leaving Cherry behind with the dogs in case Scott's party should turn up, Atkinson, Keohane and Demetri made the trip across the bay to Cape Evans to break the news of the probable demise of the Polar Party. Silas and his companions at Cape Evans had been watching for a flare from Hut Point, which would signal the return of the Polar Party. Visibility had been so bad, though, that even if the whole of Hut Point had been dynamited they wouldn't have seen it, so up to now they were completely unaware of the drama that had been taking place across Erebus Bay.

After digesting the shocking news, everyone had their own theories as to what had befallen the Polar Party. Silas was convinced that the party hadn't even made it back onto the Barrier and had fallen down a crevasse on the Beardmore Glacier.

Still at Hut Point, Cherry was having a miserable time of it, which started from a fall he took when seeing his companions off across the sea ice.

It wasn't just the cold and pain that was dragging Cherry down. The dogs started fighting among themselves, a continuous battle that went on day and night. He tried beating some sense into the dogs he suspected were ringleaders, without success. He commented that at one point he would have "gladly killed the lot of them." His delivery from canine purgatory came about on April 14, when a relief party arrived from Cape Evans to take him and the dogs back to Cape Evans, where the remaining party settled down to wait out the winter.

Terra Nova was 200 miles north of Cape Evans and making one last failed attempt to reach Evans Coves when, facing the possibility of being trapped in the ice for the winter, Captain Pennell ordered all attempts to relieve Campbell's party be abandoned and *Terra Nova* steamed north to the open sea and back to New Zealand.

On the voyage back, all hands were required to haul sail and go below to trim coal. After Griffith Taylor and George Simpson staged a small "mutiny," Pennell let them off sail trimming duties and allowed them both to work in the coal bunkers, where it was warmer than hanging off the rigging in a South Atlantic or wading waist-deep in water, hand-pumping the bilges. They were soon joined by Bernard Day and Herbert Ponting, who also preferred the warmth of the coal bunkers. The weather in the South Atlantic lived up to its foul reputation, with Taylor writing in his diary:

> The pump-handles [across the waist] are left on all the time now, and with "life-lines" they make something to grip as you sidle along the deck. Ponting didn't see the handle, and running to dodge a big wave he was knocked silly by a blow on the brow. Result—two lovely black eyes, and a thankful heart that his nose wasn't broken.

Taylor noticed that as they approached civilisation, everyone who had spent the past year on the ice came down with various ailments, such as influenza or, in Griff's case, neuralgia. This could be put down to their being exposed to the diseases that were afflicting the crew of *Terra Nova*, along similar lines to the way Pacific islanders were decimated by the crews of European sailing ships.

April 1, 1912: *Terra Nova* entered Akaroa Harbour, New Zealand. Everyone was confined to ship and forbidden to communicate with anyone on the outside, while Pennell and Drake went to shore on the launch to send a cable off to London. While they were gone, two men in a small boat circled the ship. When they got close, they called out: "Why didn't you get back sooner? Amundsen got to the Pole in a sardine tin on the 14th of December."

Taylor was the most stunned. Gran had prophesied this on December 20, 1911, while camped in the "Punch Bowl," in the Western Mountains during the Second Western Party. He woke up from a dream declaring that

Captain Harry L. Pennell.

he knew Amundsen was turning back from the South Pole. Ridiculed by his comrades, he wrote it down in Taylor's Browning.* The Browning was left at Cape Roberts on February 5, and picked up by Priestley six months later. Taylor didn't see it again until 1913, at Priestley's home in Tewkesbury, England. Sure enough, inside the Browning was Gran's prediction.

* A day calendar of Robert Browning's poems.

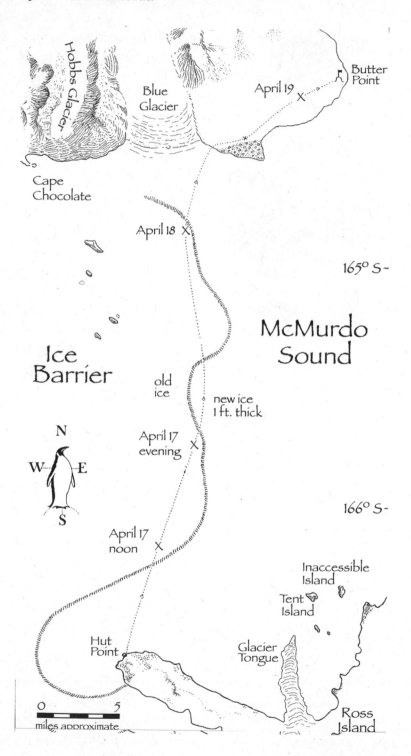

Hobbs Glacier

Blue
Glacier

April 19   X .... Butter
Point

Cape
Chocolate

April 18   X

165° S –

April 17   X
noon

Ice
Barrier

old
ice

new ice
1 ft. thick

McMurdo
Sound

N

W   E

S

April 17
evening   X

166° S –

Inaccessible
Island

Tent
Island

Hut
Point

Glacier
Tongue

Ross
Island

0   5

miles approximate

16. THE SECOND WINTER

Two chief things I am looking forward to are music
and seeing a girl's face and hair—not any particular
girl's—but just any nice face and soft hair; these eternal
beards and matted hair and grubby clothes are rather
monotonous.

—Frank Debenham

As Dr. Atkinson was now the ranking naval officer, it fell to him to take
charge of the party for the winter and, it was supposed, the next summer until *Terra Nova* returned. It was hoped that *Terra Nova* had picked
up Campbell's Northern Party as the ship passed by on their way back to
New Zealand, but in light of the number of failed previous attempts, and
the worsening ice conditions since, it was more than likely that Campbell
and his men were still stranded at Evans Coves. They knew the Northern Party
had only limited provisions and inadequate gear to last them a winter,
so Atkinson decided the right thing to do was to send a relief party to
Evans Coves.

Almost everyone was against making the trip. Debenham was the most
adamant because he was very familiar with the hazardous western coast,
but Atkinson felt they had an obligation to go and picked Silas, Keohane
and Williamson to accompany him. The plan was to make their way
across the treacherous sea ice, but if a gale blew the ice out to sea, they'd
climb onto the shore and cut across the glaciers, hopefully picking the
correct glacier to descend to Evans Coves, where Campbell's party might,
or might not, be camped. This would all be by moonlight, or possibly
no light, as the sun was close to leaving them for the winter. It was a trip
that Silas later recalled as "insane" and "doomed from the beginning."

If Campbell's party *was* stranded at Evans Coves, the worsening weather conditions meant the relief party would in all likelihood also be trapped at Evans Coves—four more mouths to feed during the winter.

On April 17, 1912, they set out across the sea ice from Hut Point.

Even in the most perfect conditions we were not able to carry sufficient supplies to maintain ourselves there for the winter or to get back again to Cape Evans. Not one of our best organised efforts. However, we four started off on April 17th to cross McMurdo sound and landed at Butter Point. Temperatures were low at night in the minus forties. We reached the Eskers by the 19th after crossing four miles of newly frozen sea ice and turned towards the depot in Butter Point. But had to camp in a warm blizzard and did not reach the depot until nightfall. Here next morning we saw the ice to the north breaking up and drifting away to sea and this put paid to our journey to relieve Campbell and his party.

—Wright memoirs

To continue the journey on land would have meant crossing numerous glaciers in the dark, which was out of the question, so they waited at Butter Point for the ice to re-form before making the return journey. Leaving two weeks's rations at Butter Point in case the Northern Party should pass this way on their own (a prescient move, it later turned out), they hastened back to Hut Point on dodgy ice, making it back on April 23, 1912, the same day the sun disappeared for the winter. With Atkinson choosing to remain at Hut Point in case Scott's party should turn up, Silas navigated for a party consisting of Williamson, Tryggve Gran and Keohane back to Cape Evans—in the middle of a blizzard with temperatures dropping to minus 31° F. It was one of the more unpleasant crossings, with Silas writing:

In the poor light I found it desirable to follow the land round to Glacier Tongue especially as the ice became so thin there was a perceptible bow wave in front of the sledge and party, while Gran actually at one time put his foot through the soft ice covering.

Atkinson, alone at Hut Point, finally had to admit the Polar Party was not coming back, and Hut Point abandoned for the winter.

Cape Evans hut snowed in after a winter blizzard.

Realising how close they had come to perishing on the futile attempt to relieve Campbell, Atkinson wrote: "Wright from the very first, had been against this journey. He had some knowledge of a previous sledge trip on the western coast. Not until after I had told him that we should have to turn back did he tell me how thankful he was of this decision. He had come on this trip fully believing that there was every probability of the party being lost, but had never demurred and never offered a contrary opinion, and one cannot be thankful enough to such men!"

The thirteen men at Cape Evans were: Dr. Atkinson, Cherry-Garrard, Silas, Tryggve Gran, Thomas Crean, William Lashly, Frank Debenham, Thomas Williamson, Edward Nelson, Archer, Demetri, Patrick Keohane and Frederick Hooper.

Both Crean and Williamson had also been on the Discovery Expedition and must have been heartily sick of the place by now. Winter duties were assigned and, in many cases, doubled up. With the departure of Simpson, Silas took over meteorological duties in addition to his geomagnetic work and his studies of atmospheric electricity, gravity, and glaciology. Much of his efforts were put into keeping the instruments running in the harsh climate. Among the problems was the outside wiring that was deteriorating because it was only cheap electric doorbell wire.

Atkinson was the ranking officer, doctor and parasitologist; Cherry-Garrard was the ornithologist, keeper of the official record and editor of the *South Polar Times*. Nelson continued as marine zoologist; Debenham remained as geologist and also took over Ponting's duties as official photographer, but not his darkroom because Silas had already moved into it. Gran was the ski expert and assistant meteorologist, and also took over Birdie Bowers's job as stores master. PO Lashly was in charge of the mules that had been dropped off by *Terra Nova*. Crean oversaw sledging stores and equipment; Hooper, the hated acetylene lighting plant; and Archer took over duties as cook. Demetri was in charge of the dogs, and Keohane and Williamson were charged with preparing for the summer sledging and filling in wherever needed.

Before life at Cape Evans settled down to the slow winter routine, Atkinson gathered the small party together and asked everyone what they should do next summer. The assembled group was shocked. They were used to Scott's more autocratic style of leadership. Atkinson, in contrast, was giving them a choice of what to do come summer:

1. Send a party out to find out what had happened to Scott's party and hopefully find their remains.
2. Make another attempt to rescue Campbell's Northern Party—if indeed they were at Evans Coves and not sipping Wincarnis cocktails on a New Zealand beach.

Atkinson put it to a vote, with everyone voting to look for Scott's party, with one abstention. (Diplomatically, no one recorded who abstained from voting, but Silas later recalled it was Cherry.)

Winter hit Cape Evans with a vengeance. Blizzard after blizzard slammed into the hut and pushed out the sea ice, which meant it was impossible for them to exercise the mules on the ice. Trotting them around on the shore was awkward, as there was very little solid and stable ground to walk them on, especially during the twenty-four hours of darkness. Inside the hut though, conditions were positively cheery—even the taciturn Demetri blossomed during the second winter.

The cheerful atmosphere could be attributed to the absence of Scott's brooding presence. Silas wrote:

Deek sheltering behind some packing cases.

We were a happy party, once we had faced up to the loss of the Polar Party and had decided what to do next summer. In fact the whole atmosphere was now different. There were no cliques so far as I am aware. The barrier of boxes between the afterguard and seamen was still there, but the passageway in both directions was used more commonly. To a large extent this was due to Atch. As a naval doctor, he was to our petty officers much more accessible than to an executive officer. We all respected him, felt for him, pitch-forked a difficult situation and, more than that, I think I can say that we loved him.

The line between the officers, scientific staff and seamen was less defined, much to Silas's pleasure. He wasn't comfortable around formality and never got used to the strict naval discipline that Scott demanded.

The weather worsened, with winds regularly gusting over 100 mph, picking pebbles up off the beach and hurling them against the side of their hut. The dogs, who were left outside, had the worst of it and habitually broke into Silas's magnetic cave to seek shelter from the wind. One dog died, and Nugis went missing on July 29. Speculation was that he had gone out hunting on the sea ice and become lunch for a killer whale. Everyone was much saddened, as Nugis was a favourite of the party due to his cheerful disposition.

Activities outside were now severely curtailed, and the group entertained themselves inside with the few games they had at their disposal.
Bagatelle was a smash hit, so much so, Silas recounted, "the little round
wooden balls were soon beaten into strange shapes which skewed the
score considerably."

The pianola, whose bulk had caused Silas so much annoyance on the
voyage down, proved to be handy for breaking the monotony, but the only
members who could play it were Cherry-Gerrard and Debenham.

May 23, 1912: Silas almost burned down the hut. He needed a place where
he could use his pendulum stand undisturbed, and had been busy constructing a hut [the "Petrol" hut] outside made out of wooden packing
cases for walls and tarred paper for the roof. Despite the fact the wind
continuously tore the roof off, and in some cases levelled it completely,
he persevered. The bitter cold was making it difficult for him to work, so
Silas commandeered a Pyrsos lamp from the main hut and tried to light
it. Regardless of how much he pumped the oil, it failed to light. He gave
up in disgust, leaving it on the mess table.

*Nelson, who was next to me at the large table in the hut, evidently thought this
was a cowardly attitude on my part, grabbed the contraption and pumped away at a
furious rate until the body of the lamp burst and blazing oil poured over the table and
on to the floor. The shout of "FIRE!" brought all hands to the recue and it was only
a short time before the fire was smothered by handy blankets, etc., grabbed up from
nearby beds. My bed was quite far away, beyond the Pianola, so my blankets were
not required; but I did notice how, in spite of the excitement, everyone was careful to
take the blankets from someone else's bed and not from his own.*

—Wright memoirs

Silas did have the foresight to grab the fire extinguisher, but unfamiliar
with how to use it held it at the wrong end, depositing its contents on both
Debenham and himself. Gran's windproof jacket was also a victim of the
fire, due to the unfortunate fact that it was closest to the conflagration.

June 22, 1912: Midwinter's Day and the day the last edition of the *South
Polar Times* was presented to the group by Cherry. He had for the win-

ter been the official biographer for the party, as almost everyone (Silas included) had lost interest in recording the minutiae in their diaries and were quite happy to let Cherry take over as official biographer.

The *South Polar Times* was a collection of contributions from members of the expedition. Everyone signed their names with a nom de plume. Submissions were made anonymously by depositing them in a box nailed to the wall of the hut, although it was always obvious who were the authors of the articles. (Silas's nom de plume was Trahnter.)

The first two volumes of the *South Polar Times* were produced on the 1901 Discovery Expedition. The first volume was edited by Ernest Shackleton, the second by Louis Bernacchi. Cherry-Garrard's edition was the third and last volume. The first two volumes were printed in 1907 by Smith, Elder & Co. (250 copies). The third volume was published by Smith, Elder & Co. in 1914 (350 copies). The original typewritten volumes are in the British Museum.

July dragged on, with the inhabitants of the hut sinking into a polar ennui. The wind blew ceaselessly, and most of the time it was impossible for anyone to get up Windvane Hill behind the hut to take wind speeds

Three volumes of the *South Polar Times*.

or temperatures. Silas noted that Cherry was his usual cheerful self but somewhat subdued by the loss of his two greatest friends, Edward Wilson and Birdie Bowers. Every time the dogs barked outside, Cherry wondered if it might be the returning Polar Party.

On July 12, 1912, the roof to Silas's petrol hut blew off—again. He was getting frustrated with trying to carry out his magnetic experiments, writing in his diary: "A man might just as well bury himself in a snow drift at once, as attempt to do scientific work down here."

Silas had been training the other members in the use of magnetic instruments and measuring longitude by occultations. Nelson took the most interest in the subject and spent hours predicting future occultations before the winter was over, Nelson had become quite an expert.

> **Occultation:** when a planet crosses (transits) the face of the sun and is eclipsed or occulted.

July 19, 1912: Atkinson gathered the group together and named those who would be going on the search party. It was pretty simple: Debenham and Archer were to stay behind at the hut, while everyone else would head south. (Debenham had injured his knee again, during a football game.)

Silas, although pleased to get another chance to poke among the rocks on the Beardmore Glacier, was not looking forward to the long march over the Barrier to get there. Atkinson proposed four teams: two mule teams of four each and two dog teams of three each. The dog teams would depot provisions at specific intervals as far as they could safely go and return to Hut Point to await the returning mule parties. As they still assumed Scott was lost on the Beardmore, one team would stay at Cloudmaker Depot, at mid-glacier, while the remaining team would ascend to the top of the glacier. If they hadn't found the remains of the Polar Party by the time they reached the Polar Plateau, there would not be enough provisions for them to go farther south and they would have to return to the coast without ever knowing what had happened to Scott's party.

Atkinson had also decided rations were to be increased this time— one extra biscuit and more pemmican as well one extra onion added per day, per man, to prevent a recurrence of scurvy.

The long winter was having its effect on the dogs, who were starting to fight among themselves. Silas noted in his diary:

August 19, Boulik has evidently done some deed which has placed him outside the pale of the Canine social order. They all make a dead set for him as soon as he leaves the annex. Been rescued two or three times already.

Hunkered down in snowdrifts with not even a penguin to chase, it must have been miserable for dogs more used to the activity of a sledge run. Silas, taking pity on the dogs, finally gave up on his beloved petrol hut and turned it over to Demetri, for a dog shelter. The crew did some cleaning up around the hut during this period, depositing a few tons of garbage—including Griffith Taylor's bed—into the Ross Sea.

August 23, 1912, and the sun finally returned! Gran noted that everyone behaved like "excited schoolboys" and danced and caroused until 2 AM. As the sun rose higher over the mountains, Silas scrambled to finish his scientific work, concluding his measurements on acceleration due to gravity by measuring the swing of a pendulum. Penetrating radiation experiments were still ongoing, along with magnetic variations, aurora observations and the continuation of Simpson's met observations. It was expected that *Terra Nova* would be waiting for them when they returned from the Barrier, so there wouldn't be much time to pack everything and get on board before the ship had to leave.

August 25 and the hut caught fire again. This time it wasn't Silas's fault but that of a chimney layered in seal blubber grease. Fortunately, the fire was quickly extinguished with handfuls of snow.

By now the weather had improved enough for them to dig themselves out from the winter snowdrifts. Atkinson took a mule party to Hut Point with a load of stores and dug out the *Discovery* hut, while Silas and the others shifted tons of snow off the roof of the hut at Cape Evans by means of saws.

To everyone's surprise the mules performed splendidly hauling the sledges to Hut Point, and were far superior in demeanour to the Siberian ponies from the previous year. For the next month, various teams went out on depot-laying trips in preparation for the trip south. The excitement during that time came when the exhaust on the kerosene battery-

Cape Evans in the winter with Erebus in the background.

charging engine got clogged by a 12-foot snowdrift and filled the hut with carbon monoxide. The only victim was Silas, who passed out and fell flat on his face and was for a time ignored by the others, as it was assumed he was drunk.

October 6, 1912: Twenty-four days before they started out on the search party, Silas was having misgivings, writing: "I have an enormous respect for the Barrier & am afraid everyone's nerve is a bit shaken now we know what we have to buck up against."

17. THE SEARCH PARTY

The naval man is very adaptable up to a certain point,
but beyond his experience is pretty hopeless.

—Silas Wright

Silas wasn't keen to go back out on the Great Ice Barrier. He had crossed
it twice and survived, and it wasn't as if their equipment had improved
since last summer—in fact, much of it had deteriorated.

At 10:30 AM on Tuesday, October 29, 1912, the search party (or re-
covery party) got under way from Hut Point. Silas navigated for the mule
party, which consisted of Edward Nelson, Tryggve Gran, Frederick
Hooper, William Lashly, Thomas Crean, Thomas Williamson and himself. Atkinson, Cherry-Garrard and Demetri started two days later with
the dog team. The plan was to follow the Southern Party's original supply depots until they came across the last depot broached by Scott's returning Polar Party. Like the previous year, they'd march at night and
rest during the day when the snow conditions were softer and more difficult for the mules.

The mules performed well, despite the fact that they were being fed
the wrong rations. Nobody realised that mules preferred a different diet
to that of ponies, and it wasn't until years later that Silas discovered mules
didn't like eating snow, as the Siberian ponies would (or had to). As it was,
whenever they did give the mules water, their appetites improved considerably, but at the time, nobody made the connection. The collars that had

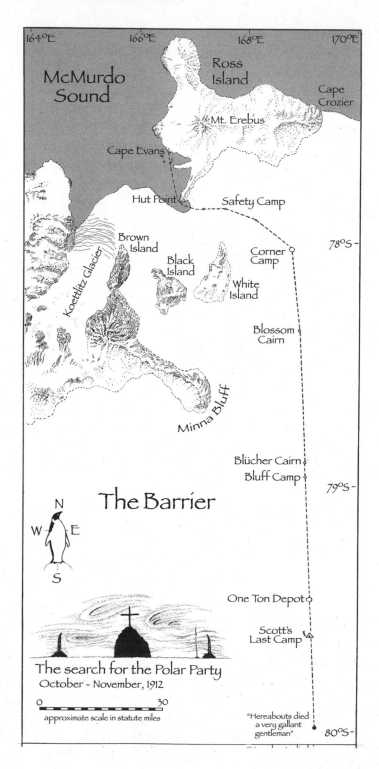

164°E   166°E   168°E   170°E

McMurdo
Sound

Ross
Island

Cape
Crozier

Mt. Erebus

Cape Evans

Hut Point   Safety Camp

Brown
Island

Black
Island

White
Island

Corner
Camp

78°S

Koettlitz Glacier

Blossom
Cairn

Minna Bluff

Blücher Cairn
Bluff Camp

The Barrier

79°S

N
W   E
S

One Ton Depot

Scott's
Last Camp

The search for the Polar Party
October – November, 1912

0   30
approximate scale in statute miles

"Hereabouts died
a very gallant
gentleman"

80°S

been used by the ponies to pull the sledges didn't fit the mules properly, with some of them suffering from chronic chafing around the neck.

And according to Silas, mules had a completely different temperament to that of the more cantankerous ponies:

Mules getting exceedingly cunning, 4 of them have learned how to unpicket themselves and they can not be left a moment to build cairns, etc., unless a bit of old rope is given them to chew in lieu of their traces.

They also tried to feed them too soon after stopping—apparently, mules don't like to eat if they are overheated. The mules that survived the journey back to Cape Evans suffered from bleeding gums—symptoms of scurvy.

Out on the Barrier, Silas was dismayed to discover his sleeping bag was near the end of its life. Holes were appearing in it, which made sleeping a rather draughty affair. If it deteriorated any further, it wouldn't survive as far as the Beardmore.

On November 11, 1912, they reached One Ton Depot. Everything was as it had been when Cherry-Garrard left it the previous autumn, so Scott had obviously not made it this far—which, as far as they were concerned, fit their theory that Scott's party had met its end on the Beardmore Glacier. Upon further examination of the supply cache, they discovered something disturbing. Wrote Silas: "Here we noticed for the first time that many of the bags of pemmican rations smelt and tasted of the kerosene fuel, which could only be due to leakage or evaporation from the tins of oil."

It turned out that the leather seals on the oil container lids had shrunk in the extreme cold, allowing the contents to leak out. In later years, Silas wondered whether oil containers had leaked their contents at depots farther south, as partially empty oil containers had been reported by other returning parties, though no one at the time had thought anything of it and put it down to "evaporation."

The search party continued south, with Silas leading the mules. The next day, on November 12, 1912, Silas found the tent. His first diary entry for that day: "Found owner, Bill and Birdie in tent."

Cherry remembered it this way:

That scene can never leave my memory. We with the dogs had seen Wright turn away from the course by himself and the mule party

swerve right-handed ahead of us. He had seen what he thought
was a cairn, and something looking black by its side. A vague
kind of wonder gave away to real alarm. We came up to them all
halted. Wright came across to us. "It is the tent." I do not know
how he knew. Just a waste of snow: to the right the remains of one
of last year's cairns, a mere mound: and then three feet of bamboo
sticking quite alone out of the snow: and then another mound, of
snow, perhaps a trifle more pointed.[1]

Later, in Silas's memoirs, he reflected further on that day:

*To me this had come as a complete surprise as I had been quite certain that we would
find they had perished among the crevasses on the Beardmore Glacier. I had been
plugging along my chosen course when I saw a small object projecting above the surface
on the starboard bow but carried on the chosen course until we were nearly abreast of
this object which I decided had better be examined more closely, but did not expect it
was of great interest so told the mule train to continue South while I went over the ½
mile or so to examine what it was. It was the 6 inches or so tip of a tent and a great
shock as I had been so certain that the Beardmore crevasses had been their downfall. I
tried to signal my party to stop and come up to me, but my alphabetical signals could
not be read by the navy and I considered it would be a sort of sacrilege to make a noise.
I felt much as if I were in a cathedral and found myself with my hat on. Eventually
it got across to the party that I wanted them to come in and went to meet them as it
seemed inappropriate to camp close to the tent, which I ordered not be touched until
Atkinson and the dog party came up. I think this was about an hour later, but am
not all clear on this point. I think the mule party behaved most properly and the usual
noises of making camp were absent. I had halted them about 100 yards away from the
tent and there was of course much speculation as to what had occurred.*

*When Atch came along and I told him the tent had been found, he took command
of the future arrangements. We cleared away the snow and opened the tent to find there
were only three occupants: Scott, Wilson and Bowers. Scott we thought was the last
to die, his diary was outside his sleeping bag and his arm half across Wilson's body.
All had died peacefully in their sleeping bags. Atch took the diaries and later read to
us all the parts that enabled us to know roughly what had happened. The five-man
party had reached the South Pole on January 17th, 1912, but Amundsen and the
Norwegians had already done so on December 14th, reaching the Polar Plateau by
another glacier. Evans had been the first to go mentally and then physically on February*

17th at the foot of the Beardmore. It was thought that he had fallen into a crevasse and was concussed. Titus Oates got very badly frostbitten feet but struggled on until March 17th with gangrene. Then considering he was a drag on the party he walked out into a blizzard about 19 miles south of the last camp of the remaining three. As my diary says: "A damn fine finish." The Owner and the other two staggered on short of oil and food until March 22nd when they made this last camp of theirs. The blizzard lasted at least until March 29th which was the date of the last entry in the Owner's diary. Cold and starvation and exhaustion was too much for them, capped as it was by the long blizzard. Atch also read Scott's last entry in the diary, which read "For God's sake, look after our people."

It has always been assumed that Scott was the last to die, but Silas was convinced that Bowers was the last survivor. He was the strongest of the party and perhaps could have carried on alone to get help. There is also a handwritten note on the back of one of Scott's notes to let the finders know where to find Bowers's diaries. "Last note to/ Mrs. Bowers/ Cardweeck/ Ardberg/ Bute/ Scotland." It was neither in Scott's nor Wilson's hand—besides, Wilson had stopped writing on March 7, 1912.

They didn't perform more than a cursory examination of the bodies, which had been out on the Barrier for six months in temperatures of minus 70° F. Even if they had wanted to do an autopsy, they would have needed a chainsaw.

The camp nearby Scott's tent.

The cairn over the tent. "There alone in their greatness they will lie without change or bodily decay, with the most fitting tomb in the world above them." —Atkinson

The men retired to their camp nearby and sat around Atkinson as he read aloud what he thought were the pertinent passages from Scott's diary, revealing what had happened since Lt. Teddy Evans's party had left them. After that, the diaries were closed and stayed closed until they arrived back in London. Silas and Cherry were given the job of removing papers and personal effects from Wilson and Bowers. Cherry did this service for Wilson, while Silas did the same duty for Bowers. They also removed the chronometer watches from their wrists. (They were on loan from the Greenwich observatory and awkward questions would have been asked if they had been buried along with the bodies.)

Atkinson read the lesson from the burial service in Corinthians and some prayers from the burial service, then they collapsed the tent on top of the three bodies and built a large cairn of snow blocks over the tent, topped off by a cross facing southwest, flanked by two smaller cairns, each with a 10-foot sledge sticking out of it.

In 1975, Silas was asked why they hadn't brought the bodies home from the Antarctic as "the British did." He replied: "No they don't. It's the Americans who like to plant them in the wrong places."[2]

We left there two 10 ft sledges on lesser cairns each side—east and west – of the grave. Shot Lal Kan and Kan Sahib, both in very poor condition and also left such food and equipment as would not be required on our return to Hut point. The large cairn was surmounted by a cross made of ski runners and a note recorded by Cherry: "A slight token to perpetuate their gallant and successful attempt to reach the Pole—inclement weather and lack of fuel was the cause of their death." All members of the search party put their signature on the note. The death of Evans on the Beardmore Glacier and the death of Oates in his pitiful attempt to ensure the safety of the three others is also in this record.

—Wright memoirs

They located and dug out the Polar Party's sledge, containing the 40 pounds of rocks Wilson had collected from the Beardmore Glacier, as well as all their scientific gear, except for the theodolite and camera. Silas also found the letter to Norwegian King Haakon that Roald Amundsen had left at the Pole, for Scott to deliver should something happen to Amundsen on the trek back. (Silas put it in his pocket and promptly forgot about it until days later on their return journey.)

The next day they carried on south, in an effort to find Oates. On November 14, at 80° south, they reached Scott's second-to-last camp, where they found Oates's sleeping bag, the theodolite and camera. But no Oates—a winter of storms had buried his body. They probably walked right over him and didn't even know it.

In the early morning of the 15th we built a cairn with a cross on it near the place where Oates walked out to his death in a blizzard, with a note lashed to the cross which read: "Hereabouts died a very gallant gentleman ... he walked willingly to his death in a blizzard to try to save his comrades beset by hardships."

—Wright memoirs

They abandoned the search for Oates's body and turned back. Silas was relieved they had located the bodies of Scott, Wilson and Bowers, but the marching wasn't over yet. Attention now turned to finding the six men in Campbell's Northern Party. Silas recalled:

We turned back to see how the Northern Party had got on. It was a terribly difficult decision Atch had to take: if the Northern Party had not been picked up by Terra

Nova and had come to grief during the winter, as they nearly did, our name would have stunk to high heaven, because we elected to investigate the dead rather than relieve the living.

Silas lost the trail a few times, but the cross over Scott's tent helped guide them back to Scott's last camp, now renamed Sorrowful Camp. There Gran put on Scott's skis. He was determined that they should finish their journey back to Cape Evans.

On the return, the mules had stopped eating their food. The men tried different diets, without success. One of the mules, when confronted with a sugar bag containing tea leaves and oats, ate the bag and tea leaves but left the oats. Silas doubted the mules would last to see Hut Point.

Mule with feedbag.

Safety Camp, November 26, 1912: They had relieved the mules of their duties and were reduced to manhauling their sledges while the mules stumbled on behind them. The next day they reached Hut Point and to their great surprise met Victor Campbell at *Discovery* hut, scrubbed clean of soot and now the ranking officer. No one was more relieved than Silas:

I for one, was quite confident that they [Campbell's Party] would have managed to get through the winter safely in an ice cavern or igloo. But I was wrong in assuming

*that they would arrange for the collection of sufficient seals for food and heating before
they disappeared for the winter until they came up in spring to rear their young ones
and to bask in the spring time sun. This was a serious error due to their confidence
that the ship would arrive to pick them up since they were able to see only open sea
within many miles. In the result the lives of many seals were saved but at the cost of
hard privation for Campbell's Northern Party during the winter.*

Silas's relief was shared by the rest of the party, because no one was
looking forward to dragging sledges 200 miles over the by now treacherous sea ice to look for the Northern Party. Campbell's men had been on
their own for twenty-one months, apart from a few days when *Terra Nova*
transported them from Cape Adare to Evans Coves (the one time when
they had an opportunity to have a bath).

The next day the search party arrived back at Cape Evans. Two
days later, two of the mules that had served them so faithfully were dispatched. Silas noted: "Atch shot Begum and Abdullah tonight. Begum
so weak she had to be dragged out of stables. Gums swollen & congested.
Believe it is pony scurvy they had." Not surprising, considering they
had been existing on a diet of rope, canvas, tobacco ash, wood, dottle
from pipes, dog shit ...

It wasn't only the mules that were in bad shape. Silas was disappointed
to find that the state of the cables between his magnetic variation hut and
the meteorological recording gear were in such bad repair that part of his
scientific work had to be abandoned.

With the excitement of finding the remains of the Polar Party behind
them, it was now just a matter of keeping busy until *Terra Nova* arrived—
assuming of course that she would arrive. Priestley, Hooper, Debenham,
Abbott, Gran and Dickason left to climb Mount Erebus, while Cherry-
Garrard, Atkinson and Archer wandered off to rifle through Shackleton's
hut on Cape Royds one last time. Silas, Campbell and Williamson joined
them in the looting a few days later, and the next few days passed with
Silas and his comrades loafing around Shackleton's hut, gorging on skua
eggs and canned delicacies such as mutton cutlets in tomato sauce and
chicken and veal pâté, all the while keeping a close eye on the sea ice. If
it didn't break up in the Ross Sea, *Terra Nova* wouldn't be able to get close
enough to take them off.

Christmas Day 1912 passed quietly. Provisions being depleted, there weren't the usual treats on the table. As there was still no sign of *Terra Nova,* the men resigned themselves to spending a third winter at Cape Evans and were loading ammunition pouches in preparation for a seal slaughter. An ice cave was dug to store the seal meat and blubber for the stove because they only had a few bags of coal left to heat the hut for the next winter.

Finally, on January 20, 1913, *Terra Nova,* under the command of the fully recovered Teddy Evans, hove into view, and the entire camp raced around preparing to abandon Cape Evans.

I think the Shore Party at Cape Evans were, on the whole, pleased to abandon their expectations for a third winter and this was true even of the scientific staff whose work was by no means completed. But I have to confess that I have a niggling regret that my looked for and expected "one day for scientific work on the Beardmore Glacier" had to be given up because we found the bodies of Scott, Wilson and Bowers so close to home. I had so looked forward to this opportunity and was so certain it would come to pass.

—Wright memoirs

Before they left, it was decided that to remember those who had died on the expedition, a large wooden cross made of Australian jarrah would be erected on Observation Hill, with the choice of inscription given to Cherry-Garrard. Along with the names of Scott, Wilson, Evans, Oates and Bowers was the inscription from Tennyson's "Ulysses":

TO STRIVE, TO SEEK, TO FIND, AND NOT TO YIELD.

The task of placing the cross was given to Atkinson, Cherry-Garrard, Debenham, Lashly, Crean, Keohane, Francis Davies (the ship's carpenter) and Silas, who remembered the event:

January 23, 1913: Terra Nova stopped at Cape Geology to pick up the second Western Party's geological specimens and three days later, at Evans Coves, where they picked up Priestley's geological specimens and visited the ice cave. From there, they headed for New Zealand.

Silas revisiting the cross on Observation Hill in 1960. "The cross was about 8 ft. high and very heavy. The sea ice was melting fast and open pools were forming, but we got safely ashore and found a good place for the cross right on top of Observation Hill, excavated a hole and erected the cross firmly with its deeply carved inscription facing south." —Silas Wright

Terra Nova was in the Southern Ocean at latitude 60° south with the pack ice miles behind it when the engine was slowed and the ship stopped its usual wallowing roll. Debenham emerged from his cabin to see what was up and was surprised to see the ship was enveloped in a white mist and only yards away was the sheer side of an enormous iceberg. Debenham couldn't understand why they would be steaming so close to an iceberg. Silas wandered along the deck and Debenham pulled him aside, asking him why the ship was so close to an iceberg. Silas replied, "Have a look at the port side and you'll see" and wandered nonchalantly off. Debenham turned to port to see another monstrous iceberg, also just a few yards off. The icebergs had created a mini fog bank, which *Terra Nova* had unwittingly sailed into, becoming trapped between the two ice castles. Eventually the ship made it to the other side before the icebergs closed up.

> Antarctic icebergs, compared with those in the Arctic, are more numerous, surrounding the whole continent. Most are flat-topped and tabular in shape, formed from shelf ice or glacier tongues. When they drift into warmer waters they become encased in fog, which makes them essentially invisible and treacherous for shipping.

February 10, 1913: Terra Nova arrived off Oamaru, south of Christchurch, New Zealand. After giving everyone on board ship strict instructions not to speak to anyone from shore, Captain Pennell and Atkinson rowed ashore to find the local telegraph office. After they'd sent the news of the disaster that had befallen the Polar Party, the telegraph operator was locked in a room until confirmation arrived that the news had reached London.

The 1910 Scott Expedition was officially over.

January 7, 2009, Hobart, Tasmania

My trip was over, too. I'm leaning on the ship's rail, enjoying the warm sunshine and admiring the green(ish) hills that line Hobart harbour. For me, the trip filled in a lot of blanks in my life. Although I always had a lot of admiration for my grandfather and great uncles, seeing the places they lived and the extreme conditions under which they worked gave me a newfound respect for them. I also gained newfound respect for the rest of the expedition members. Wilson, Bowers, Oates, PO Evans, Atkinson, Cherry, Debenham...

But to me, Scott appeared to have learned nothing from his time on the 1901 Discovery Expedition, repeating the same blunders and in some cases making up new ones. Poor Oates and Taff Evans were doomed from the moment Scott picked them to be on the final Polar Party, but if in fact Scott had told Lt. Teddy Evans to send the dogs further south from One Ton depot to meet the returning Polar Party and Evans had relayed that change of plan to Atkinson, perhaps Scott, Wilson and Bowers might have survived. Certainly Bowers would have. As Silas said, "Birdie Bowers was the toughest man I ever met." But I can't lay all the blame on Evans. Scott could have also given those instructions to Lashly and Crean in case Evans disappeared down a crevasse, or died of scurvy—which he very nearly did.

And Victor Campbell should never have assumed the Terra Nova would be able to return to pick them up from Evans Coves and should have taken enough supplies for overwintering and winter clothing.

That only five men died on the 1910 British Antarctic Expedition is a testament to the resilience of those who were there with Scott.

18. HOME

Looking back on those eventful days, I am now
surprised at the optimism which led us to discount the
choice by Amundsen of a new glacier for reaching the
Polar Plateau and the South Pole and one which could
be negotiated by his dog teams.

—Silas Wright

Silas and Frank Debenham left the *Terra Nova* in Christchurch, where
after a brief refit, the ship continued on to England. Debenham accompanied Silas to Melbourne, Australia, where Silas would check his pendu-
lums, since it was a place where gravity had already been measured—one
pendulum had changed its swing while in the Antarctic. Along with the
usual baggage, Silas was accompanied by two sledge dogs, Beallychick and
Bullet. From Melbourne they went by steamer to San Francisco, where
they were held up by U.S. Customs because they had not completed the
proper paperwork for the dogs before they left Australia. Customs was upset
there was no record of the dogs being in quarantine prior to their arrival.
Silas was able to persuade the officials that three years in the Antarctic was
probably quarantine enough and they were allowed to proceed by train
to Vancouver, Canada.

They changed trains in Seattle, Washington, and while Silas was
looking for a taxi with the two dogs on a leash, he tripped and fell. The
two dogs instinctively took on the job of towing Silas around the train
station like a sledge.

They stopped off in Vancouver, where Bullet was given to Silas's
brother Brownie, and Beallychick, the white sledge dog with one blue

eye, was given to his brother Alfred, who was working as a land surveyor farther up the coast, in Prince Rupert.

Sixty years later, Silas would meet someone who had worked for his brother Alfred and remembered the white sledge dog with one blue eye. Presumably Beallychick's descendants are still roaming Prince Rupert.

Debenham and Silas spent a couple of weeks working with Alfred in Prince Rupert, where the polar travellers revelled in the green forests and constant drizzle—a welcome relief after the monochromatic Antarctic.

On leaving Prince Rupert, Silas and Debenham took the train to Toronto, stopping off briefly in Winnipeg, where Silas gave his first lecture on the expedition to the local chapter of the Canadian Club—a lecture Silas would rather forget, as his lack of oratorical skills was noted in the local paper the next day.

In Toronto they stayed with Silas's father, Alfred, and his second wife, Emily, and her three children, Ben, Ned and Helen. While there, the Toronto city fathers presented Silas with a gold repeater watch. He rarely used it, as the mainspring was weak and it cost a fortune to get it fixed. (It's sitting on my desk.)

Silas and Debenham in Toronto with Silas's parents and aunt and uncle. Silas is in the back seat with Debenham in the front passenger seat.

The Priestley girls (from left to right): Edith, Doris, Joyce, and Olive. Mother seated.

They finally arrived back in London, England, late in the spring of 1913, tired and very broke. With nowhere to stay, Silas and Debenham accepted Raymond Priestley's kind offer of lodging at his father's grammar school in Tewkesbury. Summer holidays had just started and the schoolroom was empty.

The Priestleys were a large family, four boys and four girls, and it was not long before one of Raymond's sisters—Edith—and Silas became engaged. They would marry in June 1914. Griff Taylor, also tight on funds and looking for a place to stay, joined them in Tewkesbury, where he met Edith Priestley's sister, Doris, and before long the two of them also became engaged.

The schoolhouse soon resounded with the clatter of typewriters—Silas working on his glaciology book, reports on gravity, the aurora, and Physiology of the Beardmore Glacier, while Griff and Ray were busy on their books. Priestley's *Antarctic Adventure: Scott's Northern Party* appeared in 1913 and Taylor's *With Scott: The Silver Lining* in 1916—the first of numerous books Griff was to produce on a variety of subjects. (When their respective books came out, there was, to the amusement of Silas, some friction between Priestley and Taylor, as each felt he hadn't received enough mention in the other's book.)

Silas, Taylor and Priestley working in the schoolroom.

Although everyone had been planning their bestsellers, Griffith Taylor beat them all by having established himself as the person of record—selling accounts of his part in the expedition to newspapers on his return to New Zealand after the first winter. He had special dispensation from Scott to sell his story; everyone else had been required to keep quiet about the expedition until Scott had wrung every last penny out of his own book and lecture tour.

Priestley, Taylor, Silas and Debenham eventually drifted back to Cambridge University to continue their studies. It wasn't long, though, before the Great War broke out, and Silas, Debenham and Priestley joined up and headed over to France. Taylor was already back in Australia.

Silas in his Signal Corps uniform.

19. POLAR REDUX

It was a pity Scott was in the Antarctic before. He learned all the wrong things.

—Silas Wright

Among the last entries in his journal, Robert Scott put the failure of his Polar Party down to the following issues *(with my comments after each one)*:

1. The loss of six ponies in March 1911, which forced him to start later than he'd intended and limited the amount of supplies that he and his party could take with them.
    The ponies couldn't start any earlier, because temperatures were too cold before they set out, on November 1, 1911.

2. The weather: the long blizzard at 83° south and the weather on the Barrier on their return. Temperatures down to minus 47° F at night.
    On the 1901 Discovery Expedition, Scott had experienced similar bone-chilling temperatures at that time of year on the Barrier, and he knew that in 1907 Shackleton had endured even colder temperatures at the same place and at the same time.

3. The soft, deep snow on the lower Beardmore.
    Even if Scott hadn't been delayed by a blizzard at the Beardmore,

they still would have arrived at the Pole twenty-four days after Roald Amundsen. They had lost the race to the Pole before they even started out from Cape Evans.

Until the end, Scott was careful to pin the blame on his failure to reach the Pole first and return on everything except his own planning. Bearing in mind that he wrote his diaries with an eye to a bestseller when he got home, it would make sense that he'd try to spin the story until the end, leaving the more purple prose to J.M. Barrie.

The Numbers

Scott left on November 3, 1911, arriving at the South Pole seventy-five days later, on January 17, 1912—thirty-four days later than Amundsen.

Amundsen had four sledges—thirteen dogs to each sledge—and they left Framheim, the Bay of Whales, on October 19, 1911, arriving at the South Pole fifty-six days later, on December 14, 1911.

Cecil Meares's dog team, with two men, returned from the foot of the Beardmore to Hut Point, a distance of 360 miles, in twenty-five days—an average of 15 miles per day.

Silas's returning party of four men travelled from the top of Beardmore to Hut Point, a distance of 450 miles, in thirty-six days—an average of 12½ miles per day.

Lt. Teddy Evans's returning party of three men travelled from the Polar Plateau to One Ton Depot, a distance of 466 miles, in thirty-seven days—an average of 12½ miles per day.

Scott's returning party of five men (reduced to four on the Beardmore) travelled from the South Pole to 11 miles south of One Ton Depot, a distance of 630 miles, in seventy-one days—an average of 10½ miles per day.

The curious case of the number 17 (a prime number):
- 17 ponies were landed at Cape Evans.
- On January 17, 1911, the party moved into the completed hut at Cape Evans.
- 17 square feet was the amount of space each man was allocated in the hut.

- May 17, 1911: The first dog died of an unknown parasite.
- August 17, 1911: Dr. Edward Atkinson lectured the party on the perils of scurvy.
- October 17, 1911: The Southern Journey began, with the start of the motor sledges.
- October 17, 1911: The first motor sledge broke down.
- November 17: The Southern Party passed the exact spot where Scott would perish the following year.
- January 17, 1912: The Polar Party reached the Pole.
- February 17, 1912: Evans died on the Beardmore.
- March 17, 1880: Lawrence "Titus" Oates was born.
- March 17, 1912 (32 years later): Oates crawled out of the tent and to his death.

The Temperatures

Meteorologist George Simpson (who had left for home by the time Scott died on the Barrier) wrote a paper supporting Scott's claim they could not have expected such low temperatures on the Barrier, although it was already known that at that time of year, the airflow over the Antarctic continent reverses, with outward radiation from the core of the continent exceeding inward radiation from the warmer ocean. Temperatures on the Barrier can plunge to minus 70° F in a matter of hours.

Shackleton recorded minus temperatures on February 15, 1908. Five days later, temperatures dropped to minus 20° F. On February 21, at Minna Bluff, *north* of One Ton Depot, temperatures dropped to minus 35° F.

Birdie Bowers first noted minus temperatures on February 18, 1912, and minus 20° F on February 26. Scott recorded minus 32° F two days later.

Looking at it afterwards, one can guess from what Scott and Shackleton had in previous years, it might well be same conditions would happen again the year of the return party.

—Wright memoirs

As the temperatures dropped, the men spent precious hours in the morning trying to get frozen gear on—wasting marching hours that would accumulate as their journey wore on.

Transport

Shackleton had warned Scott not to rely on ponies for his trip to the Pole, but Scott ignored his advice and purchased old and weak Manchurian ponies. Ponies were more susceptible to cold than dogs and because they were heavier were useless in the deep soft snow that would be encountered after a blizzard. With not enough fuel to melt snow to make water for the ponies, they were required to eat snow. It's pretty certain they were dehydrated and not able to perform their best.

Scott wanted white ponies because he thought they withstood the cold better. The colour of their coats, in fact, was of no significance.

The motor tractors, which were to be his secret weapon for depot laying and supporting the Polar Party, were tested in the more benign climate in Norway and proved completely ineffective in harsher Antarctic conditions.

Scott used Russian dogs, rather than Greenland dogs, which were used to travelling on flat, featureless landscapes. Russian dogs needed landmarks to head for, and could only follow a previously broken trail, meaning they'd have to lag behind the slow pony teams, negating their speed and efficiency.

On the Beardmore Glacier, Silas (their Canadian snow expert) warned Scott that the ice was tearing up the wooden runners on their sledges and that the ice that was sticking to the badly scored runners would slow their progress on the return journey, meaning they'd be using more supplies than planned. Scott ignored him.

Supplies

The leather seals on the oil containers may well be of note. Did they really shrink in the extreme cold and were they responsible for the depletion of oil in the oil containers or did one of the previous returning parties help themselves to more oil than they were entitled to? Food supplies at depots were found to be less than expected by some of the returning parties, so that is not out of the question.

On hearing of Scott's plans for the trip the winter before they set out, Silas realised that Scott hadn't provided for enough provisions for the return journey and suggested to Dr. Wilson that they take more cooking oil to cook the frozen meat that could be cached from the unfortunate ponies that were shot on the outward journey. If Wilson did relay Silas's concerns, Scott ignored his advice.

Navigation

Silas was an expert in navigating under difficult winter conditions. He was sure that he would be picked by Scott to be on the final Polar Party and was shocked when Scott cut him out at the last minute. As things ended up, Scott got lost on the return journey, wasting days wandering on the Beardmore Glacier—days that could have meant reaching the safety of One Ton before the weather turned against them. Scott had spent very few of his navy years actually at sea, and navigation was not his forte.

Why did they waste time looking for rock specimens on the Beardmore? Especially after geologist Griffith Taylor was passed over for inclusion on the party, because as Scott said, "there was no time for science on the polar journey."

Rations

Scott had calculated the size of rations needed by the sledging party. Two pounds of dry food, per man, per day. At that time it was calculated that the average person in England consumed two pounds of food per day, with three-fifths of that water. This made no allowance for the extreme cold in the Antarctic and the many more calories required just to heat the body, let alone feed it, along with the loss of fluid due to the excessive sweating from the exertion of pulling an 800-pound sledge. Silas wrote:

I believe, with Cherry, that the food was quite inadequate for the heavy work and to compensate for the heat losses from the body in low temperatures and to melt nightly the progressive accumulation of ice at the lower part of one's sleeping bag in really cold weather. This unbalance becomes larger due to the increased drag of the sledge at very low temperatures.

Scott failed to make full use of the only source of fresh meat they had on the Barrier—the ponies. The meat from slaughtered ponies would not spoil, as it would remain frozen under the snow at various food caches, which were, as it turned out, too far apart. Amundsen placed his depots at regular 1° intervals, not haphazardly spread out like Scott's. As it was, the returning parties would invariably barely reach the next food depot just as their rations were running out.

One case which I remember so clearly, because I felt very strongly about it, was the apparent neglect in Scott's plan to make the maximum use of the meat of the ponies, the survivors of which were to be shot at the foot of the Beardmore Glacier on the way to the South Pole. I spoke earnestly to Dr. Bill [Wilson] that the use of this meat should be part of the plan even though it would mean giving up something else to take the place of the fuel needed to make full use of the meat. Even Atkinson's party, returning from the top of the Beardmore Glacier would have been very glad of additional food. I, for one, was quite hungry by then.

—Wright memoirs

Scurvy

Scurvy first became apparent on Silas's Western Party, when Frank Debenham complained of a classic symptom—sore gums. It is known that one loses ascorbic acid when one sweats, and Scott's sledging rations completely lacked anything containing vitamins A or C.

In a group interview, after their return to London, Atkinson was asked by a reporter about the possibility of scurvy but was prevented from speaking by Lt. Evans. After that, Atkinson vehemently denied there ever was any scurvy among the party—despite the fact he'd given a talk on the perils of scurvy the previous winter. "Atch lectured on scurvy—good," Silas wrote on August 17, 1911. Atkinson had also invalided out Lt. Evans because of the same illness. Later, Silas wrote: "I think maybe we all suffered from a general deficiency of the many vitamins which are now known to exist but which had not been discovered in 1910, except of course the anti-scorbutic vitamin."

Curiously, unlike the case with previous Antarctic expeditions, no medical report was issued after *Terra Nova* returned to London.

The Fifth Man

Months prior to the start of the Southern Party, Edward Wilson painted a picture of five men pulling a sledge on the Barrier. This is puzzling, because up to now it had always been just four men pulling a sledge, and Wilson was careful when it came to the accuracy in his paintings.

Who was the fifth man? The fact that Birdie Bowers left his skis at Three Degree Depot indicated he did not expect to be included on the Polar Party. From Scott's diary it is obvious that he changed his plans at the last minute, without properly thinking things through. Silas was always convinced that Bowers was the fifth man.

Suicide

Did Scott intend that they commit suicide? Upon their return from the Pole, he notes in his diary that he demanded Wilson open his medicine bag and allow everyone to help themselves to opium tabloids. Among the usual items that the search party found in Wilson's medical case (which Wilson himself made up) were eighty-two tablets of "Soloid," a corrosive sublimate of 1¾ grains each (1 grain is fatal). Did they take some at the very end?

On viewing the bodies in the tent, Tryggve Gran said Scott's face was twisted, while Wilson and Bowers looked at peace. Did they overdose on opium? Features don't change after death, so what would have caused Scott's face to be that way?

One Ton Depot

Could Cherry-Garrard and Demetri have navigated farther south to Mount Hooper Depot? (Although they surely would have met Scott sooner than that.) Even if they could have gone farther south, they didn't have adequate provisions for themselves and the dogs, let alone (they assumed) five other men.

Alternatively, if Scott and his party had made it as far as One Ton and Cherry-Garrard was there, Cherry-Garrard did not have enough rations to take all three men—besides himself and Demetri—back to Hut Point. He probably would have had to take the sickest of Scott's party, leaving one, or even two, behind, cut his and Demetri's rations and make a dash to Hut Point for a relief party. Could Atkinson have returned in time with a rescue party or would he have had to stay behind at Hut Point to tend to the sick men who were now in his care? They couldn't use the dogs on the return rescue party, because they were knackered, so would have had to manhaul sledges to One Ton Depot, which was slower, and there was no guarantee they would have even made it to One Ton. The weather was getting worse and there is every possibility that a rescue party might themselves have been trapped out on the Barrier.

Scott had to have known they couldn't make it all the way back to the coast with five men, unsupported. Tryggve Gran was convinced Scott gave last-minute verbal instructions to Lt. Teddy Evans to overrule his previous order to Cecil Meares that the dog teams only be taken as far south as One Ton and instead be taken farther south, to Mount Hooper Depot. Evans would have been the ranking officer at Cape Evans in Scott's absence and could have ordered the dog teams farther south.

The Search Party

The decision on who to look for the next spring—the remains of Scott's party, or the stranded Northern Party—was voted on by the men left behind at Cape Evans but as ranking officer, the fallout from making the wrong choice would have ultimately rested on Atkinson's shoulders.

I had the greatest admiration for him [Atkinson] both as a man and as a leader in a difficult situation.

—Silas Wright

The Science

In terms of discovering anything new—other than novel ways to kill yourself in sub-zero conditions—the 1910 Scott Expedition did advance science in mapping the area, glaciology and geophysics. Silas published what is considered the definitive book on glaciology (*Glaciology*, London, Harrison and Sons, Ltd.,1922) but was frustrated that the Royal Geographical Society (RGS) washed its hands of the Scott Expedition, which meant that funding for writing up conclusions and reports suddenly dried up. Even before that, there were doubts being raised within the RGS as to Scott's scientific achievements. On April 7, 1912, Scottish Geographer, Hugh Robert Mill, speculated that as Scott was keeping so close to Shackleton's original course, they were hardly likely to discover anything new and even if Scott did reach the Pole, he would be "tied to his line of depots for a return and can accomplish nothing except to bring his party back alive."

He kept so close to Shackleton's track that he could discover nothing unless Shackleton had never been there; but by reference to Shackleton's names he evidently found everything exactly as set down....The Northern Party seems to have done nothing except to demonstrate that Borchgrevink was not such a duffer as has been thought. From Cape Adare they did nothing more, but apparently rather less than Borchgrevink did....As regards the scientific results we must wait until Simpson returns. The whole of the collections of the Western party seems to have been abandoned....Even if Scott reached the Pole, he is tied to his line of depots for a return and can accomplish nothing except to bring his party back alive.

—Hugh Robert Mill (Geographer and Meteorologist), April 7, 1912

20. WHAT BECAME OF EVERYONE?

For scientific leadership give me Scott; for swift and
efficient travel, Amundsen; but when you are in a
hopeless situation, where there seems no way out, get
down on your knees and pray for Shackleton.

—Raymond Priestley

Although the lives of five men on the Polar Party were cut short, the remaining expedition members went home and got on with their lives, and
in some cases went on to remarkable careers.

Thomas Crean made one more trip to the Antarctic with Ernest Shackleton
on *Endurance*. He was asked to accompany Shackleton, on Shackleton's
final expedition on *Quest,* but declined. Crean served with distinction in
the Royal Navy, which ostracised him in the eyes of his Irish Republican
countrymen, who considered him a traitor to the cause. He retired to
Annascaul, County Kerry, where he opened a pub called the South Pole
Inn (which is still pouring delicious pints of Guinness). He died in July
1938. Every year, a contingent of Royal Marines turns up in Annascaul
to tend to his grave.

Harry Pennell, captain of *Terra Nova*, died aboard the battleship HMS
Queen Mary in the battle of Jutland, in the Great War.

Lieutenant Henry Rennick was navigator on HMS *Hogue* and died when
it was torpedoed by a German submarine on September 22, 1914.

Tryggve Gran flew the first airplane across the North Sea. He attempted to join the British Army Air Corps in the Great War, but because he was Norwegian, he was rejected (Norway was a neutral country). He subsequently joined under the assumed name of Teddy Grant and during the war claimed to have shot down German ace Hermann Goering. In 1928 he led a search party looking for Roald Amundsen, who went missing while searching for the Italian airship *Italia*, which had disappeared on a flight to the North Pole (Amundsen was never found). During the Second World War, Gran was connected with Vidkun Quisling's hated Nazi-puppet government in Norway. After the war, Gran was tried and found guilty of treason. Fortunately for Gran, his previous accomplishments spared him from the firing squad, but he went to prison for eighteen months. Gran openly blamed Teddy Evans for Scott's demise, claiming Evans ignored Scott's order to send a dog team south of One Ton Depot to meet the returning Polar Party. Evans, who was rising in rank in the Admiralty and the peerage, was furious with Gran for airing dirty laundry and stopped speaking to him. There is a story of Gran turning up at Evans's house in London, only to have the door slammed in his face.[1]

> Norwegians have long been embarrassed by those who collaborated during the Nazi occupation. This is especially true of the offspring of Nazi-Norwegian unions: Anni-Frid Lyngstad, of the supergroup ABBA, being the most prominent (her mother was Norwegian and her father a German officer). When Anni-Frid was two years old, her grandmother took her to Sweden to avoid reprisals from Norwegians.

Cecil Henry Meares joined the army at the outbreak of the Great War, serving with the Northumberland Fusiliers and eventually transferring over to the RNAS (which later became the Royal Air Force), where he rose to the rank of lieutenant colonel in the intelligence branch. He was posted to Japan in 1921 as part of the British Aviation Mission—where they presumably taught the Japanese how to build and fly fighter planes. He retired to Canada with his wife, Annie Christina, and died in Victoria in 1937.

Edward Nelson continued his career as a biologist and was found dead in his laboratory in 1923. On February 19, 2009, his daughter Barbara Johns, then aged ninety-three, died aboard an expedition ship that was taking her to the *Terra Nova* hut at Cape Evans. The ship encountered a bad storm in the Ross Sea and Johns fell, hitting her head. She never regained consciousness and she died—only 190 miles from the huts. The Antarctic claimed another life.

Surgeon Commander Edward Atkinson, RN. Like Silas, "Atch" never wrote books about his experiences in the Antarctic. He continued with his naval career after returning from the Antarctic, and in the Great War was with Admiral John Jellicoe on the British Grand Fleet at the siege of Gallipoli and off France, where he lost an eye from shrapnel. He was decorated for bravery numerous times, the most notable being in 1918, when aboard the sinking HMS *Glatton*, badly burned and temporarily blinded, Atkinson stayed aboard the ship to rescue crew members. He went to Russia, where he dispensed medical help to victims of the Bolshevik Revolution. Marrying in 1928, he settled in Glasgow. Atkinson died aboard a ship in the Mediterranean, on his way back from India on February 20, 1929. Silas Wright wrote of Atkinson: "Atkinson has never received any credit for that winter, [he] had a terrible decision to make."

For **Raymond Priestley,** the war came at an inconvenient time. His book *Antarctic Adventure: Scott's Northern Party* had just been published and he was about to go out to promote it when war broke out. Like his now brother-in-law Silas, Priestley joined the army and went over to France, where he was a major in a 46th signals company. While Priestley was serving in France, Fisher Unwin, the book publisher's office in London, was bombed during a Zeppelin raid and most of the copies of *Antarctic Adventure* were destroyed in the ensuing fire. In April 1915, he took time out from the trenches to marry Phyllis Mary Boyd. They had three daughters: Margaret, Mary and Anne.

In 1920 he and Frank Debenham founded the Scott Polar Research Institute at Cambridge University. In 1935 he became vice-chancellor of the University of Melbourne but left three years later after a disagreement with the chancellor. He served as chancellor of the University of Birmingham from 1938 until 1952. He was knighted in 1949.

He was chairman of the Royal Commission on the Civil Service from 1953 to 1955; deputy director of the former Falkland Islands Dependencies Survey (later called the British Antarctic Survey) from 1955 to 1958; and president of the British Association for the Advancement of Science (British ASS, as Silas used to call them) in 1956. He revisited Antarctica in 1956, and again in 1959, this time in the company of the Duke of Edinburgh on the Royal Yacht *Britannia*. His wife, Phyllis, died in 1961, the same year he was elected president of the Royal Geographical Society.

Raymond Priestley died on June 24, 1974, at the age of 87, in Cheltenham, Gloucestershire.

Griffith Taylor parked himself in the Priestley family's Tewkesbury home to write his book *With Scott: The Silver Lining*. As mentioned earlier, while there he met Priestley's sister Doris Marjorie Priestley, whom he married on July 8, 1914, in Melbourne, Australia. In 1920 he chaired the University of Sydney's geography department. His views on the superiority of the Asian race and limiting settlement in parts of Australia brought him much derision and scorn, to the point where he left Australia to take up a post at the University of Chicago. He stayed there until 1935, then moved to the University of Toronto, where he was professor of geography until 1951, when he returned to Australia.

His warnings on populating the arid areas of Australia proved remarkably accurate as the country sinks deeper into drought and thousands of acres of farmland become untenable. Griffith Taylor died in Manly, Sydney, on November 5, 1963. He was always a bit disappointed that Priestley, Simpson and Silas had received knighthoods while he did not. (Although he did have more Antarctic landmarks named after him than anyone else.)

Herbert George Ponting returned home with 1,700 photographic plates. The original plan was for Scott to use the images to illustrate his lectures to raise funds to pay off the expedition's still-outstanding debts. Fortunately, with the hand-wringing and national mourning that followed the news of Scott's death, donations from the public paid off the debts and in fact provided for legacies for widows and children left behind. For Ponting, it wasn't until after the Great War that he was able to make some money off the photographs, publishing his book *The Great White South* and releasing his cinematic footage as "The Great White Silence." Despite suspicions from other members of the expedition that he was making a fortune out of his Antarctic photographs, none of these ventures made him much money, and he never went on another expedition. He stayed in touch with Cecil Meares, a friendship that lasted until Ponting's death in London, in 1935.

Frank Debenham served as a lieutenant in the Oxford and Buckinghamshire Light Infantry during the Great War and was wounded in 1916. He married Dorothy Lempriere in 1917 and was the first director of the Scott Polar Research Institute in Cambridge—founded by a portion of the excess funds donated by the public after Scott's death. He guided the institute from a tiny room at the university to its present location, writing in a June 13, 1961 letter to Silas:

> The PRI is going strong, almost too strong, one can hardly get into the place for staff and research people in every nook and cranny. There are grand plans for enlargement but the university doesn't help much, they still regard us as something tagged on and rather a nuisance.

From the time they left *Terra Nova* in New Zealand and together made their way back to England via Canada, Debenham and Silas remained good friends.

Frank Debenham died in Cambridge, in November, 1962. During his lifetime he wrote a number of books on Antarctica, but it wasn't until 1992 that his polar diaries were published by his daughter, June Debenham Back, as *The Quiet Land*—and stands as one of the best first person accounts to come out of the expedition.

Apsley Cherry-Garrard drove an ambulance during the Great War but was unable to participate further, as his physical and mental health was never the same after he returned from the Antarctic. He retired to his family estate at Lambeth Hall, where he wrote *The Worst Journey in the World*. The book was vetted by Scott's widow, Kathleen, who demanded he make numerous changes to the manuscript before it went to press, with even George Bernard Shaw getting involved in the editing (or censoring) process. Unfortunately, by then it was 1922, and the market was saturated with accounts of the expedition, and no publisher was interested. Cherry-Garrard had to pay out of his own pocket to print the first edition. *The Worst Journey in the World* has since gone on to become a classic of polar literature.

Silas and Cherry-Garrard remained close in the years after the war, with Cherry becoming a frequent visitor to the Wright household. Compared with the others from the expedition, Cherry-Garrard was quite well off; he took on the role of "banker to the Antartickers" and was most generous with the occasional "Could you let me have ten quid until Tuesday?" inquiries. After years of declining health, he died on May 18, 1959.

Surgeon Commander George Murray Levick, RN, continued his career as a naval surgeon, pioneering the use of infra-red in medical treatments. In 1914 Levick published *Antarctic Penguins*, which is still the definitive book on penguin behaviour. He and his wife founded the Public Schools Exploring Society, where he would take boys on expeditions to Finland, or Newfoundland, teaching them self-sufficiency and science. During the Second World War he trained commandos in survival techniques, and his experience in the ice cave on Inexpressible Island led to his involvement in a plan to wall two men within the Rock of Gibraltar, if the rock should fall into Nazi hands—where they could stay for up to seven years. Levick died on May 30, 1956.

Terra Nova was purchased back by Bowring in 1913 and went to work as a sealing vessel and freighter off Newfoundland. In September 1943, the ship hit ice off Greenland and sank. Before it sank, the captain set her on fire. The only thing that still survives from the ship (besides her silverware, nicked by the expedition members) is the bell, which hangs in the Scott Polar Research Institute and is rung twice daily to signal teatime, and the ship's figurehead (removed in 1913), which sits in the National Museum in Wales.

Lieutenant Teddy Evans carried on with his naval career during the Great War. As commander of HMS *Broke,* Evans was involved in action off Dover, deliberately ramming a German destroyer, which resulted in hand-to-hand fighting. In January 1916 he married Norwegian Elsa Andvord. After the war he was promoted to the rank of vice-admiral, and he became a member of the peerage in 1945 as Lord Mountevans of the Broke. Throughout his career in the navy, he always mounted a small penguin on the masthead of any ship he commanded. He eventually retired from the Royal Navy in 1949, with the rank of admiral. There was some resentment from the other members of the expedition, who felt Evans rather hogged the limelight on their return from the Antarctic. Evans's account of the expedition was published in 1921 as *South with Scott*. He died on August 20, 1957.

Silas Wright joined the Royal Engineers in the Great War and served in France, where he developed the first trench wireless. He joined the British Admiralty and rose to become head of the Royal Naval Scientific Service. During the Second World War, he was heavily involved in developing radar and countering torpedoes and magnetic mines. He invented the protective degaussing device, which used an electrical charge run through a ship's hull to neutralise German magnetic mines that lay on the sea floor. He was part of the planning for D-Day and had much to do with the logistics after landing, including Mulberry Harbours—large floating caissons that were towed over to the coast of France, where they were assembled as artificial harbours.

When he retired a few years after the war, Silas moved with his wife, Edith, to Canada, where he was hired by the U.S. and Canadian navies to work on counter-torpedo measures. He retired a second time, then took the post of director of the Marine Physical Laboratory at the Scripps Institution of Oceanography in La Jolla, California. He retired to his waterfront home on Salt Spring Island, British Columbia, for the last time in 1970. Silas died on November 1, 1975, at the age of eighty-eight.

Honours bestowed on Sir Charles Seymour "Silas" Wright:

> Polar Medal with 1910–13 clasp
> 1914–15 Star
> Victory 1918 Medal
> British War Medal 1914–18
> Defence Medal 1939, 1945 (2)
> George V Silver Jubilee Medal
> George VI Coronation Medal
> War Medal 1939–45

KCB (Knight Commander of the Order of the Bath)—star and badge
King's Royal Rifle Corps Badge
Legion of Honour
MC (Military Cross)
OBE (Officer of the Order of the British Empire)
Royal Geographical Society Antarctic Medal
U.S. Congressional Medal of Freedom

The huts at Cape Evans and Cape Royds see fewer than two hundred visitors a year, which makes one wonder if they are worthy of the millions of dollars being spent on restoring and maintaining them. It's a question I've asked myself both before and after seeing the *Terra Nova*, Shackleton and *Discovery* huts. For selfish reasons, I'd like to see them preserved—although not at the expense of their losing their unique atmosphere. Even then, will anyone ever see them? To counter that argument, the New Zealand Antarctic Heritage Trust plans to install live webcams, so people from around the world will be able to see the huts without actually travelling there. Perhaps that is the best way, but does sitting in your ratty house-coat, peering at a grainy image of a dimly lit room at the bottom of the planet compare with actually standing inside one of the huts, absorbing the atmosphere left behind by the men who lived there roughly a century ago? Probably not, but a live webcam will allow us to experience a little of what those men went through—I'm personally looking forward to sitting in my ratty housecoat and logging on while a winter blizzard batters the hut. But if Quark Expeditions ever send another ship to the Ross Sea, go. There are fewer people seeing the huts than climbing Everest...

Silas with the sledge he turned into a bookcase. (He was planning to keep it intact, but it was too small to fit in their house in England, so he cut it in half).

# APPENDIX

List of scientists, officers and
crew of the 1910 British Antarctic
Expedition*†‡

Officers

Edward L. Atkinson, Surgeon
Commander, RN, Parasitologist
Henry Robertson Bowers, Lieutenant, RIM‡
Victor L.A. Campbell, Lieutenant, RN
Edward R.G.R. Evans, Lieutenant, RN*
Lawrence Edward Grace Oates,
Captain 6th Inniskilling Dragoons‡
George Murray Levick, Surgeon
Commander, RN
Robert Falcon Scott, Captain, CVO, RN‡

Scientists

Apsley Cherry-Garrard, BA, Assistant
Zoologist
Bernard C. Day, Motor Engineer*
Frank Debenham, BA, BSC, Geologist
Tryggve Gran, Sub-lieutenant,
Norwegian, NR, BA, Ski Expert
Cecil H. Meares, in charge of dogs*
Edward W. Nelson, Biologist
Herbert G. Ponting, FRGS, Camera
Artist*
Raymond Edward Priestley, BA,
Geologist
George C. Simpson, DSC,
Meteorologist*
Thomas Griffith Taylor, BA, BSC, BE,
FGS, Geologist*

---

* wintered over 1911 only
† joined for the winter of 1912
‡ died on return from the South Pole

Edward Adrian Wilson, BA, MB
(Cantab), Chief of Scientific Staff
and Zoologist‡
Charles Seymour Wright, BA, Physicist,
Glaciologist

Men of the Shore Party
George P. Abbott, Petty Officer, RN
W.W. Archer, Chief Steward, late RN†
Frank V. Browning, Petty Officer, RN
Thomas C. Clissold, Cook, late RN*
Thomas Crean, Petty Officer, RN
Harry Dickason, Able Seaman, RN
Edgar Evans, Petty Officer, RN‡
Robert Forde, Petty Officer, RN*
Demetri Gerof, Dog Driver
Frederick J. Hooper, Steward, late RN
Patrick Keohane, Petty Officer, RN
William Lashly, Chief Stoker, RN
Anton L. Omelchenko, Groom*
Thomas S. Williamson, Petty Officer, RN†

Ship's Party
Alfred B. Cheetham, Boatswain, RNR
Arthur S. Bailey, Petty Officer, 2nd
class, RN
Wilfred M. Bruce, Lieutenant, RNR
Francis E. C. Davies, Leading
Shipwright, RN
James R. Dennistoun, in charge of
mules on board ship
Francis R.H. Drake, Assistant
Paymaster, RN

William L. Heald, Petty Officer, RN
William A. Horton, Second Engineer, RN
Dennis G. Lillie, MA, Marine Zoologist
Fredrick Parsons, Petty Officer, RN
Harry L.L. Pennell, Lieutenant, RN
Henry E. P. Rennick, Lieutenant, RN
William Williams, Engineer, RN

Ship's Personnel
Albert Balson, Leading Seaman, RN
Robert Brissenden, Leading Stoker, RN
William Burton, Leading Stoker, RN
William Knowles, Able Seaman
Joseph Leese, Able Seaman, RN
Silas Lammas, Fireman
John Hugh Mather, Petty Officer, RNVR
Mortimer McCarthy, Able Seaman
Angus McDonald, Fireman
William McDonald, Able Seaman
Thomas McGillon, Fireman
Edward A. McKenzie, Leading Stoker, RN
Thomas F. McLeod, Able Seaman
W.H. Neale, Steward
Robert Oliphant, Able Seaman
James Paton, Able Seaman
James Skelton, Able Seaman
Bernard J. Stone, Leading Stoker, RN
Charles Williams, Able Seaman

# NOTES

Unless otherwise noted, all images in this book are from the author's collection.

Chapter 1

1. C.R. Ford, in radio interview on "Scott of the Antarctic," New Zealand Broadcasting Service (NZBS), 1960.
2. C.H. Hare, in radio interview on "Scott of the Antarctic," NZBS, 1960.
3. C.R. Ford, radio interview.
4. Robert Scott, *Scott's Last Expedition* (London: Smith Elder, 1913), 453.
5. Harold Begbie, *Shackleton: A Memory* (London: Mills & Boon, 1922).
6. R.E. Priestley, *Christchurch Evening Star,* May 10, 1975.
7. Griffith Taylor, in radio interview on "Scott of the Antarctic," NZBS, 1960.

Chapter 2

1. Silas Wright's memoirs.
2. Griffith Taylor, *Journeyman Taylor* (London: Robert Hale, 1958), 82.

Chapter 3

1. Scott Diaries, October 27, 1910. Papers at British Museum.
2. Griffith Taylor, *With Scott the Silver Lining* (London: Smith Elder, 1916), 5.
3. Frank Debenham, in BBC Television interview (no date).
4. James Lees-Milne, *Ancestral Voices* (London: Chatto and Windus, 1975).

Chapter 4

1. L.C. Bernacchi, *A Very Gallant Gentleman* (London: Eyre & Spottiswoode, 1942), 56.
2. Bowers Diary, Papers at Scott Polar Research Institute, Cambridge.
3. Bernacchi, *A Very Gallant Gentleman*, 61.
4. June Debenham Back, *The Quiet Land* (Huntington: Bluntisham Books, 1992), 57.

Chapter 6

1. June Debenham Back, *The Quiet Land* (Huntington: Bluntisham Books, 1992), 41.
2. Griffith Taylor, *With Scott the Silver Lining* (London: Smith Elder, 1916), 106.
3. Raymond Priestley, *Antarctic Adventure: Scott's Northern Party* (London: T. Fisher Unwin 1914), 41.

Chapter 7

1. Debenham Back, *The Quiet Land*, 92.
2. Frank Debenham, *In the Antarctic* (London: John Murray, 1952), 30.
3. Taylor, sledging diary, 1911.
4. Taylor, sledging diary, 1911.
5. Scott Diaries, February 14, 1911. Papers at Royal Geographical Society Archives.
6. Edward Evans, *South with Scott* (London: Collins), 76.

Chapter 8

1. Robert Scott, *Scott's Last Expedition* (London: Smith Elder, 1913), 203.
2. June Debenham Back, *The Quiet Land* (Huntington: Bluntisham Books, 1992), 124.

Chapter 9

All quotes from Raymond Priestley, *Antarctic Adventure: Scott's Northern Party* (London: T. Fisher Unwin, 1914).

Chapter 10

1. Scott Diaries, May 24, 1911.
2. Robert Scott, *Scott's Last Expedition* (London: Smith Elder, 1913), 445.
3. Griffith Taylor, *With Scott the Silver Lining* (London: Smith Elder, 1916), 272.
4. Herbert Ponting, *The Great White South* (London: Duckworth, 1921), 153.
5. Apsley Cherry-Garrard, *The Worst Journey in the World* (London: Chatto and Windus, 1952), 303.

Chapter 11

1. Robert Scott, *Scott's Last Expedition* (London: Smith Elder, 1913), 444.
2. F. J. Hooper sledging diary, 1911.
3. F. J. Hooper sledging diary, 1911.
4. Edward Wilson, *Diary of the Terra Nova Expedition to the Antarctic, 1910–1912*, ed. H.G.R. King (London: Blandford Press 1972), 100.
5. Scott, *Scott's Last Expedition*, 470.
6. Scott, *Scott's Last Expedition* (London: Smith Elder, 1913), 483.
7. June Debenham Back, *The Quiet Land* (Huntington: Bluntisham Books, 1992), 124.

Chapter 12

1. Robert Scott, *Scott's Last Expedition* (London: Smith Elder, 1913), 495.
2. Frank Wild sledging diary, December 31, 1908.
3. Scott, *Scott's Last Expedition*, 514.
4. Edward Wilson, *Diary of the Terra Nova Expedition to the Antarctic, 1910–1912*, ed. H.G.R. King (London: Blandford Press, 1972), 219.

Chapter 14

1. Robert Scott, *Scott's Last Expedition* (London: Smith Elder, 1913), 523.
2. Scott, *Scott's Last Expedition*, 560.
3. Scott, *Scott's Last Expedition*, 544.
4. Edward Wilson, *Diary of the Terra Nova Expedition to the Antarctic, 1910–1912*, ed. H.G.R. King (London: Blandford Press, 1972), 232.
5. Scott, *Scott's Last Expedition*, 560.
6. Scott, *Scott's Last Expedition*, 571.
7. Scott, *Scott's Last Expedition*, 573.
8. Wilson, *Diary of the Terra Nova Expedition to the Antarctic*, 245.
9. Scott, *Scott's Last Expedition*, 578.
10. Scott, *Scott's Last Expedition*, 587.

11. Scott, *Scott's Last Expedition*, 589.

12. Scott, *Scott's Last Expedition*, 588.

13. Scott, *Scott's Last Expedition*, 590.

14. Scott, *Scott's Last Expedition*, 594.

15. *The Hobart Mercury*, February 28, 1913.

Chapter 17

1. Apsley Cherry-Garrard, *The Worst Journey in the World* (London: Chatto & Windus, 1952), 481.

2. BBC interview, 1975.

Chapter 20

1. Geoffrey Hattersley-Smith, Foreign Office, London—Polar Regions Section.

INDEX

Page numbers in *italics* denote photographs, images or maps.
Page numbers in **bold** denote definitions or biographical details.

PHOTO CREDITS

Unless otherwise noted, all photographs, maps and illustrations are from the author's collection.

117. Dogs down crevasse. PF Wright photo.

118. Watkins camera. Mari Ogawa photo.

122. Discovery hut. Mari Ogawa photo.

123. Interior of Discovery Hut, Mari Ogawa photo.

123. Demetri and Meares. Herbert Ponting photo.

Chapter 8
126. Dog holes. PF Wright photo.

127. Vaida and Beileglas. PF Wright photo.

130. Crean and Evans mending sleeping bags. Herbert Ponting photo.

133. Nobu Shirase party. Courtesy the Shirase Antarctic Expedition Memorial Museum, Nikaho city, Akita, Japan

134. Summer sledging party. Herbert Ponting photo.

Chapter 9
136. Cape Adare. Captain Harry Pennell photo. Courtesy Pennell family archives

138. Cape Adare latrines. Mari Ogawa photo.

144. Northern Party supplies on *Terra Nova*. Captain Harry Pennell photo. Courtesy Pennell family archives

145. Evans Coves camp. Dr. Murray Levick photo.

147. Ice cave entrance, Inexpressible Island. Dr. Murray Levick photo.

153. Interior of ice cave. Dr. Murray Levick photo.

157. Northern Party returns to Cape Evans. Captain Harry Pennell photo. Courtesy Pennell family archives

159. Plaque on Inexpressible Island. Mari Ogawa photo.

Chapter 10
163. Chris and gramophone. Herbert Ponting photo. British Antarctic Terra Nova Expedition (1910–1913) Album. Alexander Turnbull Library, Wellington, N.Z.

165. Exterior of ice cave. Herbert Ponting photo. Raeside archives.

168. Preparing pemmican rations. Herbert Ponting photo. British Antarctic Terra Nova Expedition (1910–1913) Album. Alexander Turnbull Library, Wellington, N.Z.

169. Scott writing in his cubicle. Herbert Ponting photo.

170. Transit. Mari Ogawa photo.

171. Silas and theodolite. Herbert Ponting photo.

172. Nelson digging out. Herbert Ponting photo.

173. Making up a sledge. Herbert Ponting photo.

174. Midwinter party. Herbert Ponting photo.

175. Cape Crozier party leaves. Herbert Ponting photo. British Antarctic Terra Nova Expedition (1910–1913) Album. Alexander Turnbull Library, Wellington, N.Z.

178. Cape Crozier party returns. Herbert Ponting photo. British Antarctic Terra Nova Expedition (1910–1913) Album. Alexander Turnbull Library, Wellington, N.Z.

180. Blubber stove. Herbert Ponting photo.

181. Sundial compass. Mari Ogawa photo.

182. Debenham and Griffith Taylor. Herbert Ponting photo.

183. Silas and Chinaman. Herbert Ponting photo.

185. Bernard Day and motor sledge. Herbert Ponting photo.

186. Ponting and dog cart. Herbert Ponting photo.

187. The Tenements. Herbert Ponting photo.

189. Oates in pony stables. Herbert Ponting photo.

190. Vaida. Herbert Ponting photo.

Sledge tracks cross Adélie penguin tracks.

Since the death of Scott and his companions, their entombed bodies are calculated to have travelled in the ice approximately 39 miles north of "Sorrowful Camp," at a speed of roughly 0.4 miles a year (as of 2009). At that rate, they will end up in the ocean in or around 2250. Or, if the climate change scientists are correct, sometime next year.